Library of (

The knitting goddess : finc
projects, ai

1. Knitting—Patterns.   2. K

746.

1

ACKNOWLEDGMENTS

(more or less in order of appearance)

The staff of the Webster's, Art to Wear, Tzun Tzun, Crystal, the staff of Knitting Niche, Karen Young Nelson for her research, Laurie Weinsoft for knitting like me but far better, The Black Sheep Gathering, Linda Carter of the Yarn Garden for her encouragement and feedback, Maureen McLaughlin, Linda Berning and Gina Parosa of Northwest Wools, Shannon Pernetti, Sandy Sitzman, Paulette Rees-Denis, and Patrice Hawkwood Shanck for teaching in a sister format at just the right moment, Katherine Maxson-Landis and Rachael Cornell for being guinea pigs, Chelsea Miller for her research and also her superior yarn-winding skills, Linden Phelps, Beryl Hiatt, and Carol Simmons of Tricoter, Joan Contraman, Janice Merola, and Lolly Jamerson, Joan D'Arcy and John van Rees, Jenny Rideout and Aydika James for everything, the Knitting Goddess Beta Testers for early readings of the manuscript, Ellen Farr for Elizabeth, Elizabeth Farr the angel of knitting, Harriet, Alexandra, and Demetra Aposporos for being real-life Greek goddesses, Joseph M. Holzer for the pinch hit in the bottom of the ninth, the amazing scholarship of Elizabeth Wayland Barber, without which this book would have been rather more difficult to imagine, and of course George Aposporos.

Also, a special thanks to Mary Ellen O'Neill for asking me what Brigit's voice sounded like and to Geri Thoma for getting it.

VII

Introduction

On one early spring day I walked up a creek trail in a small arts community I was visiting at the time. My goal was quite specific: to complete a shamanic ritual suggested to me by a spiritual friend who is also an indigenous Tibetan shaman. My instructions were to throw ashes into the creek's running water. The intent of the action was to let go of the final remains of an important relationship. I had completed the preliminary steps of the ritual slowly during the preceding few months. The process had been not unlike cleaning out a small closet that held a variety of things I still liked but could no longer use.

When I walked out from the trailhead half an hour later, I felt invigorated, calm, clear, and lightened. The day was beautiful. I had about twenty minutes before I needed to meet a new friend with whom I would be making the five-hour drive back to the Pacific Northwest airport near my home and where she would catch a flight to her home in Europe. The two of us were part of an international spiritual practice group that met twice a year.

In the meantime, I decided to stop by the wearable art store to admire the beautiful but expensive handmade items that were sold there. I forewent the hand-dyed silk dresses with four figure price tags and settled near a sweater rack near the back, where my fingers closed around a beautiful but simple cable knit pullover in a buttery color and my size. It would cost about $75 to make it, but the sample itself was unmarked.

The woman who was behind the counter was quite young and kind of hip. I asked her how much the sweater would be.

"Oh, about three hundred dollars."

We both grimaced.

"But," she said, without missing a beat, "you could make it yourself."

"Oh. I could make it myself."

"Sure. We have this really inexpensive book."

She walked over to the rack and took down an oversized, staple-bound pamphlet. It offered simple instructions and lots of pictures, and best of all as far as I was concerned, it contained a second set of directions and illustrations for the left-handed. I had learned to knit when I was in junior high or thereabouts, but never got much of anywhere since I had to transpose everything. Consequently, I'd never become as fast or neat as the other kids. Indeed, until that moment, the word I would have summoned to best describe knitting was "ick."

When we met, my friend the shaman had also taken the time to observe how Westerners like me who follow a spiritual path have a tendency to reach our heads so far up in the ethers that we miss the next step, right in front of our noses, on planet Earth. But I did not have this comment particularly in mind when the saleswoman suggested I learn to knit.

Instead I just said, "Okay. I can do it myself."

Briskly, she helped me pick out a set of needles of an appropriate size and length and directed me toward yarn. (The needles were straight, wooden size eight. She suggested that I use a yarn that was single ply.) I was entranced with the beauty and the styling of the needles. My hands still held the vivid memory of the last needles I had used in Home Ec. class. They were plastic-coated metal, slippery, rendered in some pastel color not found in nature, and dropped stitches like nobody's business. Nobody had told me knitting could be this elegant or aesthetic. Before I cast on a single stitch, I was already, well . . . hooked.

We decided I would practice on this yarn and then begin an appropriate project.

Still in that comfortable, heightened, thoughtful state, I met up with my friend, who was a doctoral student in economics in Sweden, at the counter of a nearby lunch spot and almost bashfully showed her my unexpected prizes.

"Oh, knitting," she said. "I used to knit like crazy. It's wonderful. I used to

make sweaters and study at the same time. Before I knew it, I was designing my own reindeer and just putting them in. I'll teach you how."

A couple of hundred miles up Interstate 5, she took the driver's seat and I began to wind my skein of deep red wool and mohair yarn into a ball, using the gear stick to hold one end taut. Soon after, we pulled into a truck stop overlooking a cornfield, nosed my car between two semis, and I learned how to cast on. By the time we pulled into the big city two hours from then I was knitting and purling. Three or four weeks later I had finished my first sweater. A month after that, on the basis of nothing but a little curiosity and a desire for occasional independence from yarn stores, I decided to find out how to learn to hand spin. On a wheel. Like some fairy-tale person. I happened to inquire about lessons to a woman who worked at a local store. She turned out to be a spinning teacher. She gave me two private lessons, and let me know, in a casual but astute way, that the major yearly gathering for the craft would occur at the fairgrounds of a nearby city in several weeks. I attended.

So, as I alternated between my two new skills as I took breaks from writing, I quickly realized how well knitting and spinning balanced the physical toll of the many hours I spend almost daily in front of not one, but two computer screens—I write and do financial accounting on the desktop, and do e-mail, Internet, and astrology for clients on the sub-note. Like the physical action of using a keyboard, spinning used the hands, could be stopped and started, had an almost musical rhythm, and was capable of creating a meditative state.

But unlike the physical act of writing, it was also soft, luscious, colorful, nurturing, and yielded immediate results. Soon my professional routine and new avocation had all but married into a single practice. As I gathered my fiber together and spun it into glistening, lofty yarn I felt I was gathering together my thoughts and my imagination and my soul. As I waited for my browser to load, I futzed with patterns and colors on my knitting needles instead of tapping my pen, grumbling, or shooting off the odd desultory e-mail to a friend who would no doubt read it while doing time in a similar precinct of high-tech purgatory. When tech support put me on hold while they tried to figure out my hardware glitch, I spun some more. On about the third call, the technician of the hour

quite precipitously began to flirt with me over the phone as he fed me a string of arcane software commands. I'm still convinced this was because the magical atmosphere created by a working spinning wheel had somehow made its way over the interstate phone lines.

As time went on, I began to notice that spinning's effect on me was both stimulating and meditative. The practice of letting wool, silk, alpaca, and other fibers flow through my hands and twist into yarn that held unique blends and variations of color, texture, luster was deeply sensual and right brained. Meanwhile, the practice of knitting and planning a garment in orderly stitches and grid-like patterns was more integrating and left brained, yet also offered a deeply meditative quality. Soon, every time I began a new knitting project or spun up a fresh bag of fiber, I would almost unaccountably move a stage in my writing process as well, effortlessly getting the next idea or energy burst that would move a back burner writing project on to the front burner, and, then, to completion or developing new ones.

Though I had "beginner's mind" in knitting and spinning, I knew at least a thing or two about spiritual practice and the history of religion. So, one by one, the mythological archetypes that depicted woolwork lined up in my mind to remind me they were there. Ariadne, Arachne, Athena, Penelope, and the three Fates of the Greco-Roman world were all associated with the fiber arts as spinners and weavers. In the Middle East, Isis and Rachel, one the mother goddess of her people and the other the Old Testament beauty who became the mother of Israel, were both associated with fertility, the initiation of overcoming great hardships for deep love, and with linen and wool respectively. In the Celtic world, Brigit, triple goddess of fire and illumination and guardian of bards, was associated with handicrafts of all kinds. In the Navajo tradition, Grandmother Spider, the Weaver of Worlds, was revered and respected. And from the Hindu tradition came Maya, the Divine Mother, who wove and unwove the form of reality itself.

All of these women were, technically speaking, spinning and weaving goddesses—the art of knitting was probably not invented until the fourth to sixth centuries, by Arab shepherds, in Egypt. (The earliest knitted garments are "toed" sandal socks found in Coptic Egyptian tombs—since they may very well have endured due to the dry Egyptian climate, it is unknown whether they were the

first knitted garments or just the first knitted garments that are currently available for examination. Nordic and Celtic people also make a case for Viking origins of the craft.) Knitting was a man's trade until the Middle Ages, when it eventually made its way to Germany and Italy and then England through the trade routes that moved from the Arab world to Spain. Yet, when this occurred, women embraced and assimilated knitting just as they had, of necessity, embraced spinning and weaving in the ancient world. And some of the ancient feminine archetypes and wisdom resurfaced in the literature, art, and history of that time, using this new and newly fashionable form of needlework. These included the Virgin Mary, who was painted knitting in both Germany and Italy in the fourteenth century and the historical Queen Elizabeth, who learned to knit as a princess while whiling away the hours waiting for the tides to change while her half sister Mary was still queen. (Both of these virgin/queen/mothers displayed Isis-like qualities.) When Elizabeth became queen, one morning she was brought the list of candidates for honorary titles for her final selection as she sat knitting in her garden. She did not have a pen at hand, so she made the final selections by punching a knitting needle through the list on the appropriate lines. The custom continues into the present.

Gradually, in the West, knitting superseded weaving as the most accessible fiber work form. The power that had gathered around weaving also came to gather around knitting.

As I researched, I grew to anticipate that a heroine's ability to use yarn and a wheel or a spindle or loom—or, later, a pair of needles—would promise a story that shared wisdom about the potentials of feminine power. I was never disappointed. My knitting goddesses, as I came to call them, knew how to use passion, love, strategy, and patience to change or heal worlds and to travel between them. Their tools represented a flexible, strategic, and sometimes deeply magical power that contained much wisdom about how to access strength, work with and transform systems, heal themselves and others. The knitting goddesses were, well . . . *shamanic*. Except instead of talking sticks, drums, herbs, and animal helpers (with the notable exception of goats and sheep) they used a bit of wool and something made out of wood to shift the nature of their, and others', reality.

Recent research suggests that learning a new skill, like knitting a difficult Fair Isle pattern, can enliven and even heal the brain by creating new connections between dendrites. And an art therapist I know who works in a nursing home knows his octogenarian patients are back on track when they respond to his suggestion that they knit or quilt. Other research shows that working physically with the right and left sides of the body can harmonize the language and image centers of the brain at a new level. Also, my students and I have had the strong experience of the ancient rhythms of fiber arts literally connecting us with the experience of timelessness, or stillness, an experience which is seen spiritually as the doorway to enlightenment and deep healing.

Clearly, ancient women experienced these same benefits, which worked their way into stories about the sacred power of spindle and loom. Today, when we become able to shift our attention, even briefly, from the Pentium chip tempo of our own world to the ancient rhythms of fiber moving through two hands, something in the soul seems to heal naturally. It is not hard to see why wool had been offered to Athena at her temple by Jason, tied around an olive branch, on his way to capture the golden fleece. Or why Arachne, a mere mortal, was prevented from weaving tapestries more beautiful than Athena's. The artistry of fiber work does not only clothe and shelter the tribe. It is also a wellspring of power and creation.

This book is designed to make this explicit connection available to you through the stories of these archetypes and explorations of how their wisdom can enrich and teach us now, while we sit at PCs instead of looms and carry car keys and cell phones instead of drop spindles and bobbins. It also offers eight knitting projects, varied in use, stitches, color, fiber, time to complete, and approximate cost to make. The projects are inspired by the stories and are intended to nurture your heart, soul, hands, and eyes through careful yet playful choices of pattern, shape, and color. Yet they can also be accomplished, if need be, while you are talking on the phone, sitting in a lecture, or waiting for the kids to finish soccer practice. They create beautiful, and in most cases, simply accomplished results. The stories put the knitting goddesses into your mind and heart; the knitting has the added perk of, in addition to those other two areas, running it through your eyes and, most importantly, your hands. The book also offers the

basic instruction you need to knit any of the patterns, and lots of wisdom about yarns and the (easily solved) mysteries of sweaters, if knitting happens to be new to you. With this book you can give yourself, and anyone else you like or love, the treat of learning to knit in the freedom and privacy of your own digs. Or at the beach, or at a ballet recital, or on a commuter train, and no matter which aspects of the book you decide to enjoy.

A Note For Brand-New or Newer Knitters

If you are a prospective new knitter, you may be stymied because you are concerned you will not knit perfectly, evenly, or neatly, that you will fail or be thwarted. This is normal. As Miranda, the twenty-eight-year-old proprietor of an electrical contracting company put it, "I learned to knit from my grandmother. Kind of. She did these things with little tiny stitches that took forever and I learned a few things from her but not everything, so I got frustrated, and couldn't finish things. I hated to count and I made mistakes. She knew how to knit but she wasn't a knitting teacher."

Lots of people I've talked to who are interested in knitting but don't learn have described a version of these same challenges—as if knitting were as exacting and harrowing a ritual as tax audit preparation. And I've been there. I'm not much farther along in the curve than you are. But really, when you knit, you can do whatever you want. That's the point. You can use patterns where you have to count if you want to. You can use patterns where you don't have to count if you don't want to. In some circles, this is known as "grunge" knitting because you can do it in a meeting or on the phone. I call it flow knitting. I do flow knitting all the time when I am working out what to do next in writing or when I need to center, or in any situation when a quieter mind is called for. If you're a new knitter, you probably want to know how to make something fun pretty quickly, and how to fix mistakes if you make any (everyone does). *Knitting Goddess* patterns and instructions are designed specifically to address these questions and desires. Knitting, purling, picking up dropped stitches, how to choose yarns that don't show mistakes, and patterns that require very little counting of stitch patterns or rows are written here just for you.

Also, keep in mind that as I write this I have only been knitting for about two years. Most of what you see here is readily available by reading, asking questions in those amazing storehouses of knowledge known as knitting stores, putting yarn in your hands, and just giving yourself permission to play. A good light source, natural, halogen or full spectrum, which will allow you to appreciate the full range of color, texture, and luminosity that fiber offers is also helpful. Believe me, if I can knit, so can you.

A Note for More Experienced Knitters

The stories are offered to give you new insight into this craft you love. But I suspect you will also enjoy the designs. They don't have lace patterns or cables, or Fair Isle patterns, or ingenious shaping. In fact, they are one size or sizeless creations that have virtually no shaping at all. But the fabrics and yarns are colorful and luscious, the results are distinctive and appealing, they have all been examined or knit by experienced knitters, who, to my delight, enjoyed making and admiring them. A few of the designs are knitting puns that work the imagery of the archetype in question into a traditional technique in a new and different way. There is almost always something to enjoy about the yarn or the stitch or the combination—how they combine with each other or how simple stitches and interesting yarns combine to create something that looks more sophisticated than it is. At least one of them might bend your mind in a new way. And they make pretty stuff. They work the stories through your hands and heart.

As the fiber runs through our hands as it has for generations upon generations, an exchange that is both physical and spiritual can happen. Whether we choose to pursue knitting to explore its symbolic potential for gathering power and connecting with the timeless, to connect with the ancient goddesses to add a new dimension of pleasure to our work, or simply for the prodigious pleasure of knitting, our lives can shift subtly and sometimes deeply, as a result. We ourselves become knitting goddesses.

Table of Contents

The
KNITTING
GODDESS

Grandmother Spider and the Basic Basics

Marcel Proust once observed that love never comes when we are longing for it. Love is much more likely to come along when life is perfectly in its place, just to muss it up again.

Knitting isn't that kind of love.

The invitation to knit usually doesn't arrive when we are feeling like everything in life has achieved a measure of Parisian fullness and balance and needs to get roughed up again. Not always, but more often, it seems to be in one of those ragged, odd moments of life—when we are feeling somehow at odds, in transition, at risk, out of sorts, or just plain awkward—when two needles and a skein of something intriguing manage to present themselves within arm's reach. A voice whispers in our ear. We pick up the rudimentary tools and fiber, put up with the fleeting added challenge of learning yet another new skill, and the next thing we know we are knitting our way through our transition, ordering our life into a new pattern while we also use our hands and needles to learn to pattern yarn. We counter one transition with another, and get through both, and then some.

Marianne picked up knitting in graduate school as an accompaniment to a series of technically and psychically trying economics exams. Soon she was spontaneously knitting reindeer of her own design along the yokes of ski sweaters as she also mastered that alternate reality known as statistics. Sandra decided to knit again soon after she apprenticed to a shaman and was about to begin therapy to re-examine old issues of abuse. And although Michelle learned to knit when she was about eleven, it was while her mother drove her halfway

across the country to start college, and while one of her grandmothers was dying, that she began to knit with conviction. Not only new knitters take advantage of this special knitting opportunity. Last spring, I suddenly got the urge to teach myself how to knit lace, which I thought would be impossible but turned out to become a great passion. By that moment in my life as a knitter, I knew enough to pay attention to what happened next in the rest of my life. Sure enough, what happened next was that I bought my first house, an experience that I also thought would be either difficult or dull but actually turned out to be neither—rather, it was the beginning of a new passion.

Well, there you go. It's just something about knitting. It has a small, yet commanding voice, and what it tends to say, at times like these, is that it will help take us through the big steps with little steps. And technically, in this case, those little steps are known as stitches. Knitting takes unease and supports it with shawls the way the performers at a big top support a trapeze artist with a net. It underpins transition with a deeper sort of harmony.

We millennial types aren't the first ones to come across this clever ally through the business of rites of passage. As it happens, there is a very ancient tradition that extensively honors this quality of the fiber arts and which identifies that magical, yet practical whisper. It comes from the one called Grandmother Spider. Her tools include her web, and her specialties are creation and emergence—in other words, she presides over the art of finessing that delicate yet utterly essential threshold between one thing and the utterly impossible seeming thing that will somehow, nonetheless, absolutely for sure and no doubt about it, happen next.

Grandmother Spider

No one knows exactly where Grandmother Spider, or Spider Woman, came from. She apparently emerged on our continent with the mysterious Anasazi people, who may have brought her with them across the Bering Strait or from South America. She spread through the Native American societies, where she helped create the people with language, by singing and thinking them into life with

words. (She's certainly the ancestor of E. B. White's Charlotte, who saves Wilbur the Pig's life with words written in a web.) Once the First People are created, she keeps her eye on them from some dark and quiet crevice or other. And then, when they're in a jam, or confused, or dejected, she leads them from those places that are cold and empty and dark to those places which are warm and light and quite wondrously full. She finesses this transition with her magical and practical tool, the web, and her deep knowledge of and reverence for the power and possibilities of matter. In the Navajo tradition, these magical qualities are also ascribed to the spiritual and practical art of weaving, which in turn creates the world and the patterns of the world.

One way Grandmother Spider's power is conveyed is through the tradition of her visual representation. She is never drawn literally. Instead, she is conveyed through words and symbols. These symbols include pictographs, symbolic spiders, and the equal-armed cross that can sometimes be a symbol of emergence from one world to the next.

This tradition teaches that weaving became the provenance of women through an emergency collaboration of sorts between Grandmother Spider and First Woman. In it, the Navajo people put on sets of wings and flew upward to find a hole in the sky of three successive worlds, one after the other, as they outgrew the resources each world had to offer and mastered the lessons which were required of them to be able to pass into the next. Their journey is one of differentiation and discovery. Each successive world has more food, and more light, and more diversity than the last; each world also presents a slightly more difficult access than the previous one. As they leave the first world, they simply fly up and find the hole. Between the second and third, they must follow the wind as it makes a spiral through this awesome aperture.

The sky between the third and fourth worlds becomes so solid and strong that it cannot be penetrated. But just when the First People begin to lose hope, a human being wearing a blue mask peers around the Northernmost, Southernmost, Easternmost, and Westernmost edges of the sky. Then, each of these four humans picks up the edge of the sky he or she holds. This creates just enough space between this prohibitive sky and the next world for the First People to split

up and for some of them to quickly and gratefully slip through the gap at each corner.

Another people from another tribe already live in the fourth world. They teach the First People how to irrigate their own corn in exchange for labor, they become complacent and trusting, and cast aside their winged suits (which are what their original insect wings have become) as they gain more trust in life.

And they do live happily ever after until, one day, somehow inevitably, that universal lord of chaos and unaddressed emotions, known as Water Monster, comes home and discovers that someone has stolen his children.

In the time-honored way of water monsters, he subsequently decides to obliterate the world with his particular je ne sais quoi, which happens to be an enormous, unstoppable flood.

Since the First People no longer have their winged suits, the only way they can head for the sky this time is to abandon their beautiful fertile land and climb the tallest mountain ahead of the waters.

In this they are led by the one called First Woman, who is a member of a council of 32 of the wise.

When the tribes reach the top of this mountain, the water continues to rise. At this point First Woman takes a magical bamboo seed from her pack. Within four days it will make a giant tree. She calls the rest of the council of the wise together and they discover that each of them possesses one of these magical seeds. And so the seeds are planted, and the people chant more sacred magic over them day and night for four days and on the morning of the fourth day these 32 bamboo plants have come together to make a giant, hollow tree 32 joints high and large enough to shelter the entire tribe, with a tiny, peaked room at the top.

The people climb into this room just ahead of the flood. All creatures are represented. Each has brought a gift for the new world in her or his pack. One of these creatures is Grandmother Spider, who now travels with her own children. Her pack carries a skein of very strong silk thread for braiding rope, or weaving blankets.

As the floods begin to rise up the bamboo tree, joint by joint, the people discover that this blue sky has become more impenetrable than ever. It is, in fact, as

hard and implacable as stone. Penetration proves impossible. The birds among them rise up to make a hole, but they can do no more than crack it, because the motion of their wings does not permit stillness. So in their wake the tribe sends up Locust, who can use his wings and poise in stillness at once. Locust makes a tiny, tiny hole in the sky. So the next world has been breached, but it is still inaccessible because no one can enter this microscopic aperture, and, meanwhile, the waters continue to rise.

For the first time, the First People are at a loss. They can see the tiny hole. They can see the raging waters below them. For the moment, they are safe in the tree of their own ingenuity and prayer. But they have no method of eliding the place of their perch with the portal of their liberation.

And that is exactly when a small, quiet, sensible yet commanding voice emerges from a dark crevice in the bamboo tree.

"If I were at that opening," points out Grandmother Spider, who has been waiting silently in the shadows for her turn to speak, "I could spin a strong rope ladder back to the tree and anyone could get across. Then we could go in size order and each of us could make it larger as we go."

As the floodwaters rise joint by joint up the bamboo tower, Grandmother Spider mounts Dragonfly's back and together they ride to the hairline crack of their prospective deliverance. From there, Grandmother Spider spins a thread down to the bamboo tree, where First Woman catches it. Then, as fast as she can, which is fairly fast, and perhaps even faster with First Woman's urging, Grandmother Spider rides up and down her original thread twelve times. Next, she makes another twelve-ply thread just like the first and spins rungs across it, and her weightless web transforms itself into a strong rope ladder which grows from the magical tree to the tiny aerial hole of liberation.

The creatures traveled up the ladder from smallest to largest, each of them enlarging the diameter of the hole for the next largest of their tribe. Finally everyone had gone through but First Woman and First Man.

First Man asked First Woman to go through before him.

"No, you go," she said. "There are some treasures I want to collect first for our tribe."

And so it was that First Woman was the last to go up Grandmother Spider's ladder. As she did, she cut the silken ladder loose from the tree. She went up a few rungs, then wrapped those rungs around her like a silken placenta, and up a few more, and again, and again, until she slid through the hole in the sky.

By the time she reached the Fifth World, she was so wrapped with silk and bundles that the others needed to unwrap her. As they did, the spiderweb ladder that had wrapped First Woman shriveled to its former, tiny dimensions and lay upon the ground. And so all of them were delivered to the Fifth World as if they had traveled together through a birth canal.

"From now on," the people said, in honor of First Woman and Grandmother Spider, "the women shall do the weaving and wear woven things, instead of buckskins."

Also, ever since then, Grandmother Spider has directed the destinies and thoughts of men and women through her kindness, good advice, and tiny, powerful solutions to enormous problems.

There are many things to love about this story. For instance it speaks eloquently of the experience of transcendent faith and human fraternity, in which at some level, we are all climbing up a ladder of faith in the sky, on the way to a portal, each of us making the way easier for the next of us who in turn makes it easier for the next. This doesn't necessarily have anything in particular to do with knitting (although it doesn't exclude it, either). But other aspects have everything to do with knitting. For instance, in this story, the fate of an entire culture literally hangs by a thread, and is saved by a thread. Not only is this a resonant metaphor for faith, but a testament to the power of the small, and the healing potential of patterning. It is, I suspect, part of the magic that still invites women, and men, to pick up yarn and needles at a moment of sacred awkwardness in their lives. It also speaks of the importance of fiber arts to the survival of our species, and how humans used yarn and weaving to overcome a trial, since somewhere near the beginning of history and in climates that were not temperate, those humans who could spin and weave and keep themselves warm were often those humans who survived.

And, of course, First Woman's tribe's ascension can also be related to the very specific awkwardness and excitement of birth. The spidery silk that wraps, envelops, unwraps, and, then, finally resumes normal proportions after First Woman is freed from it has an obvious placental quality, and the confounding portal in the center of each successive sky displays the combined salvation and unpredictable nature of the birth canal. Of course, when we create anything, including a sweater, we give birth in a different way. And then, also, there is the way that First Woman can hang, alone, simply suspended by the silk, and draw herself up it, step by step, at once magically and practically, so like a spider spinning its web through the brush of our world. This also has a lot do with knitting, because, like a knitter instinctively saving every scrap of yarn, First Woman winds the ladder into a neat ball around her, rather than discarding it. She knows that the instrument of her people's transition, however evanescent, is sacred, and that to cast it away would be to cast away an aspect of their own power. Here, also, is the blind faith and courage of doing something new. Not entirely unlike the Fool in the Tarot deck, who jumps off a cliff in complete trust that he will land somewhere new and wonderful, First Woman hoists herself up through the sky with no tether to the only ground she knows. Her trust in Grandmother Spider's thread is absolute.

Just look at any spiderweb. Its efficiency and its seductiveness lie in its near invisibility. That just barely delineated wafer of patterning that shows itself only when the sun blunders through its gossamer orbs and ladders is optimally functional. Not only does the invisibility keep the spider safe while also luring prey, but also the unassuming spider silk is itself brilliantly engineered. Researchers have discovered that webs spun by individual spiders are calibrated with ultraviolet light spectrums, which attract specific insects.[1] Knitting is like that. Very unassuming. Lots of light inside. Tailors itself to the individual knitter, and sustains her.

So, just a few little stitches, easily mastered if you are willing to hang out and be awkward for a few hours or a day or two, will carry you from the world you currently inhabit and into the realm of knitting goddesses. Ask Grandmother Spider, and she might even sit on your shoulder and help. You might consider

going outside, finding a spiderweb, and rubbing it into your hands, as Navajo women do before they begin a rug in order to imbue their hands with her magic and expertise, both born from beholding the nature of exactly what is sitting in front of her. I leave the characteristics of your particular worlds to you.

Before we start to knit, here is my other favorite Grandmother Spider story.

Changing Woman, the Navajo's mysterious divine feminine creator and daughter of darkness and dawn, often wears a turquoise gown. Among other things, she has the ability to make children from herself only, and is deeply connected with the earth and the seasons. She was out walking one day when she discovered Grandmother Spider's home, in a dark hole underground. Grandmother Spider herself was inside, sitting at her loom: the loom's cross poles were made of sky and earth cords. The warp sticks of sun rays; the heralds of rock crystal and sheet lightning. The batten was a sun halo and the comb was made of white shell. The loom had four spindles. One was made out of a stick of zigzag lightning with a spindle whorl made of cannel coal. Another was a stick of flash lightning with a whorl of turquoise; the third spindle was a stick of sheet lightning with a whorl of abalone, and the fourth was a streamer of rain with a white shell whorl.[2]

Changing Woman stayed with Grandmother Spider for four days. During these four days, Grandmother Spider taught her to weave and how to take care of and respect the weaving tools. She also taught her the songs and prayers that must accompany each stage of weaving. Changing Woman brought these sacred skills back to her people. From this, it is said, Navajo weaving began and so much more. This is how Spider Woman taught the Navajo how to physically create form, pattern, structure, and symbolism. Through weaving, the Navajo literally order their world. "The weaving way holds beauty," say the Navajo holy women to the student, "the weaving way holds power."[3]

Somehow or other, Grandmother Spider teaches, when we begin with something small but well chosen we are actually making the momentous magic that will lead us from the familiar darkness of potential and uncertainty to a new and newly ordered reality. The smaller the better, really. The secret of the universe lies in those awkward places, those meek unexamined crevices where the

mother of the world is in her element. You can get there in a lot of different ways, but I submit, a knitting needle is particularly well equipped to do the trick. Besides, when you use it, you end up with something really cool to wear.

So, shall we give it a whirl?

The Basic Basics

If you are a new knitter (if you aren't you might want to go on to Chapter Two) your first assignment will be to learn to make a gauge swatch. To do this you will learn to choose materials, cast on, knit and bind off your stitches.

Choosing Your Materials

Grandmother Spider's magic is that of using exactly the correct substance at exactly the right time, and this is also the secret of knitting. Again, knitting's substances are almost as simple as Grandmother Spider's—materials are yarn, needles and a few accessories. The first step to knitting is choosing them. When you love your yarn and it feels good to your hands, and your needles do, too, knitting is pretty easy. So the first step of knitting consists of finding out what you like. This isn't a luxury. It is absolutely practical. In knitting, learning the magic of substances means learning what is technically appropriate to your project and also what your hands and eyes love. In my opinion, and knitters are opinionated, this is about fifty percent of knitting well and enjoying knitting.

Yarn

We'll start with yarn. Go to the store and purchase one skein of worsted weight yarn (this is a yarn that will work on needles size seven to nine; this will usually be indicated on the packaging). Choose a solid color yarn, or something that is only slightly variegated (changes from color to color along the yarn) or flecked. Solid or almost solid colors allow you to see your stitches the best. Choose a color you love in a medium shade if possible. White or pales will tend to get dirty

while black or any other very dark color makes it hard to see your stitches. For this exercise, choose a single ply yarn (one strand of yarn only). For this sample, I also prefer to use a 100 percent wool yarn, or a blend of wool and another fiber or fibers that is primarily wool. Very important: avoid mohair, boucle, silk, eyelash, or anything else with a halo or uneven texture. Important: take time to touch different yarns, notice how they feel on your hands, and look at their fiber composition (this will be noted on the label). Fiber blends are like gourmet sauces. They mix beautifully and subtly to give you pleasure, and to hold together, and to behave in specific and often different ways when they are made into garments. Which kinds of yarns are soft? Which are rough? Which are shiny, and which are matte, and which have a little halo (fuzz) around them? Which have some bounce and resilience to them, and which seem to hang flat and smooth? Let your hand and your eye naturally begin to learn a bit about this.

Needles

Knitting needles are made out of many different materials, including metal, plastic, horn, resin, bamboo, and different kinds of wood. Each has different characteristics. For instance, metal or plastic coated needles are known by knitters as "fast" needles, great for increasing speed, or for coddling a highly textured yarn. On the other hand, they can also feel cold, and are less flexible than wood or bamboo.

Wood and bamboo needles are warm, more flexible, hold yarn easily, and look beautiful. (Bamboo is slightly faster, more flexible, and less expensive than wood, while wood is very beautiful and may be more durable.) All other things being equal, wood or bamboo needles are the ones you want to start with. Take some time to touch the available needles, and decide which pair and type most pleases you in terms of feel and look. You might even want to hold each type in your hands and see if you can feel the difference between them. Again, sensitizing your hands is good practice and preparation for knitting, where, almost naturally, your hands will gain the attribute of becoming almost psychic, sensing

variations in stitches and fibers and fabric. Over time, this practice teaches you the magic of each substance, and the value of subtle nuances and differences between substances in terms of appropriateness to a task. This applies to needles as well as to yarns. You can choose straight or circular needles.

CROCHET HOOK

A crochet hook in size h or so because it is helpful for picking up dropped stitches.

EMBROIDERY SCISSORS

Nice to have around; not strictly necessary. It's nice to cut your yarn, but usually you can just break it off like a piece of licorice you are sharing with a friend. (Note: I wouldn't try breaking 100 percent silk with my hands, it's too strong. The occasional synthetic yarn, also.)

A GOOD ABSORBENT HAND CREAM

Both wood and wool will absorb the oils from your hands. An absorbent cream won't end up in your yarn.

A BAG TO CARRY AND PROTECT YOUR KNITTING

I like plastic sweater bags from the storage shop or the ones bed linens come in, but the zippers may tear out after a while. Canvas tote bags work too, and they don't tear. Many knitting stores sell tapestry knitting bags. I put a whole project inside, including the photocopied instructions in order to avoid carrying the weight of a book or magazine. A tape measure, small scissor, stitch holders and markers (you won't need these in this chapter) go in a small bag or a side pocket.

Knitting Stores as a Resource

If possible, patronize your local knitting store. Not only will they be able to help you with everything I mentioned above, but local shops also function as official and not-so-official knitting support teams. The employees in all likelihood will steer you in the right direction for materials, help you when you are stuck with a pattern, give you suggestions for changing sizes, special order items, and may even be happy when you come hang out and knit in the shop (a flat table with chairs somewhere on the premises is usually a telltale sign).

The only disadvantage of buying things from small local places is that the stock will probably reflect what delights the owner and this will not necessarily always reflect what delights you. Some places specialize in natural fibers only. Others love novelty yarns and shiny yarns, which often have synthetic content. If there are a few stores in your area, you will probably want to eventually check out all of them. If you can't get what you want locally, try mail order catalogues and the Internet. But for this beginning exercise, if you have a shop in your town, you should have plenty to choose from.

Skein Winding

If your yarn happened to come in a skein (also known as a hank, as opposed to a ball or a center-pull ball of yarn) wind it into a ball. The illustration below shows

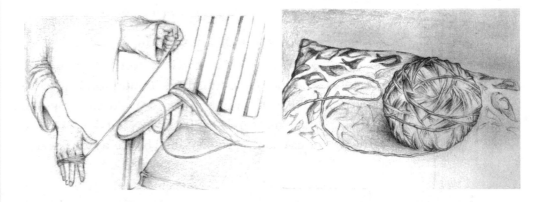

how and uses a chair to keep the yarn even and with strand separated for winding. The chair back is traditional, but not required. You can also use your own knees bent toward your chest, the two hands of another person, or a method of your own devising (I don't really suggest the gearshift of a car unless the car is not running).

Casting On, Knitting, Binding Off

All of knitting consists of three basic steps: the first, called casting on (abbreviated as CO in knitting instructions), creates a row of initial stitches on your needle. Then comes the part where you knit, or make fabric with your needles (the basic knitting stitch is abbreviated as K). Purling (Chapter Two) is close to but not exactly the inverse of knitting and the companion to the basic knit stitch. When you have as much knitted fabric as you need, you bind off your stitches (BO). When you bind off, you remove your stitches from the needle while simultaneously forming a neat bound off edge.

The countless stitch patterns of knitting—ribbed patterns, slip stitch patterns, color block, Fair Isle knitting, cable knitting, and lace knitting, and also the ones that shape the size of what you are knitting into sweaters and sleeves—are all variations on these three simple elements. Get these down, which won't take long, and then practice them until they feel very familiar to your body, and you will be able to pick up almost anything.

Casting On

First, put the label for your yarn in a safe place if you haven't already. It contains important information such as the color number, dye lot number, and gauge (number of stitches per inch on a particular size of needle), all of which you may need later. Attach a small piece of the yarn to the label (tie or staple it) for reference. If you run out of yarn during a project, having the label and a sample handy will help you to get more.

Second, get to know your needles and hands. For casting on, knitting,

purling, and binding off right and left hand illustrations are provided. After that, we lefties are on our own (we're cagey enough to transpose once we get the basics down). Put a needle in each hand. The one in your dominant hand is your working needle. In most cases, you will use this needle to make a new row of stitches out of the ones on the other needle. In the process, you will move those stitches off of that needle and onto this one. This needle starts out empty and ends up full.

The needle in your non-dominant hand is your non–working needle. In most cases, this needle starts out full at the beginning of a row and ends up empty. Then you switch hands and put a full, non–working needle into this hand and put the newly empty working needle into your other, dominant hand.

Just to complicate matters, casting on uses only one needle. Here, your hands do the work of the working needle as they create an initial row of stitches and also a non–working needle. When you are finished casting on, you will have a full non–working needle ready to go.

Follow the pictures for whichever hand is your dominant hand.

1 Measure off about 15 inches of yarn (this can be approximate—the general rule of thumb is that one inch of yarn equals one finished cast on stitch). Make a slip knot at the inner end of the 15 inches (i.e., 15 inches in from the end of the yarn, toward the middle of the skein, and

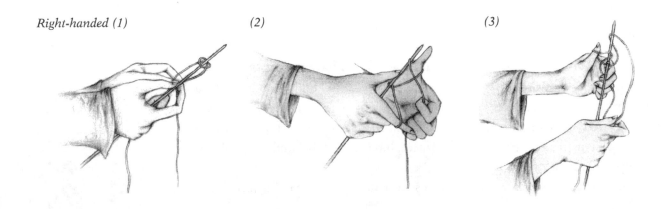

Right-handed (1)   *(2)*   *(3)*

not at the cut off end of the yarn). Slip this knot over one of your knitting needles. If you need to, adjust it so it holds the needle but moves back and forth along it, neither too loose to grip nor too tight to move.

Congratulations. This is your first stitch.

2 Now, you are going to use both your hands, one of your needles, and that first stitch to create a row of 15 stitches on your needle.

Basically, you are going to set up half a stitch, in the form of open loops or half figure eights on the fingers of each hand, and join them with each other in closed, complete single stitches on the needle.

I mention this because casting on is kind of conceptual. When you knit, it looks like you're knitting—little stitches line up on your needles, and even when you make a mistake (everyone does) you can tell what and where it is and what to do about it quite easily because what you're doing is usually regular and, dare I say it, logical. But casting on requires a leap of faith—it's much more right brained and doesn't look like much of anything except itself, or an odd rendition of a butterfly's wings, until the stitches are done. So a conceptual overview of what you are actually doing is helpful. However, once you learn casting on, it feels completely second nature, like something your hands have always known how to do.

(4)

(5)

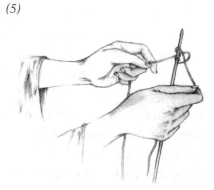

(6)

Left-handed (1)   (2)   (3)

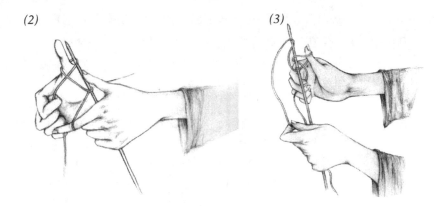

Now, hold the needle in your dominant hand and with your last two or three fingers and with your thumb, or in any combination that will allow you to simultaneously hold the needle and keep the index finger on that hand available. (Note: there is lots of fingering to casting on, like playing a flute or a piano . . . but unlike the flute or the piano, you can adjust the fingering to suit your hands. The result is what counts.) Once you are holding the needle in this way, place your index finger under the yarn that is coming from the ball of yarn so the yarn just runs over it *without* twisting the yarn into any kind of loop.

Hold the very (short) end of the yarn in your other hand, under the last three fingers. On this hand, loop the yarn around your thumb so that when you open that hand palm up, the yarn makes a half figure eight. In other words, once you are holding the yarn end taut with your last three fingers, reach your thumb over the TOP of the yarn (this will be the bit of yarn that is lying between the needle you are holding in your other hand and the thumb in question) and then twist your wrist outward so the palm of that hand is facing upwards. When casting on doesn't work, it's often because a new knitter has put her thumb under the yarn instead of on top of it. If you hold the needle down below the thumb of the non–working hand at its base, you will have a half figure eight. If you move the needle up toward the end of

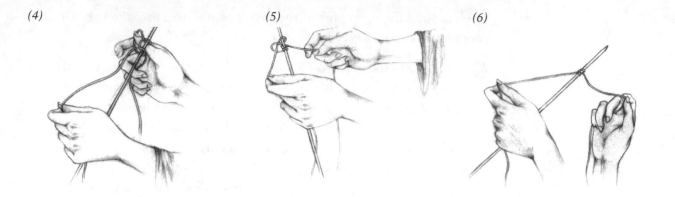

this thumb, you will have an open loop (i.e., a sideways "u" shape). Try it and see what you've got. Then, get used to this position.

Next, dip the needle into the front of the loop on your thumb. Insert the needle into the front of the loop underneath the yarn, and aim the needle toward the back of the loop. Once the needle is inside the loop, line it up with your thumb on the inside edge of your thumb (the edge that faces your palm). Illustration 2 shows finished position.

3 Once the needle is inside the loop and lined up with your thumb, use the index finger of the hand that is holding the needle (i.e., your dominant hand) to loop *its* yarn (i.e., the yarn that is coming from the ball) around the body of the needle from back to front. You now have two loops around your needle: the more closed, bottom loop that is held by the thumb of your non-dominant hand and the more open, top one that you are holding in place with the fingers of your dominant hand.

4 Next, using the thumb of the non–dominant hand that is still inside the loop of yarn, flip its loop of yarn over the top of the needle and then slide the loop off the thumb, letting it rest around the needle. The second open loop you were holding in your dominant hand will

catch around the open part of the first loop and together the two will cooperate to make a very loose stitch.

⑤ Gently pull the yarn you are holding in each hand to tighten this stitch around the needle. But don't make it too tight. It is always advisable to cast on loosely in order not to pull the bottom edge of your garment. Also, don't worry too much about the exact shape the yarn makes as it goes over the needle. Your hands will turn at their own unique angles to make this loop, which won't necessarily be the angles you see here. Casting on is a flow. If your finished stitch looks like the final illustration, you're fine.

⑥ Repeat 15 times to get 15 stitches. There will be 16 in all, including the slip knot that counts as your first stitch. See knit stitch illustrations for a row of 16 cast-on stitches.

Remember: front to back under the yarn, back to front around the needle, over, off, pull.

Try it a couple of times. If you end up with funny pieces of yarn stretching over your stitches in a mystifying zigzag fashion, just unravel them and try again. In this case, check or pay attention to the direction in which you are winding the yarn around the needle and the direction in which you are dipping the working needle into the loop. Just mess around with it, break each step down slowly, and you'll get it.

Note: At any point in this process, if you need some inspiration and have the opportunity, consider finding that spiderweb and rubbing it into your hands. Navajo women would also rub some pollen into their hands, and say a prayer to Grandmother Spider, and that way they knew her spirit was with them and she was helping them with their weaving.

Once you have the feel for this, try these refinements:

1 If you haven't already, keep practicing until you can make your cast on stitches even in tension (i.e., same size, spacing, and relative tightness or looseness around the needle). Once your tension has evened, if it hasn't already, play with keeping your stitches both even and loose.

2 Cast on your stitches over two needles instead of one. (Again, it is handy to cast on your stitches loosely so they don't pull on the bottom of your fabric and when you cast on over two needles instead of one you do this naturally.)

In knitting patterns, casting on is abbreviated as CO.

KNITTING

Now you're ready to knit. All of knitting is composed of two stitches—knitting and purling, which are nothing but mirror images of each other. In this chapter you will learn knitting.

To knit:

1 Hold the needle with the 16 cast-on stitches in your non-dominant hand. Hold the empty needle, and the yarn from your ball of yarn, in your dominant hand. Run the yarn from your ball (not the end of the yarn) through the fingers of your dominant hand in whatever way allows you to comfortably hook that yarn over your index finger and manipulate it. You might want to run it over your third finger also, or your fourth finger. Whatever works. Keeping the yarn from the skein behind the needle, put the empty needle through the first cast on stitch, dipping the needle into the stitch from under the front of the loop and pointing the needle from front to back.

2 Remembering to keep the yarn behind the needle, wrap the yarn from the ball around the point of the needle in your dominant hand

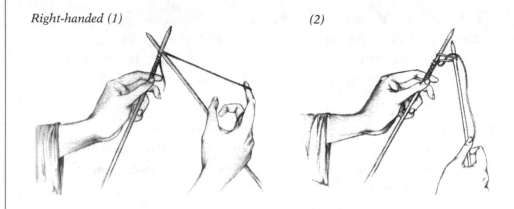

(the empty one) from back to front. The yarn will rest between the two needles and the loose strand of working yarn will end up pointing back toward your dominant side, where it came from. Again, do not worry about exactly where the yarn falls. Focus on the direction of the loop and the place you want the yarn to rest when you are finished, i.e., between the two needles, and loosely falling back toward the ball of yarn.

3 Use the empty working needle to pull the wrapped yarn through the first (top) cast on stitch on your needle, by bringing the working

Left-handed (1)   *(2)*

(3a) 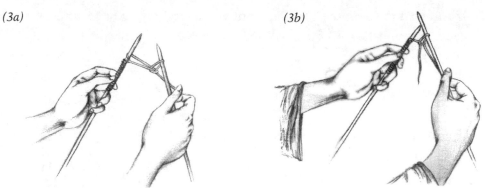 *(3b)*

needle down, under, and up in front of the other needle, catching the strand of wrapped yarn between the needles in the process and slipping the loop formed by the old cast-on stitch off of the non–working needle as the newly formed stitch tightens around the working needle. You have now knit 1 stitch.

Repeat these steps until your working hand needle holds 16 stitches and the needle in your other hand is empty of stitches.

Congratulations. You have finished your first row of knitting.

(3a) 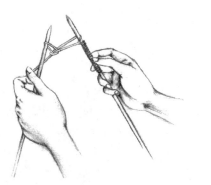 *(3b)*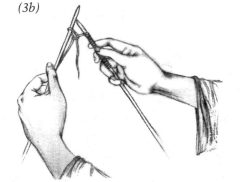

Repeat this 15 times, that is, until you have 16 rows of 16 stitches each. The finished product will look something like the illustration below:

If some of your stitches don't look like knit stitches, just pull them out and start again, being very careful to pay attention to the instructions, particularly the parts about where the working needle goes and what part of the loop it goes through (in back of the other needle) and where the yarn goes (in back of the needle). Just tinker with it, stitch by stitch, until it looks right. Then keep going. It's just fiber. You can't hurt it. Also, if you are having trouble making stitches and you are using a multiple ply or thick and thin yarn, consider trying a single ply yarn for this exercise. (Trying to learn on bumpy, sexy yarn is often the source of knit stitch learning challenges. Please, please eschew them for the moment. Don't worry, the next project is full of bumpy, sexy yarns. If this is what you like, the sacrifice is quite temporary.)

This swatch is a sample of garter stitch—a fabric made of rows of knit stitch exclusively. Garter stitch doesn't curl, makes a flat background that highlights textures and colors, and is often used as the background or foundation stitch for lace or cable patterns. Because the projects in this book are oriented toward enjoying textures and colors, there is a lot of garter stitch in this book.

This is probably a good time to talk about irregularity. The Navajo honor a quality called *hozho*, which was brought to the world by Coyote. *Hozho* is an aesthetic and inner balance that allows for the organic physical variations and flow of the natural world and specifically perfect, artificial symmetry. A Navajo rug with *hozho* will contain a beautifully balanced diamond pattern made of crosses, but perhaps each or some of the crosses will be woven intentionally in sizes that register as just barely different from each other, so they ripple across to the human eye, not unlike a flock of migrating birds. A brick wall with *hozho* will have a flow of composition and smoothness, but many of the bricks will be

slightly different in size and shape. Over time, your stitches will probably even out, like the rate of return on your stock portfolio. But, in the meantime, treasure *hozho*; because once your stitches do even out you will probably choose slightly irregular yarns to keep that look in your work. Also keep in mind Navajo women always put a tiny hole or other small irregularity into their carpets in honor of Grandmother Spider and the void she came from, and also to remind us that only the divine, whatever our personal experience of the divine may be (and whatever we may each choose to call it), is perfect.

In knitting patterns, knit is abbreviated as K.

Fixing Dropped Stitches

While you knit you may drop a stitch. You'll know because there will be extra bars (the piece of yarn that runs horizontally between stitches) between two stitches and fewer stitches on the needle than there were on the last row. Fixing a dropped stitch is easy. Just follow the illustration to your right with your crochet hook (or your finger). Put the dropped stitch in front of the bar and hook the bar through the loop 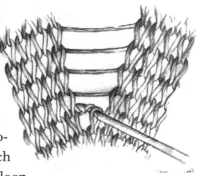 of the stitch from back to front, making a new stitch. If you dropped the stitch more than one row back you can just keep on doing this all the way up to your needle as long as the stitch pattern is regular.

Binding Off

Binding off finishes an edge and gets the piece off the needles. Sometimes an edge is finished all at once, straight across, in a single edge. Other times, with a shawl or sleeve, you'll shape an edge by binding off a specific number of stitches, which will be indicated in the instructions.

To bind off:

1 Knit two stitches onto your working needle.

2 Pass the first stitch (the one on the bottom) over the second stitch, and then off of the needle. One stitch remains on the needle.

3 Knit the next stitch and repeat Step 2.

4 Keep going until 15 stitches are bound off, one stitch remains on the needle in your dominant hand, and the other needle is empty. Cut or break off your yarn and pull it through that remaining stitch. Now you're done.

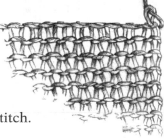

In knitting patterns, binding off is abbreviated as BO.

Congratulations. You have just made a sample or gauge swatch. Your swatch is in garter stitch. Any knitting pattern will begin with these words, make a sample swatch . . . and following will be a bit of the pattern. Then it will say, usually in large, alarmed capital letters, ALWAYS TAKE TIME TO TEST YOUR GAUGE. Gauge is the rate and size at which you yourself, with your own personal two hands, uniquely knit on one particular pair of needles. Your gauge will determine the final size of your fabric in that particular needle size, irrespective of what the directions might promise (they are based on someone else's gauge, which may or may not exactly reflect yours). Everyone knits a little differently, just like everyone speaks a little differently. A gauge swatch will let you know what your stitch gauge is (i.e., how many stitches you knit to an inch in the stitch pattern given, in this case garter stitch or knit every row) and what your row

gauge is (i.e., how many rows you knit to an inch in the stitch pattern given, again garter stitch here). This is what allows you to match your dimensions to the dimensions to the pattern and come up with something the same size. It almost always takes more time to test your gauge than you think you have to spare but doing so is very important, and could save you lots more time later. If you are knitting a project where dimensions are important (i.e., if you want the sleeves of your sweater to be 18 inches long), you need to establish your gauge and match it to the pattern's gauge and figure out where your knitting is at in size compared to the knitting of the person who wrote the pattern. Then you adjust accordingly, trading in your needles for one or two sizes up or down if needed.

So, now, just for fun, measure your swatch and see how it compares to the gauge specifications on the label of your yarn. (Remember, always keep the label that comes on your yarn.) Yarn labels will usually give you stitch gauges on a given size of needle. Sometimes these will come in the form of a square graph, representing number of stitches, with dimensions. Other times there will be a number such as, four stitches equals one inch (this is a very standard gauge) on a specific size of needles. The needles will usually be indicated in American or metric (mm) sizes, which are standard and easily converted to American sizes. You might have to multiply or subtract stitches, if the gauge dimensions are not the same as the one we have done (16 stitches × 16 rows) to get your ideal gauge. Then, again, you might not. If your gauge is much larger or smaller than the standard one given, you might want to get a pair of needles in a larger or smaller size, try again, and see what happens. Just to get into the habit. Make sure to use fractions of an inch in your measurements—4.25 stitches per inch is not the same as 4 even. Measure length from cast on edge to the bottom of the needle for row gauge. Flatten your work for stitch gauge but don't stretch it unless directed to. (A ribbed gauge swatch will sometimes be stretched.)

Left-handed

Keep in mind that as you learn to knit and become comfortable with knitting, your gauge may very well change. Also, if your life changes, your gauge may also change (see Chapter Three for more about this). Always check your gauge.

It bears mentioning that the common commercial pattern gauge ratio, 4"×4", or four stitches to an inch, and four rows to an inch, just happens to be a bit of Grandmother Spider's number. Grandmother Spider always says things four times when she is doing her magic in order to make them real. So do her people when they are doing sacred ceremonies and offering prayer. The first people ascended through four worlds before they entered their ultimate, fifth world, and 32 magic bamboo seeds, a multiple of 4, were planted. An arachnid has eight legs, four on either side.

In this tradition, four is the number of making visions reality. It delights me that in knitting, four by four is so often the magic number for determining the reality of your pattern—the grid that will provide the key to transforming inspiration into a viable knitted reality. Regardless of the particulars of our individual cultural heritage, Grandmother Spider's wisdom still runs naturally through our hearts, and through our hands.

----

[1]Sue Hubbell, *Waiting for Aphrodite* (Houghton Mifflin: New York 1999), 155.
[2]Noel Bennett, *Halo of the Sun* (Northland: Flagstaff 1987).
[3]Bennett, p. 31

Isis, Red Magic, and a Warm Stole With Wings

Isis, the great alchemist and mother goddess of ancient Egypt, appeared to me, in my imagination, wings outspread, two days before I said yes to the two wooden needles and the skein of red yarn. I had no particular interest in her at the time. But there she was, unmistakably kneeling and flying, at once, high over my head and in my mind's eye while I was focusing on something else entirely. The famous, widespread, and entirely recognizable wings were golden and white, almost puffy. They bore no hint of the brilliant, multicolored, sleek avian rainbow with which they are often rendered. The great initiator appeared to be almost playful, joyful, practically maiden-like and not at all in the grip of the unusual personal circumstances that first inspired her to unfurl her great wings (more on those in a minute). She hovered like a weather vane above me for an instant, and then she was gone. The gift of Isis' wings is resurrection. But it was only much later when I could see that she had arrived to usher me across the threshold of a new world.

At that point, as I have mentioned, I had become the proud owner of a tantalizingly empty life. Many of the different threads of experience that had once filled my time had been cut free, leaving newly emptied space. I was no longer a wife or lover after having been one for almost all of my adult life. My material needs, not enormous, were accounted for. I had settled in a new area of the country. I had stopped writing for a while. The conditions were perfect for my inner life to take center stage and for me to cultivate some true stillness.

I lived life simply and also deeply, welcomed surprises and quirks, spent

time with friends and in nature, spent quite a bit more time than usual in meditation and taught myself lots of new things. My day-to-day experience was precious, vital, fresh, fertile.

And it was also challenging. The challenges were also multi-threaded. But the changes that had occurred in my life undermined some of my most significant relationships. This was one of the threads. But one important one was that the possibility that the love I gave was flawed. The reasons that relationships dissolve are complex. How it felt to me was that, over time, as I myself matured from a maiden into a mother (a mother being, in the universal idiom of the trinity of maiden, mother, and crone, a woman who is fully actualizing her creativity in whatever capacity), the gifts I discovered were mine to offer, which had to do with increased creativity, the strength of stillness, and with leadership, would not be gifts that could nurture the relationships I had chosen to undertake. It would be nice if all relationships could weather all new discoveries, but not all of them can or should. I had entered one, and then, much later, another, relationship in a mistier, less defined state, which maidens often do. But as I almost involuntarily perceived and surrendered to my own distinctive abilities, it became clear that one by-product of such discovery would be deep change.

Days and months flowed by in stillness. Time was punctuated by the flow of feelings, the inevitable surrender to grief, the growing silence in the center of the mind, the breathtaking magic of natural seasonal change, and the good humor of friends. Slowly, I came to feel as connected to the world at large as I had to any lover. The details of everyday life, from smallest to largest, responded to my thoughts and feelings with the same quickness, intensity, and gentleness and gave me a similar feeling of intimacy and being cared for, and that I was caring for it in return. Perhaps more so.

And then, on that beautiful spring day, Isis quickly showed me her wings.

At that particular moment, I had happened to come to the point in that exquisite period where I had also noticed that part of me was missing and I was entertaining the notion of beginning to look for it. Shamanic traditions often call that something a piece of the soul. Therapists sometimes call it the lost child. Extracting it can require both ingenuity and gentleness.

From my perspective, it was a feeling of not having a firm foundation: of not quite being here or being able to easily expedite all the details of everyday life. Driving took effort. Setting boundaries took effort. Knowing what I wanted took effort. Asking for it took even more. It was clear that I had to retrieve whatever it was that would allow me to do these things and to require less effort of myself in order to go on to the next phase of life, whatever that might turn out to be. These experiences had been intensified by the other kinds of change, but were pre-existing: they had, in fact, been one of the first signs of this period of transformation.

By then, I was knitting. As I knit, my mind quieted and in my industrious solitude (knitting can create either community or solitude; it's entirely up to you, in my opinion, the most delicious version being when it creates both at the same time) I first asked, and then answered, some of my own deepest questions. Parts of the past were released, and others were rediscovered and tied together with the present like two pieces of beautiful yarn. A bit of one or two of the mysteries of the universe were also clarified (but that's another story). Without the need to pace myself against an external world and significant relationships, I started to heal and integrate very deeply and quickly and at my own pace, which I am told was often rapid, but felt glacial at best to me.

I began to wake up from unfinished sleeping dreams to find their next installments in what was clearly the waking dream of the day. One night I found myself in a small room picking out a shamanic rattle from a collection of them that was being overseen by an old woman. I wasn't able to finish choosing, but I remembered one rattle with very distinctive, odd cool earth tones I could not describe. I woke up and wrote this down. On a whim, I stopped by a mineral shop I had never gone to before on my way to buy tapestry needles (I needed to sew up a sweater). There, spread out over the diameter of a small black velvet circle, were beads in almost exactly the colors I had seen, but never seen before, and which were made from a not widely known but inexpensive mineral. It was as if the sacred gift that was the rattle had been bestowed to me physically, but in a different form.

Day and night continued to weave together in a figure eight sort of harmony that gave me answers to my deepest questions and insights about myself and my world that first challenged, and then instructed me. My fears manifested and were dispensed with equal, if not greater, ease as my desires. For instance, at the time, one of my greatest aversions was running into my former lover in the company of a new lover. A classic aversion that really shouldn't bite, but often still does, no matter how marvelously we might be otherwise feeling at the time. For a while, as soon as I discussed this fear with my guide (because through this period I had several—a main guide and several others), this precise event would occur with remarkable efficiency. I never came across the fellow under any other circumstances. Soon it didn't matter anymore, and I didn't see him anymore.

It became apparent that as I knitted yarn, I was also naturally knitting myself together and also nurturing myself with one of the most appropriate metaphors, and also physical realities, that I could have chosen for myself. I was not only knitting together a garment, but also the seen and the unseen, the solid and the evanescent, the conscious and the unconscious and light and dark in myself.

And by then I was knitting red.

I had started knitting with a white sweater shot through with pink and turquoise and gold.

"You witch," said the woman who cut my hair, quite affectionately, when she saw the thing. (She grew up in the French Quarter of New Orleans, where long departed relatives came to her room at night and gave her good advice.) She was referring to the touch of glitter, which is so beloved of the fairy kingdom.

The white and turquoise and gold were wonderful. I had bought a museum note card with a picture of Isis and Queen Nefertari on it, which had similar colors. I set up a little altar wherever I was (I traveled once in a while) and added two candles, a number of candles which Isis likes, and also a little water, and a flower, and a rock, and a flame, a combination which all altars are partial to. You can also add a little bit of your favorite spiritual text (a book is

fine) or incense, if you want. The objects had added themselves one after the next: very simple, very small, very spontaneous. But the combination was aesthetically pleasing, and I liked the way that, wherever I was knitting, I could peripherally see the little Isis setup and how its colors agreed with the colors I was knitting.

But then earth tones caught my attention (particularly a warm red shot through with brown). I combined it with more gold, and was thrilled with the way the earth and sky seemed to combine in the weaving. The red yarn became my lifeline. It focused me when I felt lost, made me pay attention when I was tempted to drift off into the blissful but sometimes disconnected space I had inhabited before I started to retrieve myself, and encouraged me when I felt listless or apathetic.

More than anything else, it was perfectly consistent and reliable. Whenever I didn't know what to do next in this wonderful yet exacting world into which I had stumbled, I knit red. And it showed me my next step.

Red thread is a gift from Isis.

Long ago, four children of the night sky came to live on the banks of the Nile. Their names were Isis, Osiris, Nepthys, and Set. Isis and Osiris were given the north side of the Nile to farm. Nepthys and Set were given the land south of the river.

Isis wove and Osiris made the earth swell with corn. Soon, in the all encompassing yet intimate way a rain cloud nurtures a parched garden, they became the nurturers of the Nile people. They also loved each other passionately.

Isis had the ability to be almost everywhere at once. She protected children and also seafarers, since part of her power came from the magnetic silvery flow of the moon. The fertile beauty who slept every night spooned against the flanks of the green god was also more than happy to fulfill well considered prayers for erotic love. And she still is.

Isis also quickly became the preeminent healer of her people. A great alchemist, she knew words of healing which were unknown to anyone else and which were said to have been taught to her directly by the great scribe and

alchemist Thoth. She became known as Great of Magic, and around the Nile centers of healing blossomed under her patronage.

As time passed she also became in many ways preeminent among gods. And when her people drew or sculpted her likeness, they began to place a golden geometric throne on the top of her head. She became a spiritual monarch of her people.

Beneath the veils, the people could glimpse a brilliant red sash that curled around her hips like the Nile in flood. The sash was said to be a clue to a deeper source of Isis' bountiful powers. So were the horns of the moon that she often wore on her head when she put aside her heavy throne crown. So was the serpent crown, the Iraeus, which was particular to pharaohs. And so was the ankh, the symbol of life that looked like a cross with a loop at the top, which she often carried in one hand.

Soon, women were dancing in praise of Isis, veiling themselves and circling hips in figure eight shapes that echoed the tie that was used to fasten skeins of Isis' fine linen yarn and also celebrated the movement of the feminine. The women also framed their hips in bright sashes like Isis', celebrating the sacred gift of fertility. Their veils were the white linen that was sacred to her, and represented, among other things, the many veils of experience and perception that lay between the seeker and the truth. These veils mystified, but they could also be lifted to clarify mysteries of the soul. The bright sashes they wore echoed the string skirt, usually first made in red, that is the first known woven garment to have been created by humans, and which was worn in cultures throughout ancient Europe and the Mediterranean to advertise a woman's fertility.[1] Isis gave it a slightly different meaning: "At the ends of the universe is a blood red cord that ties life to death, man to woman, will to destiny. Let the knot of that red sash, which cradles the hips of the goddess, bind in me the ends of life and dream. . . . Red magic courses through me like the blood of Isis."[2] This is part of a prayer from *The Egyptian Book of the Dead*.

Their dance said, among other things, that if they looked through each of her gifts and creations as if they were as insubstantial and melting as her veils,

they would at last find the sacred mystery that lay beneath. I'm not going to tell you what the mystery is. I'm not sure I know, or that it is knowable. But I know I began to discover it as I lifted the veils of my own life, and of what is often called the soul, but also has other names. And if you start to do that in your mind's eye, or as you knit, you'll solve your own bit of it, too. As we'll see in a minute, red cord or red magic is your great ally on that journey.

In Osiris, the coolness of stars and the life force of green things merged in a force that was both ardent and soothing. His presence slaked longing the way thirst is slaked by water. In part, Isis could love, heal, and protect so vastly because she herself could love, and was loved, so deeply. If Isis was the source of solutions, Osiris was, in one way or another, the solution everyone was looking for.

And Osiris answered Isis all along her dusky velvet skin and deep within her heart and loins. These two desired and respected each other, it is said, more faithfully and ardently than any other two divine beings have loved each other in any other pantheon in any other time.

Set was the god of thunder, heat, and craft. Without Set, there would be nothing sharp, no clarity, no heat, and no wit to make the art that shows us the face of the past. But none of these gifts produced water. The more parched Set became, the more closely he watched the progression of the kingdom of Osiris. And the more closely he watched it, the more deeply he desired his brother's moist, cool brilliance and easy love.

For a while Set simply sent thunder across the river to remind everyone of his existence and drank the blood of animals to slake his thirst, because he was also a hunter. But finally Set's longing to dispose of Osiris' gifts as well as his own became intolerable. It did not occur to Set to ask Osiris for some water or the means to access it. The only method he could come up with to satisfy his desire was to murder his brother.

Set built a beautiful golden coffin inlaid with malachite and turquoise. Then he perfumed his hair, lined his eyes, and went to visit his brother. He invited Osiris to admire his beautiful golden box by lying inside it to see how it would feel.

Once Osiris was inside, Set shut the coffin, and Osiris quickly suffocated.

Set threw Osiris' body into the Nile, where it was torn into 14 pieces by a crocodile.

When Isis heard of her husband's execution, she set out alone and weeping in her queenly garb to the chaotic papyrus swamps that bordered the Nile, where she wandered in search of every dismembered morsel of her beloved.

In the intolerable heat of the midday and in the sticky ooze of evenings, she wept and groped under rocks, in sand, waded through muck, and rooted among the hard and recalcitrant roots of tamarisks and reeds, as she first searched out, and then discovered, the resting places of Osiris' elongated head, his two familiar brown arms, the ripped segments of his arched torso, his strong hands, each of the long, muscled thighs that pressed against her every night, the backs of his knees and his legs, and each of his strong farmer's feet.

She did not desist until she had uncovered every piece of him except for the phallus, which had vanished.

Knowing Isis as he did, Set had fed Osiris' phallus to the crocodile to ensure that whatever healing powers Isis might have, Osiris could never again become whole.

When she saw the irreparable damage, Isis steeled herself, summoned a golden phallus from the depths of creation, and reassembled the rest of him around it.

She then bent over him, and, hiding between the long ropes of her hair she gave him a second potent life.

No one knows exactly how she did this. One version of the myth says the tears she shed on his inert body were life giving. Another says that she uttered magical words of love and power taught to her by the god Thoth.

But what is certain is that his heart began to beat, his eyes opened, and the two spent the next five days making love.

Then Osiris returned to the stars, where he became the god of the land of the dead, helping others to make the same journey that he had made, with the help of his beloved wife, into the place of light.

As Osiris died for the second time Isis stripped to the waist and also

revealed the set of great, bright, multicolored wings that always hovered invisibly around her arms. The wings were brilliant. Each row of feathers was different in color than the row before, yet all blended into a tapestry of indescribable richness. And when the wings were unfurled, whether it was day or night, every single row of feathers also shone with the light of a bright and distant sun. With these great wings, Isis spotted Osiris as he made his journey back to the stars and, from a distance, she wafted air into his lungs in that airless place so he would have the breath to make the journey.

Back on Earth, she folded these into invisibility once again. And soon she gave birth to golden Horus, who had the head of a hawk, the ability to fly, and who could also speak to his father in the land to which he had flown. And in this way Osiris lived on.

Osiris and Isis live in each of us. They represent two aspects of the soul. Osiris is the part of us that asks to be integrated, healed, and retrieved. In Osiris lies limitless potential and the answer to all prayers. Isis, meanwhile, is the aspect of each of us that is the timeless creator and healer. The Isis in us innately knows how to bring the beloved Osiris back to life.

Helpful tools for this are hidden in Isis' costumes. As the story shows us, while Isis' white veils hint at the vastness of power and bliss that we can access, her red sash gives us a literal handle on how to bring this potential into the world. All we have to do is pull.

One morning, while I was knitting myself and my red sweater together, I slipped all the way through the dream state to that place called a vision. People often have visions and call them dreams. Visions often happen in the early morning hours, after you have woken up and felt your body vibrate with the velvety, starry, and Osirian winds of the night. A vision can feel like a dream, but it's different. It's often more vivid, and it can be harder to adjust to the waking world afterward, although not always. If you will permit me to change idioms just for a moment, it is as though you put a billiard in the corner pocket with a hole in one that rolled right across the broad green feltiness of dream and landed in another precise and precisely bordered precinct entirely. And as if

once you arrived in that place you felt the porcelain of your soul reverberate with futility against the close embrace of the leather that held it where it was. The slide from dream into vision is not always dramatic, but it is distinctive, and somewhat final. Once you are there, resistance is entirely futile. You just have the vision.

In this case I found myself in ancient Egypt. Neighbors of mine came to get me wherever I was, because an emergency was occurring. In my absence, my partner there, who had been a partner in this lifetime, had kidnapped and taken a five-year-old consort, a tiny priestess. He had locked the two of them up in our bedroom. I ran to the temple house where this was occurring. I ran up the stairs and pounded on the door and demanded that he open it and give her up, that this was a sin he was committing against himself, and her, and me, and God.

He opened up the door a crack and snarled at me.

"Her parents gave her to me," he said. "And it has been sanctioned by the temple." He then slammed the door again. I stood in the hallway of that place and caught my breath. Because a tiny, beautiful, elongated, kohl-eyed child had stood to his left. She looked both inhuman and human, impossibly mature and totally innocent, all of which she was.

I came back to this world dumbfounded.

When I related this to the guide I was working with at the time her reaction was unexpected. Truth be told, she nodded her head, said little, and actually looked vaguely exasperated.

It took a few weeks to figure out that she was trying to tell me that the tiny priestess consort was the lost part of me I had been looking for. The child; the soul; the effort it took to be living in a body on the planet. I had left her with this guy (truth be told, as far as I can tell, it is true that he loved me as a priestess and as a child but not as a woman, not particularly). And now I needed her back.

She had only been in my peripheral vision, like the tiny altar to Isis, as I knocked on the bedroom door. But she was actually the point.

Soon, she was home.

. . .

Of course, Isis protects mortal children. And first she had showed me, and then she had helped retrieve, the tiny priestess. Isis had shown herself to me before I even knew that this was a development that my future held. She made herself available, and showed me the way to the knitting store, not only to find the little priestess but also for the purpose of resurrection. And as I mastered the physical process of knitting, I re-mastered the physical experience of being in the world, and recalibrated the experience of giving and receiving love. Some might say, with a vengeance.

The story of Isis and Osiris is another metaphor for the process known as soul retrieval. Each of Osiris' limbs are a part of the self that are woven together—notice I said woven, as in knitted—by Isis' healing and alchemical power.

RED THREAD

Red thread or yarn—physical, literal, red yarn, and it has to be red—helps to retrieve souls, and memories, and energy. With help of her red sash, held out like a lifeline from the beginning of time and weaving it together down into the present, I had instinctively woven together my own dismembered parts and given chaos the inevitable, yet still always miraculous ending of wholeness. So does everyone else who does this fairly universal, if messy, sort of work.

Did Isis use her red thread of life to reconstitute Osiris the way a surgeon reattaches a limb? The possibility is tantalizing. But I do know that red thread was a great ally of mine. In a simple, graceful, and very real way, with the help of red yarn and stillness, I was reborn.

Since I discovered Isis, I have gained an appreciation for the feel of linen against the skin. When the soul gets hot, linen cools and soothes. But beautiful red fibers are what thrill my heart. I collect them just a little, for my own benefit and for that of others. For instance, I have a small brilliant red Tulu rug woven by a Turkish woman for her kingly husband. Tulus look like shags made with the

raw, luminescent, and brilliantly dyed fleece of their sheep (this is prize fleece from their hindquarters which becomes chemically altered over the course of a growing season to become softer and more receptive to brilliant dyestuffs). This rug is made out of wool dyed brilliant red and shagged like a fleece. I like to take it with me when I teach to demonstrate the power of red. The nomadic tribal leaders would sit upon these rugs as a demonstration of ease and power, and although they are not all red by a long shot, sitting on mine gives me a special feeling of vibrancy and grace.

Isis' red sash also celebrates an even more vast human instinct. Many ancient Mediterranean and European populations chose red or reddish brown as the color to dye their new yarns and threads once they developed the first dyeing skills and techniques.[3] Like Isis, and like me, and like many others, they chose the red thread to hoist themselves from one level of creative mastery to the next. In this case they achieved the level of mastery in which the fiber that sheltered them from exposure began to gain the beauty and visual richness that also would nurture the eyes and the soul and become the basis for art and also to enrich the appeal of garments that celebrated fertility.

Red thread or yarn is a tremendous ally for those women who are in transition, finding lost pieces, giving any kind of birth, or needing protection of any kind. Working with or wearing something made of red yarn, preferably hand spun or dyed, and, if at all possible, worked by one's own hands, is a tremendous ally when moving from one level to the next. I often suggest this little trick to women. Generally, no sooner than I am done, they are out the door spinning red yarn, knitting it, just plain buying it, and coming up with uses I myself never dreamed of. It's been worn low on the hips to retrieve and heal experiences of abuse, sent to another city to help a good friend out of a bad relationship. The darn stuff has a life of its own. Handspun silk holds particularly good properties, but any fiber works just fine. I suggest you always keep a special bag of red yarn in your stash. You never know when, or how, it might come in handy.

Red yarn does not only retrieve lost things, it also makes new ones. Isis' epithet is Great of Magic, and part of her magic also flows from that red thread moment— the moment when intention first becomes physical in the world with all the absolute joy that color holds. Great of Magic, the epithet that is so wonderful to see strewn behind the name of a great mother goddess, as opposed to a distinguished gentleman in a beard, gives us the essential clue.

Magic is, among other things, the art of firsts. Magic is a synonym for the fiat of creation. For example, the Magician is the first image in that parade of archetypes known as the Tarot. The moment when the rabbit comes out of the hat is not that different than the moment when the desired child is undeniably conceived and the evidence is filtered into the physical reality of the blood's hormones. Or the moment when the creative project that has been steeped for so long as a careful, steely enthralling blueprint in the mind and heart suddenly locks in to words.

These moments, and others like them, effect that same nothing-to-something transition that is inherent in her red cord or yarn.

Isis goes through and performs this magical transition herself as she reintegrates and resurrects Osiris. She makes nothing (the dismembered corpse) into something (the man). And in performing resurrection, she again does something that has not been done before. Magic, Isis tells us with a veiled smile, in so many haunting ways, is only birth. Creativity. Not so complicated. Easily accessible, if you know where to look.

Magic can also simply be a by-product of intelligence. And knitting goddesses tend to get out of jams with their brains. With a few exceptions, they continually yet subtly remind us that yarn and intelligence are as intrinsically connected as yin and yang. Isis may have cleverly and masterfully used words to resurrect her husband and become pregnant. And Grandmother Spider cleverly used her thread to open the door to the world that would save her people. This may be because the practice of touching fiber sharpens the mind as it sharpens the hands. Sometimes I wonder if these particular resourceful goddesses favor

wool work (and linen work) precisely and only because it is a tool that fine-tunes their minds as they go through the disguise of using it to clothe bodies.

As we knit, we gain this characteristic ourselves. We start to notice all the fascinating little variations to our work; the way a knit stitch feels as opposed to a purl, the way bamboo needles are slightly more slippery and warm than wood, and the way a block of stockinette stitch stretches vertically as opposed to garter or moss stitches, which stay tight. All these levels of tactile observation subtly transfer to our mental processes and powers of observation as well. In this way we master another tool of very practical magic.

Fashion and the Longing for the Divine

It was soon after this that I also discovered her priestesses often spent their free time weaving and sewing their own clothing. Their discipline was worked in an environment of stillness, and the fiber work helped busy the hands and pass the time as the inner world was weaving itself. Their goals were different than mine when Isis revealed herself to me, but, as they created their own garments, they also, among other things, created their own future. What was utterly precious to me was the way this instinct had welled up naturally within me without even knowing that it was actually part of a long and distinguished tradition. Even as I sat alone, I was being nurtured and supported by a vibrant and rich thread of healing that was as long as civilization itself. Even as I suspected I did not belong, I was being embraced.

Fashion has always seemed to have magical properties. My favorite one was brought home to me at a costume party for a local art community, where I discovered that, even if you are exhausted and have nothing to contribute, you can despite yourself still seem magically interesting if you are wearing the right clothes. Even more practically, my maternal family's life was changed when my maternal grandfather designed a little pocketbook for children in the fifties. It was shaped like a flowerpot, and it became wildly successful, giving an immigrant family some financial security. Lives can be transformed when people buy, and buy into, fashion.

Fashion also becomes magical when it becomes imbued with a longing for the divine, for immortality, for perfection. Which is only a higher octave of one of our most basic human longings, since the ability to weave cloth originally evolved to protect and sustain life. And the longing for perfection, of course, is often the undertone of fashion.

The magic doesn't lie in the choice of fiber itself, or even the style. Rather, when we entertain the possibility that the substance that touches our physical body adds something to our experience aside from protection and style, our awareness of the mundane physical dimension of our experience intensifies, and the quality of our basic sensual experience of the world just beyond our own physical boundaries is subtly but unequivocally enriched. If we are what we eat, then perhaps our world is what we wear—not how it looks, so much as how it feels, and what it means.

When we knit for ourselves, or for our loved ones, we clothe others and ourselves with our own power and love and cast another protective veil of love and wisdom around them and us. We subtly invest ourselves and our loved ones with the same qualities.

PURLING

As a moon goddess, Isis teaches us how to work with magnetic flows and electricity, yin and yang. This is why you'll often see her pictured with two enormous pillars. The two make a potent combination.

So do knit and purl.

Purling is the inverse of knitting. Using the same type of single ply worsted yarn and needles you used to cast on, knit, and bind off, cast on another sixteen stitches loosely. When we knit, we hold our yarn in back of the needle and put the working needle through each stitch from front to back to knit another. Switch most of the "in backs" to "in fronts" and the "in front" to 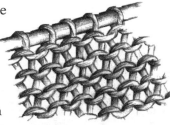 "in back" and you're purling. Following the diagrams on pp. 44–45, and holding

your yarn IN FRONT of your working needle, insert the tip of the working needle through the BACK of the loop of the first stitch on the non–working needle, inserting the needle from back to front, so the working needle ends up in front of the non–working needle (A). Loop your yarn around the working needle (first over this needle and then under it—when the loop is complete, the strand of yarn will end up hanging straight down or pointing back toward your dominant side (B). Move the working needle up to vertical and through the loop on the non–working needle, catching the newly wrapped strand of yarn on the working needle to make a new stitch in the process (C). Slip the new stitch off the non-working needle. Tighten enough so the stitch hugs the needle, but not enough that it grabs it (D). You are purling. Keep purling, row by row, until you've got it. Ten or fifteen rows are good. The fabric on the previous page is purled fabric.

To pick up a dropped purl stitch, reverse the technique you used to pick up a dropped knit stitch and hook the dropped stitch through the BACK of the stitch in the following row, as at right.

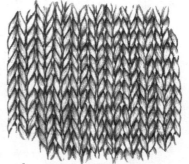

STOCKINETTE STITCH

Stockinette Stitch consists of one row of knit stitches and one row of purl stitches. It makes a flat fabric that looks like the illustration below. Stockinette, along with garter, is one of the two most common "default" stitches of knitting. If you pick up your average sweater, nothing ribbed, nothing fancy, it will probably be made of stockinette. It looks different in different textures of yarn. (This is something we are about to explore.) and provides a smooth canvas on which to paint the yarn paintings of intarsia, or color block knitting, and the interlocking beauty of Fair Isle sweaters. So, if what you want to do when you knit is explore color and

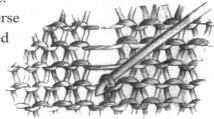

Stockinette stitch

*Purling
(Right-handed)*

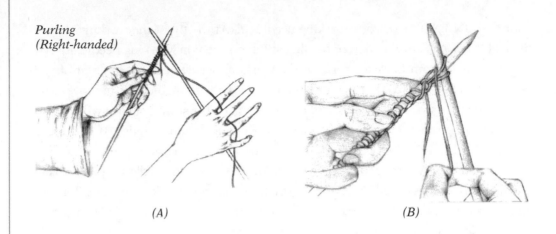

(A)   (B)

texture, you may find you prefer stockinette or garter to more complex stitch patterns, which are often better suited to single colors and uniform textures of yarn.

Stockinette curls at the edges. So, unless you want to use curl as a design or structural element (which you can do in this book if you make the Arachne Shrug or Athena Smoke Ring) you have to edge your stockinette garment with something else, such as garter stitch or one of the many varieties of ribbing, to help it lie down.

If you are a new knitter try a 16 by 16 row practice swatch of stockinette. This is how: Start by knitting two rows of garter stitch (K every stitch) so your edge won't curl. Then K (knit) all odd numbered rows and P (purl) all even num-

*Purling
(Left-handed)*

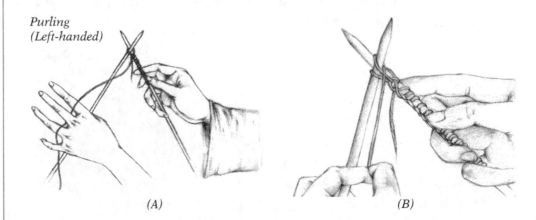

(A)   (B)

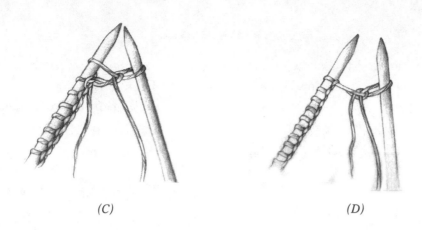

(C)   *(D)*

bered rows, starting with row three. When your K rows are odd numbered they are right side, or RS, rows. Purled rows, when they are even numbered, are WS, or wrong side rows. BO (bind off) when you have knitted sixteen rows of stockinette. If you want to double check your tension and gauge, use the same yarn and needles you used for your first swatch. If you want to begin to experiment with texture and color, try a yarn in a slightly different weight (i.e., one that uses size seven or nine needles if you started with size eight), or a yarn with a slightly different texture: one that has just a little mohair or silk and cashmere if your first yarn was pure wool, or a slinky merino wool if your first one was Shetland, or one that is a colorway, or a blend of colors, if your original yarn was a solid color.

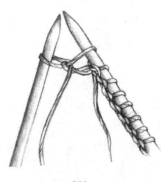

(C)   *(D)*

RED ISIS STOLE

This is a basic easy stole-style (rectangular) shawl. It combines four beautiful red or variegated red yarns to make a rectangular stole that is a testament to Isis' red sash and her great, colorful wings. The yarns include a deep red wool blend, a

red, black, gold, and teal acrylic yarn, a soft wild black eyelash (feathery—it literally looks like it has eyelashes all the way down its length) yarn sprinkled with red dots and plied with a skinny, earth-toned mohair strand, and two sleek, shiny hand painted rayon ribbons: one in teal, purple, terracotta, and olive, and one that is a dark, warm, hot pink.

If you are a new knitter it will give you lots of easy, fun practice in garter stitch, because the yarns keep changing, while simultaneously providing an engaging and changing tactile education in different kinds of yarn and how they behave while you knit them. As you knit along, their behavior (Do they stretch? Do they hang? How do they fill up the needle and fill out the fabric? How do they

blend with other yarns?) will become obvious. You will "read" them with your hands and eyes.

If you are a more experienced knitter, this is something pretty you can knit up quickly.

Lush, dramatic, and airy, the Isis stole will dress up a black or any other solid colored dress or sit easily on top of a jacket or coat while also providing you with a little warmth. Here in the Pacific Northwest, where winter is chilly but usually not snowworthy, I find it very handy to throw on over my clothes when I am traveling somewhere by car and only need to walk outside for a few blocks. It is light, plenty  warm to get me to where I am going from my vehicle, always gets admiring comments, obviates the need to throw on a heavy coat, and allows me to wear it more loosely through the evening.

This piece is also quite versatile. It has a drawstring, so you can gather it and tie it around your shoulders or fasten it with a fibula, which shows off the drape. That's how my friend Evelyn, a jeweler, likes it. But it seems like almost every woman who comes to my house and tries it finds a way to wear it that is uniquely her own. Tish, a landscaper, threw one end over her head like a hood and the other down her back and instantly turned into a very stylish Little Red Riding Hood. I like to wrap it loosely and throw each end over a shoulder, which, to me, has a vaguely Dr. Zhivago kind of look. And Laura hung it around her neck, crisscrossed it over her shoulders, and tied it around her back, making it into a very elegant (and *warm*) halter-top. Because it is so cheerful, drapes so beautifully, and has a drawstring, I also think it would make a great little improvised dirndl overskirt. In this way, this piece is a great supporter of *hozho*.

Last but not least, it also knits up very quickly. I did mine in less than a weekend. Even if you are a beginner, it shouldn't take you too much longer.

RED ISIS STOLE

Ingredients:

- 3 50g (136m) skeins of Filatura Di Crosi Sympathie in red Wool/Mohair/Acrylic, Color #941 (Main Color or MC)
- 5 50g (50–60 yd) skeins of Trendsetter Château in red and black Color 8 (polyester/viscose/mohair) (Color A)
- 2 2 oz. (94 yd) skeins of Prism Bon Bon ¼ inch ribbon in Tapestry (100% rayon) (Color B) in russets, violet, and teals
- 1 skein of Prism Bon Bon ¼ inch ribbon in hot pink Color 203 (100% rayon) (Color C)
- 2 50g (112m) skeins of Spectrum Batik in red (Acrylic/Polyester) Color 3 (Color D)
- 2 double pointed needles (DPNS) in a large size—exact size does not matter if you choose to finish the drawstring in I-cord.
- 1 pair of circular size 17 (15mm) needles. I suggest using circular (attached) needles. They allow you to put more stitches on your needles without dropping them. The plastic that attaches them, and where your stitches hang out, will probably be coiled in a circle when you buy them. If you sit on them for a while, run them under hot water, or steam them, the circles will straighten out.
- Yarn Combination #1: MC and A
- Yarn Combination #2: MC, B, and D
- Yarn Combination #3: MC, C, and D

GAUGE: ¾-1 stitch equals 1 inch in yarn combination #1. TAKE TIME TO TEST YOUR GAUGE

NOTE FOR NEW KNITTERS: Row gauge doesn't much matter in this pattern, but ballpark stitch gauge does, because you want to create a shawl that drapes and flows. A too large needle will make your shawl droop. Too small and it might

stand up straight. All of this is quite easily avoided if you knit in an appropriate gauge.

FIRST STEP: Pick up a strand of Yarn MC and yarn A and cast on 94 stitches as if the 2 yarns were just 1 yarn. This is called double stranded knitting. Because Color A has two strands, you will actually be holding 3 strands in your hand and knitting with all of them as 1. This is pretty easy, especially on big needles. If you're new to knitting, and the textures feel adventurous to your needles, just go with it slowly for a few rows. As long as you have practiced and learned on a single ply worsted, by now you will probably do fine. In fact, you might even get bored with this project by the time you finished if you didn't have the additional visual and textural interest. If you need to pull something out, all these yarns pull out fairly easily and you can start again without much fuss. If you are particularly uncertain, just practice with a small swatch of the yarns until you feel comfortable. Or go to Ariadne's Scarf, learn to rib, and do the whole scarf in one yarn (the double ply kid mohair, which is a type of mohair that is smooth).

In this shawl you will be knitting "sideways," that is, you have just cast on the length of your stole, not the width. The many steps in this simple and easily knit garment are deceptive, because they are mostly included to account for small changes in yarn. Basically, you will be holding the red wool yarn all the time and picking up and dropping the other three in regular two row intervals, and knitting in garter stitch. You will knit garter stitch and an occasional *K1 YO* row. (New knitters: in knitting instructions, anything notated between asterisks is a pattern that is repeated until further notice, or, until the end of the row, whichever come first. YO is yarn over, which is explained in *New Knitter's Workshop* at the end of this chapter.)

SECOND STEP: Knit 2 rows in MC and Color A combination. (Yarn combination #1)

Third Step: Drop Color A and pick up a strand each of Colors B and D, while still holding your MC. This is Yarn Combination #2. Just let Color A fall to the side. You'll pick it up again soon. Now, knit 2 rows with the second combination.

Fourth Step: Drop B and D, pick up Color A and add it to MC, and knit in Yarn Combination #1 for 2 more rows.

Fifth Step: Alternate these 2 combinations of yarn until the shawl measures 6 inches from the plastic needle to the cast-on end (Stretch it out a little.)

Sixth Step: Using Yarn Combination #1, knit 1 row. Knit next row in dropped garter stitch: *K1, YO* throughout the row. (See New Knitter's Workshop at the end of chapter for yarnover or YO instruction if you need it—just an extra wrap of yarn around your needle.) Knit 2 more rows in yarn combination #1. (In the row after the YO row, you will be picking up loops that are twice as big as the usual, creating a loop pattern in your fabric.)

Seventh Step: Drop Color A and pick up Color C. This is Yarn Combination #3. Knit 2 rows in this combination, then 2 more in Yarn Combination #1.

Eighth Step: *K1 YO* in Yarn Combination #2 for one row. Then K 1 row in same combination.

Ninth Step: K 2 rows in Yarn Combination #1

Tenth Step: K two rows in Yarn Combination #3

Eleventh Step: If stole has reached 20 inches in width, bind off loosely. If not, continue alternating 2 K rows in Yarn Combinations #1 and #3 until it does and then bind off loosely. If you want a wider stole and have more yarn, keep going until it's long enough for you and then bind off.

TWELFTH STEP: **Drawstring option one:** Make I-cord drawstring. I-cord is an easy form of edging and cording. Holding one strand each of any two of the yarns (a combination of one of the thicker and one of the thinner ones is good) and using your double pointed needle, cast on 3 stitches. Then knit them. Move them down to the other end of the needle WITHOUT TURNING THEM, pull the stitches tight, and knit 3 more. Repeat *K3, move to other end of needle, pull tight* until cord reaches a length that is about ten inches longer than the long edge of your stole, or to taste. This will be about 90 inches total. Bind off and thread through the loops of the fourth or fifth row in from the top (bound off) edge of the stole. This will make for a very firm drawstring; the bigger the needles you use, the more flexible it will be. If you use smaller needles, you have the option of subtracting a strand or two of yarn to create a more flexible drawstring.

DRAWSTRING OPTION TWO: Make braided drawstring. Prepare strands of yarn approximately 8 inches longer than the length of the finished stole in one each of the 3 Yarn Combinations. Braid together, knit ends, thread cord through loops of the fourth or fifth row in from the top (bound off) edge of the stole.

DRAWSTRING OPTION THREE: Just take one strand of each yarn, tie together at ends, and thread through. Simple, but effective. This is the option shown in the illustration.

THIRTEENTH STEP: Weave in ends (see Chapter Four New Knitter's Workshop).

This is a really straightforward pattern. Almost all the steps refer to changes in the yarns you are carrying. If you miss a change, you'll simply end up with your own unique design variation.

First Minor Design Variation: You can vary the Yarn Combinations, occasionally adding either yarn B or D to Combination 1. You can also vary where you place the yarn over rows, or how many of them you use, or whether you use them at all. Also, if you miss a YO here and there, it doesn't much matter—with

this kind of yarn, your slightly irregular pattern of larger loops will just look like an organic pattern and add additional interest and texture to the shawl.

Another Choice: You do not have to make this shawl red. What you need is one stretchy wool or wool blend yarn, an eyelashy-textury yarn, a variegated ribbon yarn, and one other yarn with a different texture. I based the project on the wool-based yarn and the eyelash yarn, both of these come in other colors. If you want to choose another base color from one of the yarns selected here or another yarn like one of them in texture, keep to the basic principle of texture combination, and build from there. If you do this, check your gauge.

Also, ribbon yarn is expensive. To make a less expensive shawl, subtract the ribbon yarn and add something else variegated, and preferably shiny, because the variegation (change in yarn color) is what makes this design work and what adds the multicolored, "Isis' wings" element. The shine makes the wing element stand out.

Yarn Substitution

This leads me to the general and crucial topic of yarn substitution. Although you can often find the exact yarn that's listed in a pattern in a book or magazine, you can't always. Sometimes the color in question has been discontinued. Some manufacturers change color palettes every year, or even during the season. Other times, the yarn in question is not in your budget, or the yarn can be ordered but you just don't want to wait that long. Your choices are (1) hold out; (2) choose another pattern; or (3) opt for the Knitting Goddess method, be creative, and simply substitute yarn of a similar size and type. (This method is actually pretty ubiquitous, like the Knitting Goddess herself.) Some of my, and everyone else's, favorite projects were born when we couldn't find the yarn we wanted and adventured with a readily available substitute. Yarn substitution is just a basic part of knitting, and not something that is particularly to be feared.

All of the projects in this book offer yarn choices made from readily available yarns, selected in retail stores local to me (I did use a little mail order and

Internet). But I am always going to give you the yarn *type* and *consistency*, and sometimes a few notes on how the project will turn out if you modify that type and consistency, so you can make your own informed and creative choices regardless of availability. In this sense, knitting can be like gourmet cooking. If there isn't any parsley for the herb omelet, you know you can substitute dill in a similar quantity, as long as you like the taste.

Again, in the case of the Isis Stole, the trick is to keep the springy wool blend yarn constant throughout. The wool blend bounces and drapes and gives the overall piece body and consistency. To that, add whatever you would like in combinations that approximate the same diameter of yarn, i.e., something that will look just about the same size on the needle size you are using. Try different combinations of shiny to dull, variegated to solid, textured to smooth, and even natural fibers to synthetic ones and see what you like. Keep your colors within the same basic shade (here, a warm dark red) and enrich the basic shades with complementary or analogous accents (here, variegated bits of teal, black, gold, and eggplant and a deep, warm, fuchsia) making sure that each color combination includes one yarn that maintains the basic shade in each color combination (here, the red in the wool blend of color combination A and the red base in the viscose of yarn combination B). If you don't keep the continuity of the background shade, you'll come out with something more stripey. That's nice, too.

Some stores let you sit in the store and knit up a swatch before you buy to see how you like it. If there is a store in your area that does this, patronize them. Your hands and eyes and needles and common sense will always tell you what you need to know about yarn choices and patterns.

It is particularly important to track your gauge if you substitute yarns when you are multi-stranding, and particularly so in a pattern that relies on drape, such as this one. If you decide to blend your yarns a little differently, and your final blend is more dense, you may need to move up one needle size. If your final blend is more airy, you may need to move down a needle size. Use your hands to experiment and see.

KNITTING NOTEBOOK AND RECORD KEEPING

Yarns run out. Sometimes patterns are things you want to repeat, or refer to. And once in a while, when you begin to make things to size, you will want to remember how you made them that size so you can do it again.

To this end, it's a good idea to keep a knitting notebook.

I like to use a spiral bound sketchbook, so I can sketch my ideas in colored pencil. I give each project a double page spread. I remove the label from one of the skeins of the yarn in question, and I staple it to one of the pages. This way, if the yarn runs out before the project is over I have the yarn brand, number, and color to refer to if I need to order more. This also helps if I have an idea for using a yarn in a subsequent project (it's fun to play with scraps) at a later time. I also staple or tape a piece of the yarn (or each yarn I'm using for the project) to the page. I also make notes about the pattern and any changes I make to it or the size of needles that I use for it. Then I staple the swatch to the page. As I knit through skeins, I staple the labels to the page so I know how many skeins I have used.

I also like to use a swatch board, a bulletin board where I can pin up all my swatches and regard them at my leisure. Patterns and yarns change with changes of light, like paint does, or water or anything with color. And textures look different close up, from medium distance, and farther away, as does a well choreographed ballet. So I like to enjoy my swatches because they teach me about the properties of yarn, pattern, and color, just by looking at them. This also lets me know if a pattern or yarn combination I am playing with will have the effect that I wanted, or sometimes another even better, unexpected effect.

YARN OVER

Yarn over is really easy and the basis of many fancy lace stitches. All you do to YO when your next stitch is knitted is move yarn in front as if to purl and simply knit the next stitch, creating an extra loop between one stitch and the next. When you pick up your stitch on the next row, the yarn over will unwrap into

the stitch next to it, creating a much larger loop in your fabric than the background stitch pattern you are using (in this case garter stitch) and create a special effect. To YO purl-wise, with yarn in front, wrap the yarn clockwise (i.e. around the outside) of your working needle and then purl your next stitch. This illustration shows the knit version of YO. Dropped garter stitch is one of the easiest yarn over stitches. When you use it in a contrast-ing or special yarn, as we do in the Isis shawl, it creates a beautiful dramatic design element. It is an excellent choice for easily highlighting a bit of special, more expensive, or simply leftover yarn.

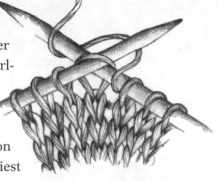

------

[1]Elizabeth Barber, Portland, Oregon lecture. (4/20/00).
[2]Normandi Ellis, trans. *Awakening Osiris*. (Phanes: Grand Rapids, 1988), 180.
[3]E. J. W. Barber, *Prehistoric Textiles*. (Princeton University Press: Princeton, 1991), 225.

Ariadne, Ribbing, and a Scarf with an Ancient Edge

i once knit a ribbed sweater with sleeves and a bodice that ended in points. I chose a rich red and rust and violet colorway, and ran a thread of gold up the center of the bodice and from shoulder to wrist along each sleeve.

The piece was beautiful but went a little slowly—anything with all that ribbing progresses more slowly than something smooth, because ribbing makes fabric shrink just a bit. But the result was unexpectedly wonderful. Women I saw on a regular basis, including the ones in knitting shops, demanded to know how it was going when I didn't have it in tow. I was both flattered and annoyed at the attention, because this sweater was slow going, and, now and then, I contemplated stashing it behind a couch pillow for a lifetime or two.

Three quarters of the way through I finally did put it down in order to attend to some important life business. When I finished, I picked up this blasted gorgeous sweater again, because of course it was still there, and in great part because my friends in the knitting stores kept bugging me about it. (Actually, I'd already lied once about having finished it.) At that point all that was left to do was the front.

About three inches in, I decided to match the front and back together and discovered that the two pieces did not match in width. The front I was working on was a whole two inches wider than the back. I counted stitches and discovered the numbers were identical. There was only one other possibility. In the middle of knitting this particular sweater, my gauge had changed dramatically. Imperceptibly, my stitches had become much larger and looser than they had

been when I started. Sometime during the interim, I had evolved from what is known as a "tight" knitter to what is called a "loose" one.

As I had eased my need to grip onto the routines and comforts of my life, I had also eased my need to grip on my yarn and knitting needles. I made new gauge swatches, and as a result switched to needles that were not one, but two sizes smaller.

I then experienced what is known as an "aha" moment. The challenge of "aha" moments is that they are internally enormous; earth shattering even, but sometimes don't look like much on the outside.

The external adjustment I needed to make was matter-of-fact. Mid-sweater gauge change is not an uncommon occurrence. Almost every knitter has this kind of war story. I once heard a knitter beg the proprietor of a knitting store to take the four inches of slipstitched baby sweater she had completed into the back room and rip it out for her, because the trauma of doing it herself would be too severe. Over the weekend, this woman's gauge had shrunk. "You got used to it," the owner had told her customer practically, meaning the slipstitch pattern, in way of positive and rational explanation. And that is one explanation. In the knitting world, familiarity breeds shrinkage. Or expansion. Depending on the individual.

But for me, and I suspect for other knitters also, there was more going on than that. This somewhat common and easy-to-rationalize shift can also, in its own way, be unexpectedly transformational: not unlike having a wild yet secret growth spurt as an adult. With it my assumptions about what could and could not be changed had been challenged and enlarged, and with this my sense of the possible became at once more tangible and more vast. The experience was also somehow erotic, in that I felt both physically penetrated and triumphant.

And all of this because of the way I moved needles through a little ball of yarn. I had changed the pattern of the sweater, and it, in turn, had changed me.

As it happens, the story of Ariadne, the ancient Minoan heroine whose power to heal others and herself and create realities, is represented by a ball of magical yarn, had something to say about that moment—in a much more dramatic, epic, and influential way, of course.

Ariadne's Voyage

Once upon a time, in the very ancient Mediterranean, the king of Athens and the king of Minoan Crete (his name was Minos, or Midas) developed a rivalry over which of the two was more powerful: possessing more riches, fertility, favor of the gods, and land. As it played out, a prince was murdered, battles were fought, and a divine bull was stolen and an unacceptable substitute slipped in its place, and, predictably, even after all of that, nothing really ever got resolved.

Instead, all of this unresolved passion and experience and frustration and resentment and longing came to rest in the womb of one Queen Pasiphaë.

Pasiphaë was King Minos' wife and a moon goddess. The mythic struggle ripened in her womb, and she gave birth to it in the person of the Minotaur, a being who had the body of a man and the head of a bull.

The Minotaur was not Minos' son. Pasiphaë had been impregnated by a remarkable white bull. So Minos commissioned his master craftsman Daedalus to create a labyrinth that would enclose his wife's bastard and hide it from the world.

Daedalus created a labyrinth that was so brilliantly, artistically, and brutally filled with twists and turns that there was no possible way for even the most exceptional human being using all of his or her wits to escape from it alive. (It wouldn't surprise me in the least to learn that Daedalus is alive and well today, writing software code.)

The Minotaur was placed in its central chamber and Crete was safe.

However, like any broken and shunned being, the Minotaur required special and expensive food, and was never permanently satisfied by any of it. He was the family secret that cost too much to maintain, but would cost even more to fully disclose.

The food he required was the human flesh of 14 tribute Athenian youths, seven boys and seven girls, in the frequency of every nine years. They were exacted from his rival king, Aegisthus, the price Aegisthus still paid for robbing the original magical bull from Minos. The boys and girls were led into the labyrinth. If they came out again, they were allowed to live.

They never came out again.

The craftsman Daedalus had actually held a single, top secret magical method of leaving the labyrinth alive in reserve. It didn't rely on human wits at all. It consisted of a magical ball of red thread. If one end was tied to the lintel of the labyrinth door, and carried to the heart of the place, it would effortlessly traverse and stretch through all of the twists and turns, and draw its bearer out from the center of the labyrinth along its path.

The ball of magical thread was a small, womb-sized three-dimensional spiral that was the antidote to the labyrinth's enormous, dark flat spiral. It was a pattern that broke a pattern.

One day, Daedalus had an "aha" moment. He came across Ariadne, one of Minos' six children, and recognized her as the being who was supposed to have the power to get in and out of that place. And he gave it to her.

Or, perhaps the young princess begged him for the yarn. It depends on which version of the story you read. I like to combine them. She asked for it, and he recognized her.

Why her? you might ask.

Ah, this is a great mystery. So often, gods and goddesses begin their eternal lives as the instant beneficiaries of the head honcho god's highlighting pen, wielded in the form of an auspicious or unusual birth. Aphrodite emerged from the ocean in a seashell. Athena was born from the head of Zeus. But there is nothing remarkable or even noted about Ariadne's birth. What is remarkable is that a special, skilled man noticed a special potential in a young woman.

Perhaps Daedalus thought it was a good idea to give the ball of thread to a woman, since fiber arts were a woman's provenance. Yarn and fiber arts were already associated with the goddess. As an historical culture, Minoan Crete is well known for its complex, dramatic textiles and sophisticated clothing designs. (They have been compared to the clothing of the court of Louis XIV.)

Visually at least, yarn in Crete may already have been allied with feminine power. Priestesses of the snake goddess, an ancient and enduring feminine force, wore dramatic and powerful ritual clothing that echoed the twist of yarn in their stark, swirling black and white patterns that breathtakingly framed their bared breasts. Their hair cascaded from their heads in black yarn-like, snake-like spiral

curls, as did Ariadne's. Serpents twined around the snake goddess' arms, providing a visual connection to fiber work and, perhaps, a clue—Ariadne has been depicted in the same garb.

Since spinning and weaving are traditionally associated with the moon, and Ariadne, like Isis, and like her mother Pasiphaë, is also known as a moon goddess, we can wonder whether Ariadne was a special priestess, and Daedalus knew this, and gave her the ball of thread in some official capacity.

This is how Ariadne first gained mythological distinction. Not by being linked with supernatural birth. Rather, in her receptivity and through her unknown, pure, young quality (her name means "most high" or "most pure"). She would have to decide when to use the ball of thread, and for what purpose. Or, she knew why she needed it already.

Ariadne made her move as the tribute of 14 youths came from Athens. Among them was the young prince named Theseus. Theseus was the son of King Aegisthus, who was the king who had warred with Minos. He had volunteered to be one of the fourteen, in order to slay the Minotaur and save them all from the curse.

Ariadne and Theseus saw each other, and they fell in love.

Imagine the black-haired Ariadne removing the carved stopper on the wide-mouthed rock crystal urn in the storage room in the back of her chambers. She reaches inside, lifts the ball and bobbin out of the mouth of the urn, and finds herself gasping the way she always does when she sees its red flash after a long absence. Red has always been one of her people's favorite colors. All different shades of red cover the walls, columns, and frescoes in her father's vast open-air palace. There is red with orange and red with coral and reds as pale as the inside of a mouth. But Ariadne has never seen red like the red of this yarn. Too lustrous for the wool that grows on the sheep that graze on the rocky Cretan coasts, too buoyant for the silk that comes on ships, it is richer than blood and brighter than the sun.

Ariadne steps out onto her terrace. The sharp turquoise sea is covered in white caps. The wind has been high since Theseus anchored in the harbor. Tonight, the 14 will enter the labyrinth. Now they stand below her, being feted by the crowd.

She touches the ball of thread again.

The choppy waters before her part, and a blond head emerges. From his throne, Minos nods his head and Theseus emerges from the water holding a gold signet ring. Minos had wanted one of the Athenian girls for himself. When Theseus stepped up to protect her, Ariadne's father had told him that if he could retrieve the signet ring from the depths of the ocean, he would leave the girl untouched. Now Theseus climbs onto the dock and holds his hand aloft. The ring catches more sunlight than any ring should. Ariadne looks closer. Theseus is also holding a beautiful twisting golden crown set with fiery gold and red gems.

As Theseus steps onto the dock, he lets his eyes pass casually across Ariadne's balcony, but their eyes do not meet. Ariadne knows that his princely powers and successes are no match for the feminine, dark, complexity of the Minoan labyrinth. The ritual is about to begin. If she does not help, Theseus and the others will die.

Ariadne throws on a borrowed ceremonial cloak, slips out the door, and intercepts the party at the edge of Minotaur's lair. Theseus leads the party. Ariadne gets in file with the party's Minoan attendants. She will enter with them and greet her half-brother. Then she will lead all the Athenians out. She is only feet from the dark passageway that goes below when one of the Athenian girls turns, and sees her.

"Help me," the girl whispers.

All eyes turn to Ariadne. She is recognized. Only one thing to do, and not much time to do it in. Ariadne looks at the ball of thread. She admires its spin, its strength, its softness, its mysterious life. Ariadne speaks a few words to it. Everyone freezes but Theseus. Ariadne says a prayer, then tosses the ball of magic thread across the corridor and into her lover's arms. As it leaves her, she feels a portion of her power fly with it. She rapidly explains what he can and must do with it. The others are released from their magical stillness and the tableau moves on.

Ariadne knows she cannot ever again return to her chambers. She is no longer safe. She has betrayed her family, and even if her father protects her, his general, Taurus, will now certainly mark her as his prey. So she will wait until morning to see whether Theseus has survived. And then she will disappear into

the network of caves below the earth's surface. Many wise ones dwell below: the snake women, who have been there since the beginning of time. They have taught her and mentored her since she was a child. They will embrace her.

At the cave mouth she has chosen, Ariadne finds a group of women spinning and weaving the garments for the upcoming sacred festivals. And so, while her heart leaps and aches, she picks up a spindle whorl.

Just before dawn, the earth beneath her feet seems to soften, and the rocks everywhere groan. Soon after, she looks up again and beholds a cloaked, blood-stained man in the shadow of a nearby pine.

The man is Theseus.

She looks toward him and he nods slowly.

Her half-brother the Minotaur has been slain.

"Come away with me," says Theseus, when she joins him. "Our ship sails within the half-hour. All of us escaped without harm. We will stop on the island of Naxos to pick up provisions. Be my wife."

Ariadne pictures the dead body of her creature half-brother, which is, no doubt, now resting in the center of his ruined lair. She considered the risks and advantages of leaving this island. Her heart breaks one way, and then it breaks the other way.

"Let's go," says Ariadne.

Where Crete was wild and craggy, Naxos is verdant, with beaches as open and smooth as a hand. By the time they set anchor, she is groggy.

"There my love," says Theseus. "Why don't you lie here while we take on our provisions? You shall be perfectly safe."

Ariadne looks at the wide soft expanse of white sand and the glassy bay, protected yet vast. Ariadne lies down and sleeps.

She wakes up slowly. The sun is still playing on her shoulders. The sand is soft. She opens her eyes. The Athenian ship is gone.

Ariadne sits up. There is an odd shimmer to the air over the ocean, one that she has only seen in the wake of the gods.

Ariadne sits on the beach for a while, waiting, and watching the shimmer disperse. The sun goes down. It comes up. This happens again, maybe two or

three more times. Ariadne grabs handfuls of sand and lets them go again. She refuses offers of food and shelter and clothing.

On the morning of the last day a ship appears.

Ariadne stands.

The ship is not Theseus'.

Ariadne sits down, turns toward the shore, crouches down like a child, and sobs.

There is something unusual about this ship. Even from far off, even from behind her tears she can see grapevines twining around the mast and exotic animals crowding the deck. A being takes leave of the ship, gets into the boat, and rows toward shore. This being is young and vital. He wears jerkins made of animal skins. His abundant hair, a color halfway between walnut shells and raisins, curls like snakes. The strange menagerie follows him, prancing across the waves.

"It is Dionysus," the villagers began to whisper. "The lord of the vine has come home!"

Dionysus comes to shore, laughing, and clapping his hands, and spots Ariadne on the ground.

Dionysus has been through his own heartbreak, and been so enlivened by it, that women pursue him everywhere he roams, but he has never before beheld a beauty who has the destiny to be laid open by her own ball of yarn and the courage to meet that destiny head on.

Dionysus kneels down, and takes Ariadne in his arms.

Ariadne allows him. His touch feels both familiar, and overwhelming in its effect.

Dionysus reads part of her mind and shrugs.

"Take your time," he says. "In the evenings, here on Naxos, we dance in the moonlight. Come by and join us if you like."

Eventually, she did.

When Dionysus and Ariadne wed, he produced the red-gemmed crown Theseus had found in the sea in that way gods have and placed it on her head. The gems matched the color of Ariadne's yarn. When the ceremony was complete,

Dionysus reached into the heavens and set the crown among the stars. Ariadne's chaplet still glows there today as the constellation Corona Borealis.

Fiber work was central to the culture of Minoan Crete. So were sacred dances, perhaps performed on the black and white tiles of labyrinths. So were womb-like patterns woven from thread in their depths. On one level, this story is a teaching on the secret wisdom of how the understanding of patterns that a knitter or weaver acquires naturally as she works can be applied to other arenas of life. This story teaches that the ability to create, destroy, or to revise existing patterns, is also the ability to create and to heal.

The spiral, a motif used often in Cretan art, which, in three dimensions becomes a ball of yarn, is a symbol of becoming.[1] When we work with yarn, we become. When we creatively tie together or repattern any of the strands of life that are available to us—social, creative, emotional, erotic, nurturing—which the ball of yarn also symbolizes, we become or make others become or other things become.

And when we turn this word "becoming" in a slightly different direction, we dissolve old patterns and create new ones in our lives, we more fully become, and we heal. For instance, my friend Angela, who was a weaver for years before she became a Jungian therapist, told me how she often relies upon the metaphors and wisdom of weaving as an important resource when she works with clients. She intentionally transfers her knowledge of weaving patterns to the sacred task of rewriting and reconnecting emotional and spiritual circuitry.

In her own way, Ariadne also heals. Her ball of thread is a three-dimensional spiral that played a pivotal role in unlocking the large, flat, stagnant spiral of the labyrinth. And once the labyrinth was destroyed, the larger patterns of power in her world, embodied in its dynasties, were broken as well.

While Ariadne was on Naxos, her father King Minos died. And with his death, the dominion of Minoan Crete on the ancient world crumbled also. (He was the one who stole the original white bull, so, in some ways, his daughter's actions embodied the re-establishment of divine order.) Aegisthus of Athens,

Theseus' father and Minos' rival king in the original dispute, also died, a suicide, when Theseus mistakenly signaled from his ship that he had died in the labyrinth. Daedalus' son Icarus fell to the ocean after his waxen wings melted. The existing pattern of succession of power and wisdom, already troubled in that world, broke open as either fathers lost sons, or sons lost fathers.

And even as the old dynastic pattern crumbled, another was gestating and was eventually born. Ariadne partners with the god of fertility and a prolific and joyous new dynasty issues. Pasiphaë gave birth to the toxicity of old Greece. Ariadne played a role in breaking that pattern, and the many children she had with Dionysus went on to seed the Helladic tribes. The small ball of magical yarn played a part in this work. Our own knitting, weaving, spinning can take us on a similar inner journey. The knitting patterns we learn and execute can literally repattern us within. A change in gauge, however classic a rite of passage, can do the trick. Perhaps it will happen, or has happened, to you in this, or another, knitting moment.

The spirit of Ariadne enters us when we get the urge to improvise on an existing knitting pattern, or change a design element, or strike out on our own. We don't really throw everything away—it's still a sweater or afghan, after all—but even if the change is tiny we come up with something that fits better, or feels better or whose colors, textures, or stitch patterns in mind or better expresses the beauty we sense inside ourselves. We inevitably begin to make such choices as the rhythm of our craft opens us and introduces us to our own natural creative and spiritual keenness.

Try it yourself sometime. Somewhere in the deep background of your soul, whole ancient civilizations of the spirit can rise and fall while you knit a sweater. Try it. You'll see.

There is not much that cannot be accomplished when you match just the right woman with just the right ball of yarn.

And now, let's knit.

Ariadne's Rib

The edge of a piece of knitted fabric won't lie flat by itself if you use the same stockinette stitch you use in the body of the garment. As those of us who sometimes ignore sound advice have already learned, it will result in an untamed edge which delicately and stubbornly curls, not unlike the edge of a piece of newsprint burning in a fireplace (but with a much more lasting effect).

Curling gives a nice effect, if that's what you want. (It looks good on some sweaters and the edge of a hood. See Arachne's Shrug, for example.) But not everyone does. There are a few tried and true methods you can apply to the edge of something to calm it down. Ribbing is one of them. Ribbing gives elasticity and shape to a piece, as well as giving it what it needs to stay flat. Ribbing looks interesting and neat, and is simple to accomplish. If you take a close look at the edges of most sweaters and socks, you will notice that they are ribbed.

Ribbing

Choose some knitting needles that are two sizes smaller than the main body of whatever you want to make. (If you choose to make the project in this chapter, it will be a scarf. But if you are new to knitting, ribbing is something you will need to know anyway.) Loosely cast on an even number of stitches that is a multiple of four, plus two more. Eighteen, 22, 26, and 30 are all good choices. (The two extra stitches ensure that the ribbing still matches up when you sew the edges together.) Make sure to cast on loosely. (The looseness prevents the edge of the garment from pulling tight later. This looks odd and feels uncomfortable.) Knit two stitches, then purl two stitches. Repeat this pattern (*K2 P2*) all the way back to the end of this row, then add two final knit stitches. The notation for the whole row is, *K2 P2* K2.

Your knitting will begin to crinkle almost instantly, and the pattern will become quite visible in just a couple of rows; i.e., every other two stitches will protrude, while the intervening two will shrink back, forming narrow, textural vertical stripes. Soon, the whole thing will begin to resemble, well, a set of ribs.

At the same time, the width of the fabric you are creating will shrink slightly in measurement. The extra two knit stitches on the end help the ribbing to match up to itself when it gets sewn to another piece. Regular ribbing looks like corrugated rib (see below) without the color change. It also looks like the cuffs and lower and collar edges of the Moirae pullover. (See next chapter.)

To practice, keep ribbing until you have an inch, or two inches, or two and a half inches of knitting. Now you have a nice ribbed border. This would be where you would start the main body of your garment. Go ahead if you want, using an easy sweater pattern, such as the one in the next chapter. Or, label and pin your sample and put it up on a knitting bulletin board for future reference, because it looks cute, and because you did it.

CORRUGATED RIB

Corrugated rib is a variation on the basic rib. It uses one color for the stitches that stick out, i.e., the rib, and another for the part of the pattern that hangs back.

Corrugated rib is fun and isn't so hard to do. One of the reasons it's so much fun is that, like a lot of interesting design, it is not only pretty and adds a strong design element, but it also makes a kind of subtle visual pun. To wit: if the protruding rib is knitted in a lighter color (e.g., white) and receding rib is knitted in a darker one (black), you will be reinforcing the rib pattern with color, since lighter colors attract light and seem larger and closer, while darker ones seem smaller and recede. And if you switch your colors (i.e., black in front and white in back) you will be working against the rib in a variation. So, either the color reinforces your pattern, or slyly works against it, reinforcing it in a different way.

Either way you choose to do it, people who look at your corrugated rib will like it, partially for this reason, but they won't know exactly why.

Corrugated rib is done exactly the way regular ribbing is done, except with two colors. All you really have to learn is how to switch them.

Cast on all 20 or 24 stitches in one color, in the needle size that is appropriate for the yarn (something that works on size six to nine needles is always a

good start). This will make a solid color at the bottom of your rib. (You can also cast on in alternating colors by making a slipknot. Tie each two stitches of one color to the next two stitches of another color. This is also kind of interesting, but requires you to twist your yarn when you cast on and overlaps the colors in the back. Try both and see what you like.)

Next, begin your rib with the color you used to cast on. Use this color for the first two stitches of the *K2 P2* pattern.

Now, pick up your second yarn (the yarn in a second color). Let's call it Yarn B. Leaving a tail of about three inches (more or less according to your taste, which you will discover as you work with switching yarns—a shorter tail is tidier; a longer one is safer and easier to hide later), loosely slipknot this new yarn to the first one, using the same knot you used in the basic cast on. Purl two stitches. Then, pick up your first yarn, pull it loosely behind (i.e., to the wrong side) of your work and behind the stitches in the contrasting color, and then "snake" or twist this first yarn around the second yarn, wrapping it twice in a spiral fashion. Then knit your two stitches.

The accompanying illustrations, which are right-handed, explain all of this visually.

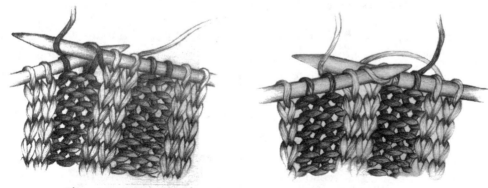

Changing to yarn B   *Changing back to yarn A*

Keep going in this fashion until you finish the row.

Matching colors, knit the knit stitches and purl the purl stitches on the

wrong side row. This time, you can keep the "carried" yarn to the same side of the fabric.

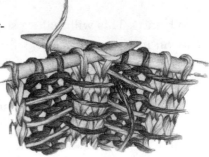

The point of carrying yarn is to prevent "holes" or gaps from forming between yarns. It can seem a little awkward and slow at first, but once you get the hang of it it becomes almost instinctive. Unless you use a bobbin (a technique of cutting a length of yarn and tying it behind the section where it will be used, which

"Wrong side" view of corrugated rib

is not necessary with ribbing) or knit Fair Isle style with one color in each hand, the yarns will naturally wrap and spiral around each other. You will probably end up separating them by instinctively placing your thumb and forefinger between them, which allows you to twist your yarns easily. This works fine with this simple pattern. If you want to work extensively with color, you will learn how to use bobbins or knit Fair Isle sometime later in your love affair with knitting. These techniques prevent this twisting. There are notes on using bobbins in Chapter Seven.

Work this pattern for about five rows or so.

Ariadne's Rib and Ariadne's Scarf

Even though they had flush toilets and bathtubs, ancient Minoans would probably not understand a lot about us. But I do suspect that the visual punnery that contributes to the simple delight of corrugated rib is something they would understand perfectly. As we have seen, in both their stories and their designs, Ariadne's people demonstrate a great love of patterns. You might even say they wrote the fresco on them. Minoan art is well appreciated for containing simple geometric design elements that playfully repeat, vary, and pun. Fresco borders, wall decoration, decorative arts, jewelry, textiles, and clothing (depicted in the frescoes) all bear the same simple, yet sophisticated designs. Spirals, quatrefoils, and floral motifs interlock, reverse, and execute other variations that both reinforce and work against the original pattern.

One of the most common and simple of these is what textile scholar E. J. W. Barber calls the four-color barred band pattern. In this motif, a row of alternating narrow vertical bands of black and blue is topped with a similar or identical row of alternating bands of yellow and red. The result is two rows of bi-color vertical banding. The four-color barred band edge pattern often finishes the edges of frescoes and clothing, including a well-known fresco where two girls and a boy are performing acrobatics with a bull, and which has been associated with the myth of the Minotaur (and also, possibly, with ancient fertility rites). Here, all three dancers' loincloths are decorated with an even four-color bar motif. Uneven lengths and widths of each of the two differing rows of colors can also be discovered in Minoan art, creating a variety of different effects. The pattern has also been found on the edge of a sarcophagus.[2]

Barber, who is also a weaver, noticed that the four-color barred band pattern closely resembled the way a four-color belt can look while it is being woven on a loom. She set up a makeshift loom with pencils and four colors of yarn, and reproduced the effect herself. She hypothesizes that the pattern was used to decorate clothing, and also frescoes, because it was already so common in daily life, since weaving was so common in daily life. You may already have noticed that this mimics what happens in Ariadne's story—the same pattern is reproduced in many realms of life.

As it happens, the four-barred pattern lends itself perfectly to corrugated rib. When we rib a little in black and blue, and then red and yellow, the result looks both regal and playful, and it's very bold. But because of the classic design, it is also elegant. And as we practice it, we become very Minoan, as we "jump" that pattern into yet another realm.

Because it is strong and simple, Minoan rib shows off the look and feel of different fibers while also harmonizing the variety in their size and textures. Big and bulky or handspun, in a soft yarn like merino with something shiny like silk or alpaca thrown in, the kind of thing you'd put on a pair of size ten needles or up, it knits up into something that looks both like a fairy-tale costume and at the same time is incredibly modern—just like the vintage Minoan stuff. In supple kid

mohair, it's reminiscent of the loincloths in the fresco. These two combine in an interesting way. And in cheerful worsted, it's good for kids.

Here are some suggestions that combine fiber types, use some double stranding, and will make a really great scarf with a broad appeal. My mother, who likes Burberry raincoats, really likes it. Along with my classic trench I do own a white vinyl raincoat, and I really like it.

Unlike many scarves, because of the corrugated ribbing at the ends, this one will have a "right" side and a "wrong" side. The wrong side is not unattractive in itself. If you want the same look on the front and the back, knit two more sections of regular ribbing and stitch them over it. It will give the ends a little more weight than the middle, like weights in the bottom of a curtain, but because the pattern is ribbed it shouldn't really droop.

ARIADNE'S RIBBED SCARF

Ingredients:

- 1 50g skein of Tahki Tweed, black (Color A)
- 2 50g skeins of Cynthia Helene Kid Mohair, in russett Color 47 mohair/wool blend (Color B)
- 4 50g skeins of Cynthia Helene Kid Mohair in black (Main Color)
- 1 100g skein each, Manos de Uruguay in blue color x and golden yellow color W (handspun pure wool), or worsted to light bulky (size ten-ish needle) yarn of your choice in these colors or similar. I used a double ply, thick and thin handspun merino, more or less the match of the Tahki black tweed in weight in mine. These are Colors C and D respectively.
- One pair of size ten needles, or size that makes gauge.

GAUGE: 4 stitches to an inch, 3½–4 rows to an inch in Ariadne's rib (gauge will vary depending on yarn) and 4 stitches and 5 rows to an inch in Main Color in 2 × 2 rib, doublestranded.

In honor of the theme of this chapter, gauge doesn't matter that much in this pattern. (The scarf will either be slightly less or more wide; less or more long and you can add or subtract units of ribbing in four stitch increments to get the width you want. You can also simply knit fewer or more rows in the main color in order to get the length you want.) If, perchance, you want your scarf to match my dimensions closely TAKE TIME TO CHECK YOUR GAUGE.

FIBER NOTE: This is a soft kid mohair/wool blend, but to some necks it may still not be soft enough. For a true luxury experience, try black cashmere, merino, or pashmina appropriately stranded to match the gauge. Or, choose skinnier accent yarns and do the whole scarf on smaller needles and with more stitches.

CAST ON 36 stitches in black, Color A.

STEP ONE: Work 5 rows in 2 × 2 corrugated rib, beginning with Color A and alternating with blue (Color C). Exception: Do not use two extra knit stitches at the head of the row. (Because scarves are not seamed, these stitches are not used.)

STEP TWO: On your sixth row, using the same 2 colors in the same color pattern, knit all the way across.

STEP THREE: On your seventh row, change colors to yellow (Color D) and red (Color B). Hold 2 strands of each color in your hand, using them as if they were a single yarn (as we did in the Isis wrap). Purling all the way across, and beginning with yellow, alternate colors every 2 stitches.

STEP FOUR: On your eighth to eleventh rows, work *K2 P2* in corrugated rib.

Step Five: On your twelfth row, keeping the same color frequency, knit all the way across. The purled red section of this rib will be raised a bit from the connecting knit stitches, creating a little decorative "knot."

Step Six: On your thirteenth row, change colors to Main Color, and, holding two strands of this yarn in your hand, and purl all the way across.

Step Seven: Rib in black for approximately 40 inches, which is how many inches four skeins double stranded will get you, or the length of your choice. You can make the scarf longer or shorter to taste.

Then, simply reverse the corrugated rib pattern. To wit:

Step Eight: Changing back to yellow and red (Colors D and B) knit all the way across for 1 row.

Step Nine: Rib for four rows, matching purls to purls and knits to knits to continue the existing pattern continuously.

Step Ten: Knit all the way across for one row in the same color pattern.

Step Eleven: Change to black tweed and blue (Color A and Color C) and knit one row, changing color every two stitches.

Step Twelve: Pick up the corrugated ribbing, alternating Colors A and C and beginning with Color A for five rows.

Cast off loosely in Color A.

A Variation

Ariadne was inspired to play with patterns, and her ribbed scarf is easy to vary as well. A strong, simple pattern like this can withstand changes in texture and even size of yarn within the same garment without looking busy, or requiring much planning to work out right. You can also add white or cream to the pattern, either in its own band or in a ribbing pattern with black or any of the other three colors, with good, pretty safe results. I recommend trying this so you can see how easy and fun it is to design yourself. Here are some suggestions to get you started:

Work part of the pattern (for instance, the red and yellow stripe) without the ribbing, i.e., in straight stockinette.

Add a narrow cream-colored stripe between the red and yellow stripe and the main body of the scarf (the silky black ribbed part). Try it on both sides or only one side.

Add a long black and white section of ribbing (5 inches or so) just to the right or the left of the center of the scarf. Measure to find out where this would be, or just go on instinct.

Combine any of these variations or make up your own. Again, the colors are so good and the design so strong, it's hard to go wrong. It's a good exercise in design, and it's never too early to start. As you go along, you may want to keep in mind how and where the scarf might wrap around your neck and which colors and patterns might show. Then again, you might want to follow your intuition. Either way, if you don't like the result, all you have to do is rip it out and try something else. This is a pattern that's hard to ruin.

Another Variation

Once you feel comfortable with the basic technique (i.e., counting your stitches and twisting your yarn) you might even want to try a second, wider piece with more variation and experimentation in pattern (you decide how wide and how varied), which would make a dramatic shawl/stole.

Blocking

The bulkier gauge and corrugated rib texture of the ends of this scarf will flare out farther than the more supple black body as done in these yarns and in this gauge. I like the flare, but if you would like to spread the body of your scarf out to meet the edges, block it to shape. To block, put your garment on a blocking board (or on top of a towel on a rug or a couch or anything else that will tolerate being slightly dampened and stuck by pins) and pin it to its desired final dimensions. Spray with water until damp. Let it dry. It will keep these dimensions until you wet it again.

Steamers also make great blockers. Just keep steaming your garment until you get the shape you want.

Once you have a basic understanding of the mechanics of knitting you will be able to make up your own ancient-modern patterns just by looking at old art, using a bit of common sense, a bit of patience, and futzing until it works. What I like about this one is that it playfully brings the Minoan shuttle loom pattern out of the past and into the present in a very common form. When we create it, a part of us enters ancient time and partakes of that pattern making-breaking magic that was Ariadne's. At the same time, we bring that same pattern and activity into the present.

I suspect the Minoans would have approved.

---

[1]Marija Gimbutas, *The Language of the Goddess* (Harper & Row: New York, 1989), 293.
[2]E. J. W. Barber, *Prehistoric Textiles* (Princeton University Press: Princeton, 1991), 324–325.

The Moirae, the Art of Finishing, and a Multicolored Pullover

Somewhere deep in the Las Vegas of your mind there is a Greek-owned diner that serves breakfast all day. The coffee is good, the takeout is fast, and there isn't a slot machine in sight. You like it because they don't mind if you knit while you wait for your order. The owner's wife often sits in the window knitting afghans in stripes.

You could swear that every time you go in the same three women seem to be sitting at the four top in the window.

"Do you ever think about that little philosopher in the cave?" says the one in the middle this morning.

At that moment, you are wondering why it is that the owner's wife cuts her yarn, instead of carrying it, when she is done with each stripe, posing to yourself one of those minor but intricately fascinating questions one poses to oneself while waiting for things, but that line got your attention.

The one who is speaking usually wears some kind of hat with a pink flower and a jean jacket, and always carries a ruler, which she uses to measure this brilliant pink yarn that flies across her table. Whatever it is, it looks very mod against the purple and silver speckled formica tabletop. Almost hallucinogenic. She is a beautiful woman in the prime of life, not an innocent but not an elder either, and speaks in a distinctively optimistic voice—a sort of trilling light opera soprano that carries. When she hits a high note, all the guys behind the counter either smile or shudder.

"Which little philosopher?" asks the woman to her left. "They were a dime a

dozen." She is the youngest of the three, sweet looking, with a big mane of red brown hair. She must be a dancer or a magician's assistant, because she wears stretch jeans and sparkling T-shirts. She might be the youngest, but always sounds incredibly rational and always appears to be surrounded by a white aura of calm.

"Oh, you know Clotho, the one who used to write about us. Back when we wore robes and wore those little crowns on our heads."

"Chaplets," says Clotho.

"Right, chaplets. When we wore chaplets."

"That was quite a long time ago." With long fingers, Clotho picks a handful of fresh red cherries from a bowl to her left. You are positive this item is not on the menu.

"Plato!" cries the one on the right. She always wears leopard, and she's got this Ethel Merman growl, and she must be at least 50. "I can't tell you how many times I told that guy, we don't live in the stars, and we don't orbit."

"We do too orbit," Clotho speaks calmly. The cherries have turned into pomegranates.

You also notice for the first time that she is holding and spinning from a drop spindle, which she manages to keep spinning while she eats the fresh cherries, because they are cherries once again. The wild pink yarn Hat Woman measures comes off of this spindle.

A waiter serves Leopard Woman a steaming plate of scrambled eggs.

Leopard Woman, meanwhile, has begun to tap a large sewing scissors against the edges of the table.

"I wanted them runny!" she booms.

The waiter, already five leagues away, turns and dashes back to get Leopard Woman's plate. Then he dashes away once more at double speed, facing her and scraping and bowing until he reaches the counter, where he scowls and mumbles, "Atropos, Atropos, Atropos."

The guys behind the line scowl and mumble, "Atropos, Atropos, Atropos," and push a fresh plate of eggs over the line, which he immediately serves her.

Atropos' face breaks into a smile.

"Delicious! Thank you!"

Then she dives into her huge white pony skin tote bag, pulls out a grape lollipop, and foists it into the waiter's hands.

He smiles very sweetly with pained eyes, puts the lollipop in his shirt pocket, turns around, rolls his eyes, and runs five leagues in the other direction.

"You know, about those lollipops," Hat Woman murmurs sweetly. "He's probably a little old for them."

Atropos thinks for a moment. "I believe I am EXACTLY three hundred and seventy-two thousand years older than he is."

"He's a man, you're a Fate," says Clotho, spinning industriously. "No comparison. Not only a Fate, but a crone."

"Speak for yourself, maiden."

"Maybe I can't have kids, but I have a license to start whatever I want. And everyone finds me desirable."

"Well, you know dear," says Hat Woman, "eventually that gets just a little bit old. It's nice to have just one person desire you. Then you get to see what happens next. And make things."

"Things? You mean babies." Clotho spins her spindle just a little more slowly.

"Babies. Or money. Or make the world go round. Or enough corn to feed everyone on Crete."

Neighboring patrons admire her pink thread.

Atropos picks up the scissors and pounds them on the table.

"Of course I'm a Fa—"

Eyeing her scissors, the same patrons recoil in horror.

"Oh, right then." Clotho speaks calmly. "We orbit in their minds. Not around some great big drop spindle in the sky. Although that was fun while it lasted."

"I liked the rainbow light colored spheres," says Hat Woman dreamily. "I liked spinning around on them."

Clotho frowns. "Well, Lachesis, to my mind, that was like riding on a carousel all day long. Or an LP."

They are pomegranates again. The fruit is changing identity every six seconds.

The Moirae,
the Art
of Finishing,
and a
Multicolored
Pullover
80

"And look what happened to them!" says Atropos joyously, and raising up her scissor. "Snip, snip!"

"Oh, you mean the spheres spinning around the giant spindle? Yes, well," Lachesis sighs. "They are gone. I do have the utmost respect for you, Atropos dear, but sometimes I have to wonder why you snip some of my threads and not others. I liked those spheres. I awfully liked gryphons, too. And why you don't dispense with thermal paper and styrofoam once and for all, I can't imagine. And about the lifespan of Princess Diana . . ."

"Oh, let's not go *there* again," moans Clotho, spinning pink yarn with perfect evenness. "Plato's version of us, it was too predictable, really. I'm glad she cut it. And since when did we get responsibility of the lifespan of human inventions? I thought we just did the beings."

"Inventions are beings, too," says Lachesis. "Why, Zeus gave me control of vowels, after all."

"I always wondered about that. Why vowels?"

"Because vowels are the wombs of words."

"Didn't *cut* Plato's vision . . ." Now Atropos is working on the home fries. "Just thinned it. Considerably."

"That's true, dear," says Lachesis. "I was measuring it just last night. We help them begin, continue, and finish everything. What about the fellow himself? What happened to him?"

"Cut that one a long time ago."

"Ah, yes."

"Can you slow down just a minute?" asks Lachesis. "I'm just a little behind."

Sure enough, a pile of pink yarn is piling up on the table.

"Oh, pardon me." Clotho slows the motion of her hands.

"Thank you," says Lachesis, "because this is an important matter." Her voice and appearance might be exuberant, but she measures the yarn carefully against her yardstick, length after length. "Okay. Keep going."

"Yes," says the long-haired young spinner. "When it comes to those tricky subheadings known as life and death, what's doable and what isn't, what should

be worked on a little more and what is already done to perfection, we are the ones they want on their side."

"Hallelujah," bellows Atropos, so loudly that all the guys behind the counter stop cooking, and in the window, the owner's wife lets her scissor hang momentarily in midair. "When it comes to deciding whether or not there will be ANY raw material, in the form of breath and heartbeat, to do deeds, slay monsters, change into animals, and have one's way with comely mortals, we are the babes in charge!"

"I don't think people need to turn into animals anymore to have sex."

Clotho tilts her spindle as Lachesis speaks.

"Oh, really?" Clotho bends, and then straightens the spindle, for emphasis, then she balances it in one hand. "I'm not so sure."

As she tilts the spindle, a woman swoons at the next table. As she straightens it again, the woman's companion rushes to fan the swooning woman, who recovers summarily.

"I think it was the maple syrup," she tells him. "I'm allergic."

"Speaking of Plato, that was too bad about Orestes," says Clotho. "Did you really have to do it, Atro? I mean, the guy was just trying to avenge a murder."

"Too much hubris, had to go."

The other two eye her balefully.

"Business end of a spindle for him! Don't worry, just kidding. He had a better lifetime waiting somewhere else, you know."

"Lachesis and I really liked working on that thread."

"All silver and blue," says Lachesis. "You're going to scare them, you know. They're going to think that we are up to no good when actually we are their helpers."

"Ah, sorry, just my crazy sense of humor," says Atropos.

"Atro," says Clotho. "What could possibly be better than being Orestes?" She thinks a minute. "Oh."

"Now don't say it out loud!"

"I won't. But that's good! They call you the smallest and most terrible, but, really, I must say, you're the most inspired of us three."

THE MOIRAE,
THE ART
OF FINISHING,
AND A
MULTICOLORED
PULLOVER
82

"Thank you." Atropos shovels a heap of scrambled eggs into her mouth. Then she grins and pinches a little girl on the cheek as the child walks by with her mother. The mother promptly yanks the little girl away and marches her child outside, glaring back in Atropos' direction.

"Everyone thinks we're so scary, but actually we're funny," Atropos continues. "When all the damsels are being abandoned and the kings are being murdered, we provide just a bit of comic relief. I mean, really. Who could take it seriously? Three hags called furies pursuing Orestes with rolling pins and bopping him to death? Pure farce!"

"They weren't rolling pins," says Clotho.

"They would have been in this century."

"In *this* century," sniffs Lachesis, "they would be Uzis."

"I liked the sixteenth century," remarks Clotho.

"Double double toil and trouble fire burn and cauldron bubble." Lachesis puts down her yarn and yardstick, takes a dainty bite of tuna surprise, then folds her hands demurely. "You just don't get lines like that anymore."

"Go on! Measure!"

Lachesis gives Atropos a look then picks up her stick.

"What are these/So withered and so wild in their attire,/That look not like th' inhabitants o' the earth,/ And yet are on't. Live you? Or are you aught that man may question? . . . You can look into the seeds of time./ And say which grain will grow and which will not." Clotho is silent.

"That Banquo. He was dreamy."

Lachesis wipes her mouth with a napkin. "We sure didn't wear white there."

"Not so basic black." Clotho spins.

"I liked Richard Wagner!" says Atropos.

"Yes, you let him live a long time." Lachesis, measuring, casts a quick admiring eye over Atropos' scissors.

"Well, he dressed us as Valkyries and let us sing arias about yarn in front of our cave!"

"I always like being in fairy tales," sighs Lachesis. "Fée, fate, fairy, it's all the same. Don't you just love that? When we get to wear those beautiful pastels, and

give gifts or cast spells upon heroes and heroines, and come back later to rescue them?"

"Or torture them," says Clotho dryly.

"And how in Greece," Lachesis continues dreamily, "we still appear on the third night after a child's birth to direct the course of his or her life."

Atropos burps.

"Why do you think I eat so much? That's a lot of kids!"

"Excuse me," interrupts an unfamilar voice. "I couldn't help but notice your conversation. But, why don't you guys have your own story? You're always monkeying around in someone else's. And why are you still using a drop spindle? I mean, don't you know that this is the twenty-first century and women have been knitting for over five hundred years?"

Just then, the expression on Atropos' face changes. She becomes abstracted, thoughtful, even Buddha-like.

Clotho turns to face the unknown intruder. He is a tall, skinny guy, about twenty-eight, wearing square glasses. The smallest cell phone imaginable is attached to his ear and instead of waiting for an answer he is already busy whispering back sweet nothings which seem to consist entirely of strings of numbers into his telephone while waiting for his coffee.

Clotho turns to her sisters.

"Hey? Who let the dot com dude in here? Not *that* kind of thread," she says, turning back to the fellow, who is wearing a black T-shirt sporting the image of a pair of white electrified wings. "Because we spin. We just spin. That's where the yarn comes that you knit from and—"

And, it is at this precise second, that Atropos' scissors close around the pink yarn and cut, removing you from the diner, relieving you of the Las Vegas of your mind, and trading it for something entirely more serene, such as the high desert outside Tucson, or Cincinnati, and leaving no trace but the sound of three voices laughing.

THE MOIRAE,
THE ART
OF FINISHING,
AND A
MULTICOLORED
PULLOVER

84

The Three Fates

Moira means fate in ancient Greek. The Fates, or Moirae, were Zeus' older sisters, and not even he could change their will. Even the king of the gods knew that there was something to this fate thing: the mystery of becoming, being, and ending. All creative processes, teach these three, ever colorful ones (afghans, lives, loves, and ideals among them) have their ideal proportions of substance and time. The Fates are tangential to mythology, and yet they also occupy a portion of center stage. They both suffer from and enjoy what I call the obliquity factor. They move sideways through the story and out again. Their activity is powerful, but they remain mysterious; vivid to our senses, and influential to our lives, yet out of our immediate range. It's a classic seduction model. But there is another one that's just as interesting.

In astronomy, an oblique or eccentric orbit is one that does not move in a round circle. In our solar system, Pluto has one and so does Neptune. Because it does not maintain the same distance from the earth at all times, it is out of range for a long period of time, to the extent that we may not even know of its existence. It comes within range for a while, shows us its face, and is gone. This makes it mysterious to us: more work to predict its orbit and to gather other data that are less available when the body is out of reach.

We can't tug a planet from its orbit. Not yet, anyway. But archetypes can be a little more accommodating. If you look at them straight on, which you can do because they may direct the physical forces of the universe but are not actually governed by them, they tend to help you out. Instead of being pursued by the Fates, we can actually invite them out of our peripheral vision and into the light of our awareness, where they are quite pleased to become our allies. They seem mysterious and awesome and cause for fear. But, actually, they sit quite convivially and predictably close to the edge of our world, quite willing and able to take a hands-on approach to help us out.

You can do it with a drop spindle—the original yarn maker. Or, with a spinning wheel. But you can also use the yarn that either of these tools make. Although we don't necessarily believe in fairies, the long-term viability of social

security or reassurances that global warming is not at hand, the power of holding a spindle or its yarn-y issue in your hand is not something to be discounted. Held and used with intention, it has been known to create, prolong, and close down possibilities—or seal the deal, when something good needs to get officially done. Some might call this the power of positive thinking. I prefer to call it a mystery.

Is it us, is it them? It doesn't really matter. In either case, the assistance comes rather naturally.

Making the Fates Your Allies

You can work on any stage of any project. This is a thing that can be done very simply. It is done in ritual. Ritual is defined many ways. For me ritual is simply a way of formalizing your connection with something that is larger than you or, alternately, a deep and powerful part of yourself, which you don't necessarily contact in everyday life. It's performed with the stuff of this world, which creates a connection with that other world (again, whether that zip code called ritual summons your own resources or someone else's, or both, is up to you). Once you make the contact, and offer acknowledgment (in the form of small symbolic gifts; see below) requests can be made.

Start by choosing your Fate. I call in Clotho to speed and solidify tenuous beginnings: to a chapter, to a garden plan, to organizing your tax paperwork. I don't enlist her aid unless the beginning at hand is something that is already slightly in the works, because she is not a magician, she is a manifestor. She doesn't necessarily supply vision or opportunity. She facilitates the physical birth of something that already exists on paper, by agreement, or in the mind. Lachesis helps me when I'm in the middle of something and I just want to take a nap or forget the whole thing, because the distance between here and there seems too daunting. And Atropos is my woman when it is time to stop futzing with something forever and let it be done. In this category, creative projects, decisions, and once in a while, getting dressed all come to mind. Note: The Fates don't really

The Moirae,
the Art
of Finishing,
and a
Multicolored
Pullover
86

care if the request in question concerns something big or small. Their concern is, that whatever it is, it comes completely into form, continues, and ends at the most propitious time. They are a kind of cosmic assembly line.

Next, invite your fate. I often see them clothed in shimmering white, with a little gold somewhere, although the character and period of their dress varies. They can also just be forms of light. Even though they are maiden, mother, and crone, to me they don't look always look that different from one another, although whatever she's wearing and whatever time period she seems to reflect Atropos always does seem more intense and concentrated than the other two. But Clotho and Lachesis are just very slightly different in the face. Of course, yours may vary. Feel free to see them however they appear, because over the centuries everyone else sure has.

Third, have a gift to offer your fate and a special place to put it. As for the place, some folks have an altar, and that is simply a place that is special to them. A shelf is good, or an undisturbed corner of your favorite desk, or the lower shelf of the bedside table where no one goes but you. If you're feeling sprightly, make a special place even more special by pulling out that volume of Greek tragedy you haven't dusted off since college and placing it there as a base. Alternatively, you could tie up your offering in a little drawstring bag and place it in your yarn stash.

For me, Clotho is easy: I use an empty bobbin from one of my spinning wheels, with a leader fastened on and ready to accept yarn. Other ideas are a set of knitting needles with a token small ball of yarn at side or just a small length of yarn.

The imagery I get for Lachesis varies, and usually tells me something about the state of the project or situation for which I am requesting assistance. This is a personal matter, and you may very well see Lachesis differently, but I tend to see the length of her rod, with the yarn extending out to one side, as Grandmother Spider's staircase, vaulting crazily yet sturdily into the sky. For me, the middle of anything is a question of emergence: when will it happen, and will I have what it takes to do it when I get there? So I might use a piece of silk yarn,

strong and tensile like spider silk, to represent Lachesis. Or a piece of picture hanging wire, which, to me, evokes the steel spans of a suspension bridge, and brings strength and stamina to my project.

The kind of image that comes to me gives me a hint about the state of my project and my energy. A silk thread request requires delicacy and tact. Something in the suspension bridge category tells me there is lots of strong, even energy available, even though the project may look daunting (like closing the gap between two sides of a river).

Atropos is easy: a pair of scissors. The fun lies in choosing exactly what kind of scissors: a tiny pair of golden German embroidery scissors? Florist's shears? Or do you need a razor blade? Child-sized paper scissors? An exacto knife? A toe nail clipper? Or a meat cleaver?

Put your symbolic gift there. Add a token that symbolizes more specifically what you want. Greet the Moira of your choice with her name. Then, tell her what you would like to have done. Just have a conversation with her, either in words or in your mind, and listen to her response.

The answer could come in words. It could also come in the form of an insight, or a feeling, or a snatch of lyrics from a popular song. Sit a minute with the vision or feel or sound or touch of what you want for a moment. Tell her you would like outcome for it to come to you in the most balanced and harmonious way possible, regardless of how that might look.

When you feel as though the exchange is finished, tell her that you would like its outcome to benefit as many other beings (people, animals, plants, minerals, you can add to the list as you like) as possible aside from yourself. Then thank her for coming, and release her to her own activities.

Then, forget almost all of what you just did and pay attention instead to what happens.

Sometimes when we do ritual we have to wait patiently for the result to materialize. But I've found that the Moirae, like claims made about over-the-counter medications, are fast acting. When I contact them I usually feel a shift almost immediately. However, because their gift is deeply technical, be prepared to have the shift come in a form you were not necessarily expecting.

THE MOIRAE,
THE ART
OF FINISHING,
AND A
MULTICOLORED
PULLOVER

88

For instance, I was once in the midst of a writing project where I was excited about the inspiration but became anxious about the outcome to the point of sleeplessness about two-thirds into the book. One night, before I went to bed, I asked for Lachesis to help. I envisioned myself writing piles and piles of clever pages in the style to which I was at that moment accustomed. The next morning, which I had planned to be one of my few days off, I woke up with an unexpected new slant on the material which intrigued me so much I sat down to explore it immediately. It came out a little differently than the previous material had. As I wrote from this angle, despite the urgency of my deadline, I was unaccountably filled with calm and a sense of ease and freshness that persisted until the project was completed. I am still convinced it was skillful Lachesis who provided me with the ability and confidence to see the new angle, which was already in front of my face, and also with the consequent ease and tranquillity which was the fast-acting magic that I needed.

I wrote the pages, but, skillful technician that she is (as any good spinner has to be) she easily maneuvered me into the conditions I needed to do what needed to be done.

The Moirae Pullover, Increasing and Decreasing, and Cutting Your Losses, er, Yarn

The Moirae pullover alternates three distinctive and beautiful yarns in a basic garter stitch to create a sophisticated pattern. It changes color every three rows

or every two rows. I offer both versions because they create slightly different effects and the garter stitch blends the colors on the right side so the effect is blendy and variegated and sophisticated. Will you carry your yarn or cut it? This is a debate that rages among knitters, and I list their pros and cons below. These are beautiful, juicy, textural designer yarns that create a distinctive pattern and color effect that both "pops" and blends. One yarn is a wild black eyelash that tames enough but not too much when it is woven in with a slightly wavy variegated synthetic in soft greens, gray greens with touches of bright, soft pink, and a chunky, light silk cashmere blend in grays, pinks, and a little soft violet.

The sweater looks sophisticated, but fun, has its understated qualities (believe it or not) and the technique is really easy. The design is a classic, boxy pullover, which adds to versatility. If you're a beginner you'll appreciate the ease of it, and if you aren't, you appreciate the look and speed of it. If you are a new knitter, this is a good choice for a first sweater because it is knit in garter stitch (easy) but has lots of variety and interest because of the way you change yarns, and how they combine together.

Each yarn maps to one of the Weird sisters. The wriggly pink and green yarn is very Clotho/maiden. The soft, lofty silk cashmere changes color as smoothly as Lachesis' rod extending reliably through space, and the intense black eyelash, well, that's Atropos all the way. Like the Isis stole, it's also an entertaining and instructive project.

The sweater is designed to be hipbone length. If it isn't on you, and you want it to be, just add or subtract rows to the front and back somewhere before you get to the armholes. It also looks great slightly cropped. Again, just subtract the length you need to subtract to crop the sweater before you get to the sleeve decrease.

The two row stripe version blends the three yarns in a very interesting way and does not really require cutting (more about this in a minute). The colors blend together more in this version and it reminds me of a brilliant spring garden somewhere under intense southern light, like Provence, cast in the dappled black shadow of an old stone building. I love the experience of knitting of the two row stripe technique, and watching other people use it because you get to watch the

THE MOIRAE,
THE ART
OF FINISHING,
AND A
MULTICOLORED
PULLOVER
90

textures and colors change the way they blend as you knit along. It's a very pleasant experience, the knitting version of walking down a river or listening to jazz or Debussy (depending on the types of yarns you choose) or, if you're very brilliant in the way you choose your yarns, Mozart. Also, even though it's not particularly difficult, no one will be able to figure out how you did it unless you tell them. The two yarn version also gives a fairly sophisticated result and is very easy to achieve. The three row stripe version gives you a slightly more bold and contrasty stripe. The three row technique gives you this neat combination of the joy of blending and the interesting lines you get whenever you use a bold design. It is bold and also vaguely painterly, kind of a cross between an impressionist painting and a dainty rugby shirt. My artist friend Jenny loves the way the pink pops out from the wavy variegated yarn on this version. And when I went into the knitting store to trade in the black yarn for something white, Gina at the counter (who was *selling yarn,* mind you) begged me not to, because she loved the way the black made the other colors stand out. So I gave up.

If you scaled it down, and even though you do have to hand wash this sweater, the three row stripe version, in particular, would look great on a child. So I've included a child size version with a slightly bolder color choice that will look great on boys and girls.

Note: if you are newer to yarn blending, or even if you aren't, consider swatching up the two- and three-stripes versions to compare the difference. Then, choose your own yarns and let your mind go wild.

Speaking of which, if you can't find one of these yarns, just substitute one of your own that blends but also looks different. And when I knit this way I like to have one of the three yarns be almost a solid color, because this creates a background that helps the other two to stand out.

And, of course, you can just use two yarns or one yarn or four yarns, for that matter.

Moirae Pullover Pattern

Ingredients:

For smaller size:

- 3 100g (94m) skeins of Colinette Zanziba in Pierro (pinks, greens, pale blues) Color 102 (wool/viscose/nylon) (Main Color)
- 2 50g (100m) skeins of Noro Silk Garden in grey, pink, charcoal, violet (silk/kid mohair/lamb's wool) Color 1 (Color A)
- 5 50g (50–60 yd) skeins Trendsetter Château in black, silver, light golden brown Color 6 (polyester/mohair/viscose) (Color B)

For larger size: add one skein each of Colors A and B.

- 1 pair size eight needles, circular or longer straight (You may want a smaller one to pick up the collar.)
- 2 stitch holders
- 1 darning or tapestry needle

GAUGE: 3 to 3½ stitches to an inch and six and three quarters to seven rows to an inch. Take time to check your gauge, but note that since you are knitting in inches, row gauge is not critically important to your finished piece. Row gauge becomes more essential in color and pattern knitting like Fair Isle, Intarsia, and entrelac, which are not covered in this book. However, correct stitch gauge is ESSENTIAL, therefore, TAKE TIME TO CHECK YOUR GAUGE.

If you don't know how to increase or decrease, or pick up stitches and knit a border (which we do around the collar here), flip past the pattern to find instructions for simple increasing and decreasing in the New Knitter's Workshop. This is also where you will find a lively discussion of whether or not to cut or carry your yarns and a trick that works for this pattern.

THE MOIRAE,
THE ART
OF FINISHING,
AND A
MULTICOLORED
PULLOVER
92

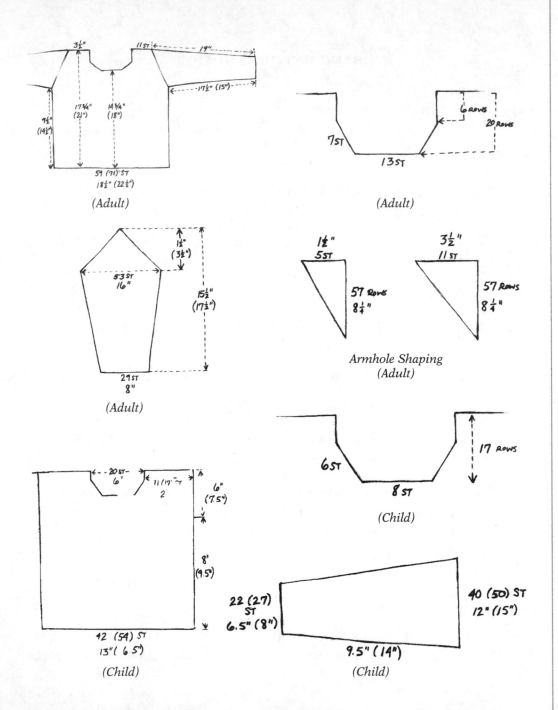

3½"

11 sт ← ——— 19" ———→

17¾" (21")   14¾" (18")

← - -17½" (15")- - - →

7½" (14½")

59 (71) sт
18½" (22½")

(Adult)

6 ROWS

20 ROWS

7 sт

13 sт

(Adult)

1½"
5 sт

3½"
11 sт

57 ROWS
8¼"

57 ROWS
8¼"

Armhole Shaping
(Adult)

1½" (3½")

53 sт
16"

15½" (17½")

29 sт
8"

(Adult)

6 sт

8 sт

17 ROWS

(Child)

- 20 sт -
6"

11 (17")
2

6"
(7.5")

8"
(9.5")

12 (54) sт
13" (6.5")

(Child)

22 (27) sт
6.5" (8")

40 (50) sт
12" (15")

9.5" (14")

(Child)

Three Stripe Version

First Step: Knit Back of Sweater.

Larger size is in brackets. See diagrams for finished dimensions of each size.

1 CO 59 [71] stitches in Main Color (MC) for a width of 18½ [22½] inches.

2 Rib *K1 P1* ending each right side (odd numbered) row with K 1. For ¾ inch.

3 Purl one row.

4 Change to Color A and knit 3 rows in garter stitch. Cut off your yarn, or carry, according to your choice.

5 Change to Color B and knit 3 rows in garter stitch. Cut or carry.

6 Change to MC and knit 3 rows in garter stitch. Cut or carry.

7 Keep repeating this pattern until your sweater back reaches 9½ [14½] inches in length. Adjust length if desired.

8 Shape armholes. Decreasing one stitch every 11 rows [1 stitch every 5 rows] on each side, knit 57 more rows and 8¼ more inches in the same garter stitch pattern for a total decrease of 1½ [3½] inches on each edge of the garment.

9 Continue knitting until piece measures 17¾ [21] inches in length.

Second Step: Knit Front of Sweater.

Larger size is in brackets. See diagrams for finished dimensions of each size.

The Moirae,
the Art
of Finishing,
and a
Multicolored
Pullover
94

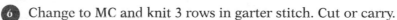

1 CO 59 [71] stitches in MC for a width of 18½ [22½] inches.

2 Rib *K1 P1* ending each right side (odd numbered) row with K 1. For ¾ of an inch.

3 Purl one row.

4 Change to Color A and knit three rows in garter stitch. Cut off your yarn.

5 Change to Color B and knit 3 rows in garter stitch. Cut.

6 Change to MC and knit 3 rows in garter stitch. Cut.

7 Keep repeating this pattern until your sweater back reaches 9½ [14½] inches in length. Adjust length if desired.

8 Shape armholes. Decreasing one stitch every 11 rows [1 stitch every 5 rows] on each side, knit 57 more rows and 8¼ more inches, in the same garter stitch pattern, for a total decrease of 1½ [3½] inches on each edge of the garment.

9 AT THE SAME TIME, when your garment reaches 14¾ inches [18 inches] in length, begin neck shaping. Bind off center 13 stitches and work each shoulder separately, binding off one stitch every other row at neck edge for 14 rows (total of 7 bound off stitches) and then knitting remaining stitches for 6 more rows, for a total of 20 rows, as you also continue to decrease along each armhole. Finished piece will measure 17¾ [21] inches in length.

10 Put shoulders on an extra pair of needles or a stitch holder.

THIRD STEP: Join Shoulders. Bind off shoulders together. Instruction if needed in New Knitter's Workshop below.

FOURTH STEP: Pick Up and Knit Collar Ribbing. Pick up 70 stitches evenly around collar and rib for ¾ inch.

Fifth Step: Sleeves

1 CO 29 stitches (8 inches) for both sizes in MC.

2 Rib *K1 P1* last stitch K1 on right side rows for ¾ of an inch.

3 Purl one row.

4 To shape sleeves, knitting in pattern stitch, alternating colors A, B, and MC every three rows, increase M1 (or using increase method of your choice) 1 stitch each side every sixth row 9 times and then 1 stitch each side every eighth row 3 times until sleeve measures 15½ inches and you have a total of 53 stitches. (**New Knitters:** the simple M1 increase is taught in New Knitter's Workshop at the end of this chapter.) Make your increase 1-2 stitches inside the edge of the sleeve.

5 To shape top of sleeve, bind off 4 stitches on each side and 6 stitches on each side every other row for 10 rows. (Bind off 2 stitches on each side of sleeve 12 times for 24 rows.) Bind off remaining 5 stitches in center of sleeve.

6 Repeat.

Sixth Step: Set in Sleeves, Finish Seams, and Weave in Ends (Instructions in New Knitter's Workshop below). Pin center of sleeve to center of shoulder. Pin edges of top of sleeve to bottom edges of armholes. Begin seaming at sleeve cuff, sew up to shoulder, and work down the side. Weave in ends.

THE MOIRAE,
THE ART
OF FINISHING,
AND A
MULTICOLORED
PULLOVER
96

TWO ROW STRIPE VERSION

Same as three row stripe, except you change yarn color every two rows. And you don't have to cut your yarn because the rows end evenly, i.e, you will pick up the new color at the side of the fabric where you let it drop.

THREE-YEAR-OLD SIZE AND TEN-YEAR-OLD SIZE VERSIONS

Quantities:

- 2 100g skeins (94m) Colinette Zanziba in pinks, greens, pale blues (wool/viscose/nylon) in Pierro Color 102 (Main Color)
- 1 50g skein (100m) of Noro Silk Garden in grey, pink, charcoal, violet (silk/kid mohair/lamb's wool) in Color 1 (Color A)
- 2 50g skeins (50–60 yd) Trendsetter Château in black, silver, light golden brown (polyester/mohair/viscose) Color 6 (Color B)
  (Or try Color 8, Mostly red and black, for a particularly bright, cheerful, bold child's sweater.)

Note: Directions for Three Row Stripe and Two Row Stripe are the same. See above.

Fɪʀsᴛ Sᴛᴇᴘ: Knit Back of Sweater. Larger size is in brackets. See diagrams for finished dimensions of each size.

 CO 42 [54] stitches in MC for a width of 13 [16½] inches.

2 Rib *K1 P1* ending each right side (odd numbered) row with K 1. For ¾ inch.

3 Purl one row.

 Change to Color A and knit three rows in garter stitch. Cut off your yarn or carry.

5 Change to Color B and knit three rows in garter stitch. Cut or carry.

6 Change to MC and knit three rows in garter stitch. Cut or carry.

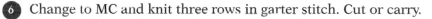 Keep repeating this pattern until your sweater back reaches 8 [9½] inches in length. Adjust length if desired.

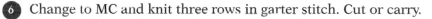 Place a marker on each side for armhole. Continue to knit until piece measures 14 [17] inches in length. On last row, bind off center 8 stitches and put shoulders on an extra pair of needles or a stitch holder.

SECOND STEP: Knit Front of Sweater

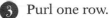 CO 42 [54] stitches in MC for a width of 13 [16½] inches.

② Rib *K1 P1* ending each right side (odd numbered) row with K 1. For ¾ inch.

③ Purl one row.

④ Change to Color A and knit 3 rows in garter stitch. Cut off your yarn or carry.

⑤ Change to Color B and knit 3 rows in garter stitch. Cut or carry.

⑥ Change to MC and knit three rows in garter stitch. Cut or carry.

⑦ Keep repeating this pattern until your sweater back reaches 8 [9½] inches in length. Adjust length if desired.

⑧ Place a marker on each side for armhole. Continue to knit.

⑨ When your garment reaches 11½ [14½ inches] in length, begin neck shaping. For both sizes, bind off center eight stitches and work each shoulder separately, binding off one stitch every other row at neck edge for 12 rows (total of 6 bound off stitches) and then knitting remaining stitches for 4 more rows, for a total of 16 rows. Finished piece will measure 14 [17] inches in length.

⑩ Put shoulders on an extra pair of needles or a stitch holder.

THE MOIRAE,
THE ART
OF FINISHING,
AND A
MULTICOLORED
PULLOVER
98

Third Step: Join Shoulders. Bind off shoulders together. Instruction if needed in New Knitter's Workshop below.

Fourth Step: Pick Up and Knit Collar Ribbing Pick up 56 stitches evenly around collar, rib for ¾ inch and bind off collar.

Fifth Step: Sleeves

1. CO 22 [28] stitches for 6½ [8] inches in MC.

2. Rib *K1 P1* last stitch K1 on right side rows for ¾ inch.

3. Purl one row.

4. To shape sleeves, knitting in pattern stitch and alternating Colors A, B, and MC every two or three rows, increase M1 (or using the increase method of your choice) 1 stitch each side every 6 rows 9 times for three-year-old version and 1 stitch each side every 8 rows 11 times for the ten-year-old version until the length of the sleeve measures 9½ [14] inches, you have a total of 40 [50] stitches, and the width of top of the sleeve measures 12 [15] inches. Make your increase 1-2 stitches inside the edge of the sleeve.

5. Bind off top of sleeve.

6. Repeat.

Sixth Step: Set in Sleeves, Finish Seams, and Weave in Ends. See New Knitter's Workshop if necessary.

Carrying Yarns

If you knit this sweater in the two row version, you will change yarns every two rows. And the right and left edges of each piece you knit will become seams. This

means you have two options. You can cut the yarn off every two rows, and weave the ends in later. Or, you can leave the yarns attached at the side (they may tangle a little) and pick them up when you need them.

The down side of cutting is that weaving in ends takes a while.

The down side of carrying, is that if your yarn is bulky, the seams will bulk up when the garment is finished (if it has seams).

When you knit, you do actually have to think about these things. They actually become interesting. In a subtle but fateful way, your decisions affect the final form of the garment. In this way, you actually become one of the three sisters.

A small survey among knitters reveals the following: Becky tries never to cut her yarn, because she feels she wastes too much of it that way. Her take is, carried yarn is an easier and more economical technique.

The practical Julie points out that you can't carry your yarn if you work in odd numbered stripes, because the yarn will end up on opposite sides of the piece each time from where you will need it to be the next time. Also, if you are working in more than four row stripes, the seams may get loaded up and bulky with yarn. This may also crop up if you are working with thicker gauge yarns in general. But fine yarns you can carry fine.

And the technically crafty Celia, quite the granddaughter of Spiderwoman and knitter of beautiful lace, adds that it is easier to control the tension of your yarn as you knit if you cut it, rather than carry it. She reminds us that you can get little pulls at the margins of your project if you carry your yarn, and that if you carry, sometimes, the last stitch on a row will end up with a different tension (i.e., it will be looser or tighter) than the other stitches.

And then there is the easy argument. Carrying your yarn is easy. So if you aren't in an Atropos sort of mood, just pick a project where you can carry your yarn. The only problem is, if you carry it, it will just naturally tangle a little, and you'll have to occasionally stop and untwist it. Which may be why Atropos started cutting those strands in the first place.

In the three row version of this sweater, you can actually use an interesting trick that allows you to carry yarn, saving yourself some time weaving in ends

The Moirae,
the Art
of Finishing,
and a
Multicolored
Pullover
100

later, without adding too much bulk to the seam. As you work your three row stripe repeats, you will notice that after each repeat you will end up with one color yarn on each side of your fabric while you work with a third. Which yarns are on which sides will vary, because the repeat is three rows, which is an odd number, but you will always end up with one yarn on each side alternating because six rows (or two repeats of one yarn) is an even number. So, simply wrap working yarn around the "dropped" yarn on each side at the end of each row or every other row (as if braiding your hair but only two sections and one wrap), to pick up the "dropped" yarn and carry it along the side parallel to the seam. It doesn't add much bulk and circumvents the process of weaving in ends. Try it and you'll see.

New Knitter's Workshop

To knit this sweater you'll just need to add a few new basic skills. There isn't any reason not to start with the sweater, instead of Isis wrap, if you are looking for a first project. If you can knit, purl, stockinette, cast on, bind off, and do a gauge sample you're ready for whatever the Moirae sweater has to offer. Some people prefer a simpler initial project (although the yarn stranding gives the Isis wrap a lot of interest) and some like a little more to do because it keeps them interested. Like most aspects of knitting, it's your choice.

M1 or Make (increase) one stitch

There are various methods of increasing the number of stitches in a row, and a lot of reasons to do it (such as, shaping the front of a sweater or increasing the stitches in sleeves to create fullness around the arm). Some slant the stitches to the left or right to follow the line of a sleeve, some create a noticeable (decorative) visual border at the edge of a garment. None are particularly difficult, but this one, which just adds a stitch almost invisibly to a row, may be the easiest of all.

1 Between the stitches in a row is something we knitters call a "bar." The "bar" is the piece of yarn in the knitted fabric that appears to run horizontally across the bottom of the row you are working on. There is a visible bar under the stitch being worked in the illustration above. To increase by making one (M1), pick up the bar with your non-working needle from back to front.

2 Then insert the working needle through the "loop" as if it were a regular stitch. You'll know you got it right if the stitch twists as it comes off the needle. This is what makes the increase almost invisible. This is an M1 knitwise.

3 To M1 purlwise, insert the non-working needle into the bar from back to front and purl through the front loop rather than knit.

DECREASING STITCHES

The art of decreasing stitches also has variations. The one we use is this:

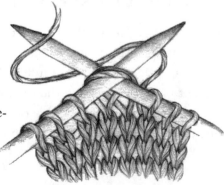

1 Insert the working needle into the next 2 stitches on the non-working needle as if to knit them (i.e., from front to back). Then knit them. This one is called K2TOG.

THE MOIRAE,
THE ART
OF FINISHING,
AND A
MULTICOLORED
PULLOVER
102

2. To decrease this way on a purl row (which we won't be doing in this pattern) put your working needle through the next 2 stitches as you would to purl and purl them.

Bind off shoulders together

Instead of binding off the front or back of your sweater at the shoulders, put the last row onto a stitch holder. When you are finished with both pieces, keep the front on the needle and do not cut off the yarn. Put the other piece back on a needle. Hold those two needles together and parallel, making sure that the RIGHT SIDES of the fabric are facing each other. (This is important, because, as you are about to see, in knitting garments are usually finished with wrong sides together.) Slip a third needle through the first stitch on each of the other 2 needles, knit them together, and slip the resulting single stitch off the 2 main needles and on to the third needle. Then do this again, so you have 2 stitches on the third needle. Slip the first stitch on the third needle (the one closest to the point) over the second stitch and off the needle, as if binding off normally. Keep going until all the stitches are bound off. This will always work as long as the number of stitches to be bound off together is the same on each side (e.g., you can also do this with the back and the 2 front pieces of a cardigan).

Pick up and knit

Pick up and knit is a method of adding a contrasting border or an additional element to a finished piece: i.e., ribbing around a collar, a turtleneck, or a few additional inches on the underside of a sleeve. Basically, when you pick up and knit,

you use the edge of your garment as your non-working needle and, with your working needle, add a row of stitches along the edge of something which you can then use to add whichever new element you like. (Here, we rib around a collar.)

Picking up and knitting sounds kind of impossible when you've never done it before. But actually one of my favorite moments of knitting comes when it works like magic, making something nagging in its slight unevenness look perfectly finished. Sometimes, a not insubstantial leap of faith is required to believe that all this strange in-ing and out-ing is going to result in an even, finished border. But then, it does.

1 Using a needle one to two sizes smaller than the one you will use for your pattern, dip the needle into the center of a stitch just below or near the edge of the bound off edge. If your stitch fabric is tight and even, use the row right below the bound off edge. If your fabric is looser and made up of different textures, you may want to go two rows below the bound off edge in order to avoid pulling the fabric and to create evenness all the way around. Your fabric will show you. It's the row that is stable enough not to pull. Use common sense, and if you aren't sure, just pick up a few stitches, knit a few rows of whatever you have to knit, and test the result.

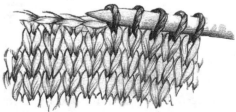

2 Wrap your yarn knitwise around your needle, and draw it through the bound off edge (This is the part where you are using the edge as your non-working needle). Continue to pick up stitches evenly as you go around your edge.

THE MOIRAE,
THE ART
OF FINISHING,
AND A
MULTICOLORED
PULLOVER
104

Stitch distribution: If your pattern specifies the number of stitches to be picked up around the edge in question, measure the area you need to cover and separate it into smaller areas with stitch markers or even safety pins or little pieces of yarn, and using seams as guidelines. If you have 100 stitches to pick up along a 32-inch edge, you might try sectioning off your collar into 4 equal 8-inch sections, and then subdividing each of those 4 sections into 5 more, and picking up 5 stitches per section. The subdivisions can be approximate. This will keep stitch distribution even and also eliminate suspenseful questions such as, what will happen if I arrive at the last inch of my edge and still have 20 stitches to pick up?

When you have picked up all your stitches, replace the smaller needle with the one you will be using (Picking up with the smaller needle ensures you won't be leaving any big stitch holes in your fabric.) and start to knit.

Evening out your fabric: You can use picking up and knitting to even out an uneven fabric. Looser, drapier fabrics knitted in more than one textured yarn can sometimes look uneven. If you see what looks like a big "hole" (i.e., a loose stitch or a stitch made in a thinner part of a novelty or thick and thin yarn) in your fabric pick up your next stitch after the "hole" rather than in it. This will camouflage and diminish the unevenness, and give firmness to the edge of your fabric. Again, you don't have to be absolutely even in your stitching for this to work. In fact, if you are using a thick and thin or novelty yarn it will probably be impossible for you to pick up stitches with 100 percent technical exactitude. Remember *hozho*, or the ideal of harmony without exact symmetry, based on the example of the natural world. Approximate is fine.

Picking up and knitting is also a great trick for making a garment wider (in the sleeves or around the bust) if it comes out too small. You simply pick up stitches along one or both edges (in this case, these would be the edges of the sleeves or bodice) and add a few rows in the stitch and color of your choice. Changing color or yarn here creates an interesting, clean design element, as you can get a clean contrasting stripe under the arm or along the side.

Finishing Seams

There they were, the two sleeves, the cardigan fronts, and the back of my very first sweater. In theory, they all looked fine. But would they fit together as promised? I knew the width of one sleeve was smaller than the other one—I'd made a small error in decreasing somewhere, but since the discrepancy was small, I'd brazenly decided it wasn't worth the trouble of ripping the thing out. But when I was ready to sew the final product I lost my nerve. Would it look like a sweater or an unintentional cubist study in wool? And what about this sewing together thing? Heck, I couldn't even cut a straight line. How was I possibly going to pull this one off?

I sought professional guidance. I brought in my sleeves, right and left cardigan fronts, and back and sat down with Rose one evening for the price of an hour instruction plus a tapestry needle for finishing.

Rose reassured me that the source of my unease was common. She herself had knitted all the separate pieces for various sweaters, and put them aside without finishing them, before she actually mustered the nerve to sew one up.

Not only did this revelation put me instantly at ease, it also went so far as to give me the mild suspicion that I might just be ahead of the curve. (The mark of a really good teacher.) Next, Rose told me that finishing a sweater required nowhere near the neatness and precision of sewing a dress. The stitching was done with wrong sides together (unlike binding off shoulders together), nothing got turned inside out, it wasn't much more difficult than basting, it only had one step, and you could use the technique to hide your mistakes.

And, as it happens, she was right. Finishing starts out fine, and as you get more practice with it, it gets better. Plus, as a last resort, you can always block your sweater to get the desired shape after you finish it.

The Moirae,
the Art
of Finishing,
and a
Multicolored
Pullover
106

Finishing a Sweater:

Mattress stitch

Lay the two pieces flat and edge to edge with right sides up. Thread a tapestry or darning needle and bring it from back to front either one or two stitches in from the edge. Insert the needle into the corresponding stitch on the other piece of fabric. Thread the needle under the loops of one or two rows of stitches then bring it back through the front, cross over to the other piece to be joined, and put it back into EXACTLY THE SAME HOLE it came out of the first time. The only trick to this is to make sure that your needle zigzags like this along the edges of your garment as it does in the illustration.

Make sure that when you cross the seam from piece to piece that your needle goes back into the same hole it just left to go to the other side.

Pull the yarn tight (but not too tight) every 3 or 4 stitches or so.

You'll know you have the stitch pattern right if the yarn pulls through. Otherwise just thread it out and try it again.

One of the advantages of this method is that the zigzag pattern gives you the option of evenly matching two slightly uneven pieces (i.e., a sleeve that came out just slightly too big for the corresponding armhole shaping on the body of the sweater). All you do here is make the stitches on the larger piece slightly closer together than the stitches on the slightly "too small" piece and all is forgiven. Also, if you are using a highly textured yarn that leaves big holes, you can work your stitches on either side (not through) the large hole to tighten it and make the overall texture more uniform. Kind of like cosmetic surgery for your sweater.

Bar to Bar

Some people think this one makes for cleaner seams. (The previous version can leave some bulk in your seams, depending on the garment.) If I am finishing something with a very even, geometric stitch pattern and that fits closely, I'll use this version. It can leave a cleaner edge. I'll use the other one on a textured, looser fitting piece. You'll come up with your own preferences. In this version of finishing seams, you match the stitches together exactly and put your needle through the bar between stitches on each side.

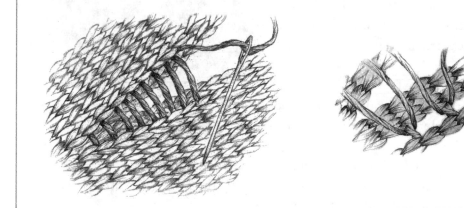

Other, more nuanced versions of finishing are available in some of the books listed in the bibliography.

WEAVING IN ENds

Thread an end onto the same large tapestry or darning sized needle you used for seaming. Whipstitch them through a seam or baste through a few nearby stitches. Bury "slippery" yarns farther into your garment. "Sticky yarns" do not have to be fin-

THE MOIRAE,
THE ART
OF FINISHING,
AND A
MULTICOLORED
PULLOVER
108

ished as deeply. Some knitters recommend weaving in ends before finishing. Others begin to seam, and weave in ends as they become annoying during the seaming process. Others weave in as the final step. It's a matter of personal taste, and of the particulars of each garment—sometimes you can't get at an end after its been seamed, in which case you finish it first.

Rachel's Wild Patience, the Secret Life of Fleece, and a Precious Pillow Cover and Bag

Fact: it is going to take you longer to knit a sweater than it would take to open a tasteful mail-order catalogue and order one right now. It is probably going to take you longer to knit a sweater than to go to the store and buy one, even if you have to try five different stores on three different weekends. It takes a wild kind of patience to be a knitter. Not that it's so difficult or challenging to be this wildly patient. When we knit, we become patient almost by accident. Almost despite ourselves, because we also want to finish and wear whatever we are making in the next five minutes, and this is part of what keeps us going, we notice that even as we hasten toward the next stitch, the next row, the next decrease, the end of the collar, we are also entering the deep warm sea called slowing down. We are surrendering to this obvious but odd sort of alternate universe where waiting is not only acceptable, but pleasurable. And going there is as easy and as impossible as falling in love.

Wild patience is a particularly fertile and creative state. It takes a simple or scarce resource, applies to it way too much time to be accounted for rationally, and makes it into a whole lot of something. Wild patience is powerful. Once discovered, it can be handily and easily applied to other areas of a life.

I call it wild because it is innovative and traditional at the same time. On the one hand, it is entirely impractical, and can even cause hardship or inconvenience on the everyday level. At the same time, it is eminently practical to the long term sustenance of the heart and soul.

In one of its lives, it is born in the story of the great romantic beauty and matriarch of the Old Testament, Rachel.

The Story of Rachel

Rachel is not a goddess. She is a woman born out of the tradition that stripped away the pantheon of deities of the Ancient Near East to make the point that each individual can have a direct, personal, and intimate interaction with the divine or sacred source, without any intervention from go-betweens. But she is a knitting goddess nonetheless.

The story goes like this. Rachel is a young marriageable girl and daughter of Laban, a farmer. She is out alone shepherding her father's flock toward the local well where the shepherds gather together during the day to lift the large, flat, heavy rock that covers the communal cistern so that they can water their animals. The day is hot and the hills of Haran, the land north of Jacob's home in Canaan, are dry, desert-like, and almost barren. Canaan is that pivotal, ancient land named after the mollusks found on and off of its coasts, which yielded the precious deep violet dye that colored the kingly linens of that entire region. As Rachel approaches, she can see that a few shepherds are already gathered there with their own flocks.

Rachel's aunt, the matriarch Rebecca, who lived near an oasis in the southern part of Canaan, was also a shepherdess. Still, some have written that it is unusual for a young marriageable girl in the society of the Ancient Near East, especially one who is also quite a great beauty, to be herding sheep alone. Perhaps she must have been unusually robust, or self-sufficient, or clever to have been a young shepherdess among shepherds, or even to do the herding on a day that none of her brothers were available. In any case, Rachel's first appearance is unconventional, and notable. Did Rachel the beautiful shepherdess have dark honey hair with startlingly black eyes and pale skin? Or was she auburn, with golden skin, regal profile, and eyes to match? We do not know. You are invited to come up with your own description, or to choose someone else's. Over the centuries, she has been described and painted these ways and more.

RACHEL'S
WILD
PATIENCE, THE
SECRET LIFE
OF FLEECE,
AND A
PRECIOUS
PILLOW COVER
AND BAG
112

In any event, as she approaches the well, beautiful Rachel looks up to see an unknown man standing at the well along with those who are known to her. From a distance, she can see that this unknown man is handsome, dark, and dressed in foreign clothing. As she gets closer, she can see that he is covered with traveler's dust, and looks tired. He is watching her with a posture that suggests some sort of certainty, a single upright figure growing gradually larger against the vast frame of desert hills. She walks forward, watching, accompanied only by the gentle chaos of sheep, the perceptions of her own body, and the scent of fresh water.

As she reaches the well, the stranger's face fills with joy. And, inexplicably yet entirely explicably, Rachel feels the same joy in her own heart.

Next, this man, laughing with delight, and exhausted as he is, is single-handedly removing the enormous rock that covers the well and watering her entire flock of sheep.

And then, smelling of dates and the dust of the road, and without saying a word, he kisses her.

For perhaps one hundredth of an instant, Rachel is astonished. Her astonishment has the duration and the nature of the surprise you might feel after you see the first bolt of lightning in a storm but before you remember what lightning is. But this kiss is not only lightning, it is also the darkest and richest of honeys.

And so once that instant has passed she is not astonished at all.

When they part from this kiss, which has the distinction of being one of the few, if not the only, passionate kisses recounted in the pages of the Old Testament, the man who has kissed her is weeping with joy.

"I am Jacob," he says through his tears. "You are Rachel. You are my cousin. My mother, Rebecca, has sent me to you to ask work from your father, Laban, my uncle."

She runs home and tells her father. And Laban runs to meet Jacob, who, on the previous night, fleeing from his own home to escape his brother's wrath, had lain on the ground with a stone for a pillow and dreamt of angels at the top of a ladder.

Laban is a shrewd farmer with far too much hard land to till and far too many sheep to herd. He briefly sizes up the handsome stranger and his story,

which includes the fact that Laban's nephew Jacob is penniless. Jacob has received the blessing that transmits the sacred covenant of Abraham and his father, Isaac, in place of his older brother Esau and has had to leave his southern home as a result. By the end of the conversation, Jacob and Laban have struck a deal. Jacob may have Rachel's hand in marriage after he puts in seven years of labor on his land as dowry.

Luckily, this is Biblical time where the span of a lifetime can easily stretch for one hundred and fifty years. So Jacob works and Rachel works, side by side, and as the seasons of the year wheel around and grain is grown and harvested flocks of sheep are born and lambs are shorn and are slaughtered for food, they love each other and wait, one imagines, with wild patience. The writer of Genesis states that Jacob loved Rachel so much the seven years of labor seemed to last but a few days. Wild patience can yield that particular gift.

One can only imagine the depth and complexity an unfulfilled yet constant love can achieve enriched by the passage of seasons and the careful, constant, detailed tending of land and animals in a harsh but fruitful land. This work becomes even more poignant here in the high desert hills, against the backdrop of a love whose progress is both harsh and fruitful, as the obvious physical bond between the lovers is denied although together they help the land give birth. This love is like so many other loves, but more so: at once fertile and arid; abundant and scarce; promising yet restrictive. Rachel waits, patiently, and wildly, for the stricture established by her father to be released.

Meanwhile, the rest of the family gets to know Jacob.

Leah is Rachel's sister. Unlike Rachel, she is, by all accounts, no beauty. She has one mysteriously weak or blind eye. But she runs the tribe and the farm while Rachel is out with the sheep.

Leah also falls in love with Jacob.

The seven years pass, and the wedding day finally comes. Laban is loath to lose such a fine worker as Jacob. The wedding feast is celebrated as planned.

But on the wedding night, the most onerous and apparently cruel of subterfuges occurs. With Laban's help, Leah, disguised and veiled as the bride, takes

RACHEL'S
WILD
PATIENCE, THE
SECRET LIFE
OF FLEECE,
AND A
PRECIOUS
PILLOW COVER
AND BAG
114

Rachel's place in the wedding bed and, unknowingly to a slightly inebriated Jacob, consummates the marriage in her sister's place. An anguished Jacob does not discover who shares his bed until the morning. By now, according to the law of this tribe, it is Leah who has become his wife.

Although Genesis does not include this part of the story, the rabbis of the Talmudic and Midrashic period say that Rachel knows what Leah planned to do and has done nothing. And Laban comes to Jacob and explains that Jacob can marry Rachel in another seven years. Instead of complaining, Jacob becomes indentured to Laban for another seven years.

So there it is, that first brutal turning point in the story of perfect, promising love. Why didn't Jacob realize? How could Laban be so cruel, and Leah so calculating and desperate? When I shared this story with an early reader who was discovering the story fresh, she wondered whether these people were better suited to the environment of an afternoon TV talk show than they were to the exalted and pivotal environment of the Old Testament.

And in a way they have made such an appearance, because, over the ages in rabbinical discourse, this astonishing development caught the hearts and souls of rabbis in a special way and inspired fascinating and creative speculation on the nature of compassion and patience. Bigamy is a notably unusual solution to any problem, no matter how enormous, in the highly monogamous Hebraic tradition, which specifically and harshly prohibits any marriage structure aside from monogamy. For instance, it is speculated that, torn between her compassion and concern for her sister, who may have been promised to Jacob's difficult and even wicked brother Esau, and her love for her husband, Rachel chose compassion over her own, and her beloved's, fulfillment.[1] And Rachel is much loved for this highly unusual and unconventional yet traditional choice.

What does the young woman who silently gives away her beloved after seven years of waiting have in common with the robust young shepherdess who appears alone with her flock at the well? Both reflect a young woman who is capable of combining very traditional and highly unconventional or surprising behavior. This shepherdess and her beloved fulfilled a conventional social role,

and a traditional agricultural role, but her choices, and her life, were innovative and even surprising. They still make us think, and question, and piece together who she might have been, and why she might have acted, and whether or not it is possible for one person to be both that bold and that gentle. They also begin to embroider this quality of wild patience—patience so deep and sweet and radical that it bypasses the inner architecture of ordinary emotions and wounds toward another, impossible-to-articulate location of inner freedom and poise. Rachel eschews a situation that other women might consider tragic, drastic, limiting, victimizing by exploring a traditional female attribute (patience, compassion) to an extreme. In a tiny way, the creative process behaves in a similar way. It eschews both the potential satisfactions and losses of conventional response for a more open, fertile state. It says, I can wait. I can be contrary. I can trust. Once it is slipped into, it's worth it. The act of knitting partakes in this quality just a bit also, and without the great sacrifice. The best of both worlds. This secret, inarticulable, yet understandable poise and balance may be the same one that the learned rabbis aim for when they praise Rachel. And what they, and we, may be praising is a creative resource and source of wisdom that can manifest on a number of different scales.

Another answer to this provocative question may lie in the way sheep are best handled. Samuel Dresner, in his wonderful book *Rachel*, observes that her identity as shepherdess suggests the quality of mercy because shepherds must care for their charges.[2] A backyard shepherd and fiber artist I know told me that the best way to handle sheep is gently. When they are handled quietly, which, in this case, means without dogs herding them and with soft voices and human whistles to guide them, the personalities of sheep, often assumed to be among the duller of animal personalities, can blossom. Sheep become friendly, put their head in one's lap, and follow one around like a dog, given such treatment over a period of time. So it's at least worth wondering whether it was actually the shepherdess who got out of her sister's and father's way; who saw, somehow, that no other solution was tenable, and that if she handled them gently, they would mellow over time. Such a person would have to be very secure in herself, and in the degree to which she was loved. Such a person would have to have faith. All of the

Rachel's
Wild
Patience, the
Secret Life
of Fleece,
and a
Precious
Pillow Cover
and Bag

116

Old Testament matriarchs had a special relationship with Yahweh. Rachel's is less filled out than, for example, her grandmother Sarah's. Sarah and Yahweh used to talk, and when he told her she would conceive and bear a son in her nineties, she laughed. And then he made it so. But one wonders if Rachel and Yahweh were not having a private, unreported conversation.

But Rachel's trials continued.

After Rachel's wedding, Leah and Jacob gave birth to six sons and a daughter. Meanwhile, Rachel and Jacob had no children at all. The most difficult of all challenges for the classic Old Testament matriarch, whose mandate and joy is to expand the tribe, and also one that is undergone by four out of the five of them. And so for seven more years Rachel had no choice but to develop even more depth and wildness. The first time may have been intentional on her part. This second time seems more like a forced march.

As Leah bore sons, Rachel reverted to more desperate options, including taking mandrake to improve fertility. The mandrake root was dug from the fields by Leah's son Reuben, and Rachel could only obtain it by trading it to Leah for one of her own nights with Jacob. During which, of course, Leah became instantly pregnant while Rachel still went barren. In the meantime, both Leah's and Rachel's handmaids, Bilhah and Zilpah, also bore Jacob sons in the Biblical tradition. Only the beloved remained childless.

And through all of this, Jacob loved only Rachel, and impossibly compassionate, softhearted Rachel waited.

Seven more years of wild patience, suffering, vulnerability, and faith passed. As they pass, this initially instant, bold, simple and wildly fertile love gains the patina and depth of something strong, like a tree, or a stone bench, or a rose hedge that has been left to weather the alternately stringent and lavish treatment of the seasons without protection on the one hand or recourse for moderation on the other. (And, in the case of the rose bush has been severely pruned in some seasons and allowed to grow free in others and has become entirely more beautiful and hardy for it.) And finally Rachel conceives. As the writer of Genesis 30 relates, "And then God remembered Rachel, and opened her womb."

And when Yahweh opens the womb of an Old Testament matriarch, he

opens it big time. Rachel's first-born son with Jacob is not just any run-of-the-mill wonderful son. Her son is Joseph, he of the beautiful countenance, the prophetic dreams, the robustly Machiavellian mind, and the coat of many colors, all of which are qualities that will help him save his own life and with it the future of his precious lineage, and protect his people deep within the heart of Egypt during his lifetime.

And this is the way of wild patience. It eventually produces wildly fertile, prolific, and precious results. This result is particularly precious in the context of her culture, which prizes the ability of women to bear sons of achievement for what is perceived to be a precious and scarce tribal line, and whose express purpose is to transmit a sacred agreement from generation to generation. Because of the desert environment in which it grows, it also demonstrates the sacred art of creating abundance from apparently meagre resources. Rachel's children are few. (After Joseph, she will bear only one more son.) Rachel would not be seen as God's favored sister in the fertility matriarchies and cultures of the Ancient Near East. Leah, who bore the mark of fertility, would be the sister who earned that distinction.[3]

But in the nomadic desert culture of monotheism, Rachel is featured as the inspirational figure of the story. She is distinguished not only for her patience, her complexity, her mysterious yet eloquent sacrifice and her motherhood, but also for her unconventional method of cultivating and shepherding her family through the boon of her great, romantic, passionate love fed by what appears to be a naturally soft, and also quite strong, heart.

A number of years later, Jacob and his clan fled their home after Jacob's sons by Leah placed the family in danger by violently avenging the rape of their sister, Dinah. They fled back to the southern land of Abraham and Sarah, where Yahweh had promised Jacob he would some day return. At this time, Rachel was pregnant for the second time.

Near Bethlehem, the entire party stopped as she went into hard labor, gave birth to her second son, Benjamin, and died on the road.

There she was buried under a hastily erected pillar, and the clan moved on again quickly.

RACHEL'S
WILD
PATIENCE, THE
SECRET LIFE
OF FLEECE,
AND A
PRECIOUS
PILLOW COVER
AND BAG
118

All the other Hebraic patriarchs and matriarchs are buried together in a single cave. At the time of Rachel's death, Abraham and Sarah were already buried there, and Isaac and Rebecca. Jacob and Leah would be buried there in time. But on the road to Bethlehem, tyrannized by the expediencies of survival, with little ceremony, and no sweetness or time for reflection, Jacob, out of necessity, abandons his great love without ceremony.

When he met her, he moved a great stone out of her way so she could drink and water her flock on a parched day. And as he buries her, he and his clan cover her with another show of stone all must have known was at once insufficient and also extravagantly expensive, in terms of potential cost to their own safety.

And here the core specialness that seemed to have been bestowed on Rachel by her beauty, sound constitution, and deep wild patience seems finally to have run out. On the other hand, her death is consonant with the scarce few, yet complexly arranged strokes of her character. She lived unconventionally, and she died unconventionally, shockingly even, and with little of the ceremony that was so important to her people. One of the rabbinical explanations for the unconventional marriages explains that Jacob's situation was permitted as long as he lived beyond the borders of the Promised Land. But that once he returned, the law had to be obeyed, and this was why Rachel died before they crossed the border.

Regardless, after Rachel's death Jacob is never the same. The vibrant patriarch who followed God's instructions and became prosperous even as he was indentured to his canny father-in-law and wrestled with an angel, subsides from substantial view until he is eventually reunited with Joseph to bequeath the covenant to Joseph's younger son, Ephraim.

But Rachel. Rachel!

We know already that her unconventional behavior and life yielded abundant fruit, and traditional results that greatly nourished her tribe as a whole. In a way, in hindsight, Rachel's unconventional and painful choices resulted in the conservation of her entire clan. Her first son was Joseph, and her second, Benjamin, became the father of the tribe that settled Jerusalem and Israel. And, thus, after her death, the wildly patient, selectively fertile and loving, courageous, and tragic Rachel became known as the mother of Israel.

Today, it is said that no Old Testament figure receives the outpouring of affection that Rachel still inspires. Near Jerusalem, she is said to rise up out of her grave and help travelers along the highway, and that this is why she has been buried there. For similar reasons, passionate prayers are said to her as the protector and hope of exiles who long to return home. The Zohar, a major source of mystical Judaism, identifies Rachel with the Shekinah, or the feminine presence of the divine. Once again anchored by a monument of stone erected at a spot that is convenient to travelers she continues to succor her vast and more symbolic flock.[4] At her tomb (a pillar still stands, along with a white domed tomb building that was built during the Ottoman Empire, although the real burial place may be elsewhere) women perpetuate the tradition of tying red cords around the building to seek her protection in childbirth as Rachel brings the sacred life impulse of the red thread into the present.

Thus, in death, in myth, and through the genetic and inspirational spark she provided to an entire spiritual tradition, the bold, innovative, and impossible to categorize shepherdess of lambs becomes symbolic and mystical shepherd to an entire people. Her soft-hearted wild patience, as brutal and inexplicable and disturbingly acquiescent as it may seem, was sufficient to spiritually gestate an entire nation.

Wild Patience as a Model for Creativity

The matter of wild patience, on a different scale, is particularly appropriate to knitting. However we interpret the story of Rachel, most of us will probably agree that the story shows that you can do a lot with a little; that depth and faith can literally or metaphorically open a closed womb. Among other things, wild patience is the realistic experience of creativity, as opposed to idealization of the creative process. Very few creative events flow as effortlessly and regularly as one of Johann Sebastian Bach's Brandenburg concertos. More often, they are characterized by the stops and starts, triumphs, reversals, sacrifices, and innovative choices, as is the story of Rachel the shepherdess. The story remorselessly clocks the ups and downs of any creative process, which characteristically contain

RACHEL'S
WILD
PATIENCE, THE
SECRET LIFE
OF FLEECE,
AND A
PRECIOUS
PILLOW COVER
AND BAG
120

stages of ambiguity, imperfection, discomfort, and sacrifice. It quietly demonstrates how the experience of creative achievement does not have to occur consistently through a project or process in order to achieve a desired result. Constant satisfaction is not an indicator of an ultimately satisfactory result. More usually, our most cherished creations withstand and even benefit from a little weathering.

In the first impulse to knit a project, or write a book, or conceive a child, we are lightning and honey happy; madly in love. We have the strength to move any stone tablet from the top of a well single-handed. When the first flush fades, the reality sets in, and reversals of fortune, and inexplicable sacrifices and compromises, frustrations, disappointments, realizations of our own shortcomings and inadequacies, long lulls, patience, serenity, become almost routine. In her "Chant of the Mothers," Rabbi Lynn Gottlieb calls Rachel "Soft Heart Woman."[5] Having the courage to dispatch stop-and-go circumstances such as these with a soft yet measured heart is a formula that more realistically expresses the optimal progress of creativity and love. It's chunky and unpredictable. It has hits of brilliance, and the occasional teeth-gnashing, heartbreaking setback. And still it lives. And the setbacks temper the love, and the creativity, and the final product, rather than destroying it. The softness and the ability to be both gentle and bold yields fertile results. When we knit we can access some of these feelings. We work slowly while, to the untrained eye, life apparently passes us by. But we know better.

Putting this into knitting terms, if you happen to drop three stitches ten rows back into the pattern, think of Rachel. If your yarn runs out because you miscalculated, and it takes a week or two to get some more in, think of Rachel. When the pattern you charted that looked so easy in principle becomes labyrinthine in execution, know that this is part of the process. Sure, throw your project under a couch pillow for a day or two—or a year or two. Then, treat yourself to that soft love, and pull it out again.

And, likewise, when, unexpectedly, you toss off the prettiest little cardigan possible, and wonder how you ever came up with exactly that blend of shine, drape, color, and pattern, think of Rachel, and tip a metaphorical cup of sweet red Sabbath wine in her general direction.

"Rachel" means lamb in Hebrew and the Sumerian word for sheep also means vulva. All of the matriarchs and other early Hebraic heroines had names that tied them to the great spirits of the animal kingdom. Rebecca, for instance, means cow, and the cow is an ancient symbol for joy and fertility. So she was strongly allied with this seminal animal that provided so much of the sustenance of the ancient Near East which, in turn, has culturally sustained our own society since its inception. The Canaanites kept warm with sheep, and ate sheep, and drank their milk, and sold them. They were core to their sustenance as they were to so many people. Another clue that Rachel and her traditional yet innovative choices were ones that supported core sustenance and nurturing of a tribe.

One of the reasons that imagery of lambs, sheep, shepherds, and shepherding are core to Judeo-Christian teachings is that the animal sustained the people who gave birth to them. They were, if you will, the stars of popular culture, in their ability to sustain and to bring abundance, the repositories of the hopes and survival of the people; the metaphors the prophets reached to bring home their points. If productivity software had existed in Biblical times, it probably would have been designed to track, propagate, sell, and protect sheep, not sales contacts. And if self help books had existed in Biblical times, many of them probably would have been about how to amass flocks instead of how to perfect the body or become powerful by using your mind.

So Rachel is also attached to core sustenance. The wife and mother of prophets, their treasure, who is also a literal shepherd in the family, loves, tends sheep, longs, waits. So, very simply, one of the invitations the story gives to the reader is to reconcile or explore the way core abundance and wild patience and a soft heart can go hand in hand.

Some contemporary shepherds are very familiar with this grouping of qualities. There are those who raise their herds on the range in large numbers. And then there are "backyard" shepherds, which includes everyone from handspinners who go to shows and come back with a Shetland sheep or mohair-producing Angora goat or two in the back of the pickup (a couple of sheep aren't so hard to

RACHEL'S
WILD
PATIENCE, THE
SECRET LIFE
OF FLEECE,
AND A
PRECIOUS
PILLOW COVER
AND BAG

122

take care of, although goats are clever), to small fiber producers who hand pick and breed their own small flocks to produce, process, and sell their own fiber, not unlike the way boutique vintners hand produce and sell their wines. (They also keep fiber and yarn to design and make their own creations on the wheel, and the loom, and on knitting needles.)

Backyard shepherds report that the ability to appreciate fiber is a very nourishing, enriching experience. Unlike rangers, they tend to have small enough flocks that they know each animal personally, and also know each animal's fiber. When you go to a fiber show and buy pure fiber from an animal, the producer will often have the name of the animal written on the packaging. There are practical reasons for this. Especially with a colored animal, like an alpaca, the color and quality of the fleece or fiber affects the price. Also, sometimes buyers want more fiber, and this way they can call the breeder and ask for some of the fleece from that particular animal by name from the next year. Although the quality of the coat can vary year by year (young fleeces are finer and brighter, and grow somewhat more coarse and dull with age, just like human hair), the color will probably match.

There are also emotional reasons. A backyard shepherd recently told me that what she and her partner love most about raising their animals is that when they make a garment, they personally know the animal it came from. The emotional connection, believe it or not, enriches the process immeasurably. Sheep follow them around, ask to be scratched under the chin, and lay their heads on their owners' laps. Contrary to popular belief, sheep are not stupid, but catty and doggy in their intelligence. Gentle handling brings this out.

Becoming Familiar with the Range of Fibers

Fiber choice, in terms of both suitability and feel is essential to fulfilling knitting. A good analogy is wine. You can drink the wine and enjoy it and know what you like without knowing what that is. But spending at least a few minutes to learn what a good "nose" is and how to taste wine enriches your experience immeasurably. This way, you will also choose a wine that complements your meal and is

lovely to drink. As a result you will be more likely to enjoy wine with your meal again and again.

Likewise, the right fiber can either make or frustrate a project. And it can also enrich us in a subtle, yet powerful physical level and as a result our emotional and spiritual lives can also benefit and become more vibrant.

In some ways, our stop and start lives are not that different from Rachel's. And knitters who work with commercial wool don't necessarily develop a handspinner's relationship to and sensitivity for fibers. But developing this sensitivity is easy to do and a great pleasure; so I don't know why anyone would want to avoid it. Part of this *is* a basic knitting skill: different types of fibers lend themselves to particular kinds of finished garments, and making fiber choices is an important part of knitting. And part of it is just plain pleasure.

The Secret Life of Fleece

A good "hand" is one of those mystical yet utterly pragmatic qualities that is at the same time universally and instinctively understood and also a matter of personal taste. But at the same time, it also gives us a window into the secret life of fleece, and how a certain feel can nourish or sustain us the way a favorite piece of music can calm or enliven us. Over time, knitters develop distinct and distinctive preferences for particular fibers, and for particularly individual reasons. They also develop sometimes metaphorical ways of describing these feelings, which transmit to someone else who works with yarn the way words like "oaky," "peppery," "berry overtones," or "acid" transmit to someone who drinks wine.

The tactile preferences, and the words used to describe them, are both as quirky and as evocative as the adjectives used to describe an oeneophilic's good nose. But, unlike wine, there isn't really any consensus about which fiber or type of yarn is superior, nor do fibers fluctuate in price as a result of their rating. To us, they're all good. You will have your own description, based on the taste of your own two hands. And the words will only be an approximation of something you feel most precisely with your palm and fingertips.

A wool yarn with a good hand can be soft, bright, and crisp. It can feel al

Rachel's
Wild
Patience, the
Secret Life
of Fleece,
and a
Precious
Pillow Cover
and Bag
124

dente, like a strand of spaghetti, in your hand, or soft and puffy like a cumulus cloud. All of these are descriptions I've heard used by knitters who like the stuff. There is also the knitter who rather charmingly confided to me that, she knows it isn't politically correct to say so, but to her hands most wool feels like "crinkly permed little old lady hair." Some spinners find silk to be an incredibly difficult fiber to spin because of its strength (wonderful to have in a finished garment, but, in the spinning it is difficult to break and can cut against the hand), fineness, and slippery quality. Others love its speed and softness.

My own hands recoil when they touch any yarn with a noticeable acrylic content. Even taking into account with the utter practicality and freedom that the fiber offers in terms of washability and affordability (not to mention the fact that it is entirely hypoallergenic and is used for premature babies in hospitals), I can't finish a garment made out of this sort of yarn. Many knitters have come to same conclusion. But it is extremely popular with many others.

Beyond personal preference, fibers can be divided into three categories: exotic and fine grade fibers (what a fiber producer I know calls "Cadillac fibers") medium grade fibers, and rug or coarse fibers.

Cadillac (or fine and/or exotic) Fibers

In most cases, exotic or fine fibers are what you want to put close to your skin (with the exception of socks and sometimes hats). If you are making an inner wear sweater, a scarf, a spring or summer weight shell, a dress, a skirt, or anything else that touches your skin, use a fiber that is going to feel good against it. These fibers include, but are not limited to:

Alpaca
Angora
Cashmere
Fine wool (Merino, Rambouillet, etc.)
Kid mohair (the silkiest hair that comes from the young Angora goat, not to
    be confused with the Angora rabbit)

Qiviut or musk oxen, a prized arctic fiber which is said to be softer, warmer, and lighter than cashmere

Silk

Rayon

Tencel

Viscose (Contrary to popular belief, these three are all natural fibers; tree fibers including sustainable rainforest fibers from different parts of the world that are processed with a solvent—no, that part isn't natural. They give you the drape and shine of silk without the price tag.)

Yak (Yes, yak. It's really soft and warm. You can't get it easily commercially, but it is readily available for hand spinners who know where to look.)

Blends of the above and some blends that include the above and some medium grade fibers so it pills less.

Fine fibers have a wonderful hand and are more expensive than other fibers. (Often, they are also warmer.) On the down side, because fine fibers are softer than other fibers, they will pill more (alpaca will pill somewhat less) and you have to hand wash or dry clean them. Exceptions include superwash merino (check the label), which you can throw in the machine. As far as pilling is concerned, you can carefully use a dog brush to remove the pills from your garment. Merino, which many find to be the softest wool available, will always pill and you'll always have to brush it. It also gets little pulls. If you work with merino a lot, and you very well may because it's so wonderful, you may develop the same philosophy my master knitter friend Laurie espouses. To wit: "Accept fact that it will pill and eventually you'll have to replace it. But it feels so good, soon you won't care."

Nonetheless, the odds are that your fine fiber garment will not last as long as a medium or coarse grade garment. How long is that? It depends on how much you wear it and how you wear it.

Because of their softness, creatively speaking, fine fibers look particularly great when what you are after is to blend colors and textures into a flowing color pattern or a single, interesting, texture. They can help to make a knitted garment look almost woven.

Note: One distinction that needs to be made here is "fine" in terms of texture and softness versus "fine" meaning the diameter of the yarn. Most fine or exotic fibers are produced in fine yarn diameters because they are very warm and insulating, and a thicker, worsted yarn would result in a radiator-quality garment. A silk or cashmere or merino yarn that is worsted weight is likely to be blended with a synthetic or with a variety of wool, cotton, or linen. Nevertheless, these are two different forms of measurements.

MEDIUM GRADE FIBERS

Worsted wool
Aran (fisherman sweater) wool
Adult mohair (including the fuzzy kind)
Worsted Wool, including but not limited to:
   Romney wool
   Shetland wool
Many wools described as "pure wool"
Many wool/acrylic blends, or wool/acrylic/nylon blends, or wool blends
   with cotton in them
Lamb's wool (sometimes categorized under fine wool; test it yourself and
   decide).
Border Leicester, Corriedale, and other sheep blends

Medium grade fibers are the fibers of choice for outerwear (i.e., a winter weight pullover or ski sweater) because they are strong, durable, and less likely to pill than fine fibers because they are harsher. They are more suitable to wear on the outside because wool insulates and repels water and they also require less maintenance. Medium grade fibers are also the fibers of choice for socks and for garments with color patterns. These yarns are firmer and crisper than Cadillac fibers; i.e., their stitches hold their individual definition more crisply and distinctly than stitches executed in finer fibers, which, as mentioned above, tend to blend. So they are more ideally suited to show off distinction between colors in a

pattern. Medium-grade fibers are wonderful for colorful argyle socks, Fair Isle and intarsia (two forms of color pattern knitting). They are often more affordable than fine fibers, and can be easier to launder and more durable over the long term. Because they aren't quite as dense and warm as some of the fine grade wools and exotics, they excel in worsted weight yarns.

A word of warning: More than one brand-new knitter has told me how she stopped knitting almost immediately after choosing a medium grade worsted wool to knit a scarf. Easy, accessible, reasonably priced yarn; easy accessible project. Should be a no-brainer. Instead, the finished scarf feels scratchy and awkward on the neck and, instead of draping, kind of ties stiffly around the neck like a ribbon, not quite and not really. Not scarf-like at all. A scarf needs a soft fiber that drapes, or flows. This means a finer yarn and/or a softer fiber. Cashmere, merino, an Angora wool blend, a silk or silk blend, or a soft, silky kid mohair are examples of yarns that would be favored by and favor this type of project. They are ideal for projects like these because not that much yarn is required, so even though they are more expensive they are often quite affordable in these quantities. You can also read patterns in knitting stores and see what type of yarns they use and go from there. If you do find something worsted weight that feels good on your skin, make sure to check the drape of the finished fabric in your swatch. If the fabric is stiff (i.e., doesn't flow like a scarf) try trading up a few needle sizes until you get the drape you prefer.

Coarse grade fibers

Navajo Churro
Jacob
Some Icelandic (Icelandic fleeces range from fine to coarse.)

These are harsher than fine or medium grade yarns, very durable, intended for rugs, hats, and sometimes purses, and will almost invariably feel itchy and scratchy against your skin. But their textures can make them fascinating to work with. For instance, Icelandic wool, which has short, softer hairs and longer,

RACHEL'S
WILD
PATIENCE, THE
SECRET LIFE
OF FLEECE,
AND A
PRECIOUS
PILLOW COVER
AND BAG
128

darker, kempy hairs, offers very rich texture and color combinations. And if you make a jacket or sweater out of one of these, it will last a very, very long time. We may eschew them as being coarse and scratchy, but other cultures prize them for their durability. For instance, the fiber expert and master teacher Judith MacKenzie relates how, when she went to Pakistan, she discovered that Pakistanis actually discard the soft, warm, dull fibers that we prize as cashmere grade fiber because they aren't strong enough. And it is true that they aren't strong—you have to ply at least three strands of cashmere to get a durable yarn, and commercial cashmeres go as far as twelve ply. But the coarse, longer hairs grown by these goats were both warm and strong. So they wove their cloaks out of the long hairs and send the soft stuff off to factories where it was used to stuff mattresses.

You can, by the way, also have someone custom spin, honest-to-gosh, the hair of your dog. It has to be washed really well, but dog fiber from some breeds makes amazing lofty, textural, warm, gorgeous sweaters. The aforementioned Laurie made her son an afghan to take to college. It was knitted in the colors of the university in question, and commercial wool, handspun wool, and handspun yarn made from the young man's dog were all worked together into the design. So he got to go to school and take his dog along. Whether dog hair comes out fine or medium grade would depend on the breed and how it is processed and spun. The hair of the Great Pyrenees dog makes wonderful fiber. No offense to German Shepherd lovers, but dog hair yarn experts tell me that this breed's coat does not have a high aptitude for becoming a pleasing yarn.

Cotton and Linen

Cotton and linen are vegetable fibers that fall into a category all their own. They breathe better than wools and other protein fibers. They make wonderful warm weather garments. At the same time, they are also less absorbent than wool and don't have its bounce and memory. There are knitters who like the hand of cotton and linen because they don't like the feel of wool. Both cotton and linen come in a variety of weights. Some knitters love knitting with linen yarn and spinning flax, the long, stiff fibers of the plant that make linen, which must be spun while

wet. One very experienced knitter told me that her latest discovery was very fine lace weight linen yarn which she discovered makes particularly beautiful traditional shawls, because the stitches knitted in this fiber achieve such beautiful definition. The final effect of a hand knitted linen sweater is also spectacular. But neither fiber is as sensuous to work with as wool, silk, or a luxury fiber. As a yarn, linen's hand can be very harsh, even cutting. And some knitters will take all lengths to avoid a "cottony" hand. But there are also knitters who are passionate about cotton yarns. They love the way the finished garment feels to wear, its washability, its breathability, and its lightness. They find it perfect for baby garments, also, for the same reasons. One even took me to a shelf in the store where a matte cotton hand spun (slightly uneven) two ply yarn was placed to show me how beautiful a cotton yarn can be. And it was very beautiful. I may even make something out of it one day soon. If you love wearing cotton too, you may end up enjoying the finished product to such an extent that its not particularly distinctive hand becomes insignificant to you.

Other Considerations

As I mentioned briefly above, all fibers can be separated into three other categories: as protein, cellulose, and synthetic. Protein fibers are fibers that are made by an animal or insect. These include silk, which comes from silkworms. Cellulose fibers are vegetable or plant fibers like flax that makes linen and cotton. Other fibers, like nylon and acrylic, are man-made. Some fibers you might think are synthetic—rayon, ramie, tencel, and viscose among them—are actually farmed wood fibers which are processed with a solvent.

Yes, there is a reason why this technical distinction is vitally important to you, the yarn end-user. That is that many protein fibers, such as wool and cashmere, have what is called memory and resilience. That means they will retain and hold the shape you knit them to. Others, like alpaca, which are hairs with none of the curl or wave of fleece, don't have memory. Vegetable fibers like rayon, ramie, and viscose have little or no memory. Neither does silk. None of these fibers snap back, but lie flat. Used alone, without a very elastic or dense sort of

RACHEL'S
WILD
PATIENCE, THE
SECRET LIFE
OF FLEECE,
AND A
PRECIOUS
PILLOW COVER
AND BAG

130

stitch, they will droop. However, they do have wonderful shine and because of the droopy quality, drape and flow beautifully, which makes them very appropriate for scarves and shawls, or a garment with a very lively mesh stitch or all over ribbing that makes a very naturally stretchy garment anyway. They also make wonderful stripes or other design features within another garment. (This is often a good idea because they can be more expensive to use.)

Another choice is double stranding silk or similar yarn with a wool yarn, which gives you the visual and textural texture of the cellulose fiber combined with the bounce and hug of the protein fiber. If you use the silk the garment will be rather more costly to make. If you use the alternatives, it will be less costly. The great advantage of silk and cellulose and synthetic fibers that produce a similar hand and sheen is that they are comparatively lightweight for their volume. One of my favorite sweater tricks is to combine a wool yarn with a blend yarn that is loaded with lots of silk. This way you get a sweater that is at once luscious, light, and a little luminescent.

Another consideration is warmth. Fibers like Angora, cashmere, alpaca, and qivuit are exceedingly warm. If they are not blended with other fibers or spun fine, they will be too warm to wear next to your skin. You don't really want to double strand them with each other. Aside from the expense of double stranding so many precious yarns, and the contrariness of using something used for warmth and softness to create texture and big open spaces, you will roast in your sweater or under your toque.

But they are often wonderful blended together. A merino and silk blend will be soft, slightly shiny, and have the memory you need to make a shaped garment—a happy and balanced marriage of fine fibers and qualities. A wool, silk, and cashmere blend will be soft, slightly shiny, warm, and lightweight, even in a bulky yarn spun on size ten or ten and a half needles.

I used to be disappointed when I would pick up a luxurious sweater in a department store and find out it was only twenty percent Angora. Once I read the label, the garment that had felt so good to my hands seemed somehow suspect. Now I appreciate the wisdom and practical artistry that goes into creating fiber blends, and that the label that seemed to play a trick was actually not dis-

appointing at all. A one hundred percent Angora item, unless it is very light-weight, will be very warm, won't breathe as well, and will probably pill or shed more than a wool blend, which will lighten the load and give the garment some structure. Handspinners typically card no more than 10 percent Angora into a blend that is mosty wool.

You can actually forget everything you just read and still do fine. The way to educate yourself and to find out what you want to use to knit is to look at yarn labels, ask questions about wear, washing, and elasticity, and always use and trust your hands, your hands, your hands. Something that feels good to your hands, or your cheek, is going to feel good against your skin as a finished garment and be a pleasure to work with.

Rachel Pillow Cover and Shaggy Bag

This pattern makes two exuberant, precious little accent pillows, 5" by 7½", just perfect for the back of a cane-backed chair, or in a boudoir at a vanity table. Tactile and combining a classic, pale yellow, loopy wool boucle with an edgy, smoky, soft violet and chocolate metallic eyelash nylon and a matching, paler nylon chenille, it blends colors and textures to create a sheepy, yet also elegant charm. It also makes a fabulous, easy little evening shoulder bag, if you forego the stuffing, decline to seal the fourth side, and add a simple strap.

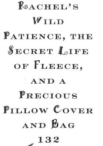

The idea was to be able to hug something that felt sort of like a sheep, but was also more fancifully textured and colored—a magical sheep, if you will. It also celebrates the feeling of fleece between the fingers (the loopy boucle and the stitch, which looks like a sheep's fleece when completed) and the deep violet dye of the named land of Canaan.

I only wish Rachel had had sparkly eyelash and chenille to help her while away the hours of her multiple seven-year trials. My friend Aydika, who came by while I was finishing this one, recognized it immediately as the pillow on which Pan's nymphs used to rest their heads after they had finished with their bacchanals. The bag has a similar quality, with a certain subtle added chic schoolgirl je ne sais quoi. It looks *wonderful* over the Penelope sweater (next chapter) whose matte, white halo texture shows off the shine, texture, and darkness of the bag to perfection.

There is more than one version of this loop stitch, which is great for collars and sleeves and for making little shaggy rugs for your bathroom or whatnot. This version of the stitch, which is very easy, comes from Lee Raven's *Hands on Spinning*.

Bonus option: If you decide to make the Arachne Shrug, you will have plenty of the two variegated yarns left over. Either of the variegated yarns blend with these colors, giving it a more casual quality. If you use these yarns, or ones in the same color range, you could substitute either or both of them for color D on the back.

Or, you could get a little more chenille and split the yarn and knit with a friend.

If you go with the friend you better talk fast while you knit, though. This pattern in either version is the knitting equivalent of a bon bon; easy, instant gratification; over way too fast. The only part that feels time consuming is winding the skeins.

Rachel Pillow Cover Ingredients

Ingredients:

- 1 pair size 11 needles
- 1 pair size 10 needles
- 2 oz. (75 yd) skein of Ironstone Yarns Big Loop pale yellow color 810.4 (mohair/wool/nylon blend bouclé) (Color A)
- 1 oz. (116 yd) skein of color one Prism Dazzle in Smoke (violets, chocolate browns) (nylon metallic eyelash) (Color B)
- 1½ oz. (88 yd) skein of color two Prism Soft in Smoke (medium to pale violets, gray blues, taupes, and brown) (nylon chenille) (Color C)
- 100g (138 yd) Manos de Uruguay in Color 38 (dark violet) (pure wool) (Color D)
- Fiberfill to stuff pillows (available from fabric stores)
- Tapestry needle
- Optional for Shaggy Bag version: some satin, silk, or a strong, shiny blend or synthetic to line the bag.

Rachel Pillow Cover Instructions

GAUGE: 3 stitches equals 1 inch and 2 rows equal one inch in triple stranded stockinette in yarns A–C.

2½ stitches equals 1 inch and 2 rows equals one inch in triple standard stockinette in yarns A, B, and D.

Again, gauge doesn't matter that much in this pattern unless you like your dimensions to be exact. In which case, check your gauge. The exuberant texture of the pillow is, in my opinion, best displayed within the sort of tight, tiny, crisp measurements shown here. But that's just my opinion. You can make it bigger if you want.

Pattern Stitch (Loop Stitch)
Foundation Row: K all stitches

RACHEL'S
WILD
PATIENCE, THE
SECRET LIFE
OF FLEECE,
AND A
PRECIOUS
PILLOW COVER
AND BAG
134

- Row 2: K1, *Make a loop in next stitch: Dip needle knitwise into stitch, wrapping yarn around working needle as if to knit, then wrapping the yarn around two fingers of the non-working hand AND the working needle as if to knit, then completing the knit stitch. This will create a total of three loops on your working needle when the stitch is completed, one smaller and two larger (these are the ones that had your fingers in them). K1* repeat from * to * across row.
- Row 3: K1, *K3 loops together K1*.
- Row 4: K all stitches.
- Repeat for pattern.

Note: Of course, everyone has different sized fingers. To make larger, shaggier loops, separate your fingers as you wrap them or hold them farther away from your needles. To make smaller loops, hold your fingers closer together and/or bring them closer to the needles while you wrap them. Smaller loops will make the pillow look like a glittery Persian lamb. Larger ones will make it look more like a precious gem version of a full grown sheep. A combination looks nice, too.

Front

1 Holding one strand of each of the color A–C, and using size 11 needles, cast on 13 stitches.

2 Knit pattern stitch for 5 inches

3 Bind off.

Back

1 Using colors B, C, and D and size 10 needles, cast on 18 stitches to make 7 inches. Knit stockinette for 2½ inches.

2 On your next knit row, purl instead, then purl as usual for a total of two consecutive purl rows.

③ Resume stockinette until piece measures 5 inches.

④ Bind off. Finish the two long sides and one short side.

⑤ Stuff with fiberfill, or a pillow form in this size if you can obtain one.

⑥ Finish the other short side.

To display pillow most artfully, turn on its side, i.e. so short end is up. This makes the loops fall against the grain and the effect of this stitch looks more organic this way.

RACHEL SHAGGY BAG (VARIATION)

STEP ONE: Make front as in pillow cover.

STEP TWO: Make back as in pillow cover.

STEP THREE: Turn work so short sides are at top and bottom and long sides are at the sides. Sew together on three sides, leaving one short side open.

STEP FOUR: Make strap. Cast on three stitches triple stranded in colors A–C and knit loop pattern stitch for twenty inches, or however many inches will allow you to cross the shoulder strap over your chest and wear the bag at the top of your opposite hip, minus a couple of inches, because the strap will stretch out over time. (You can always take it off and shorten it later if you need to.)

STEP FIVE: Center each end of the strap at one side of the bag and sew on.

RACHEL'S
WILD
PATIENCE, THE
SECRET LIFE
OF FLEECE,
AND A
PRECIOUS
PILLOW COVER
AND BAG
136

Optional: Cut lining fabric to two pieces of one half inch larger than bag dimensions, put right sides facing, seam around the two long sides and one of the short sides, turn inside out, iron seams and tack into inside of bag at the four corners.

Optional: Knit a little flap in pattern stitch in the exact shape and size of your choice, seam it on to one side, and attach a snap to the underside or a button to the bottom edge and a raised elastic buttonhole to the purse itself. Or, just fasten a snap to the center point of the inside of the top of the bag on each side about ¼–½" down.

---

[1]Samuel H. Dresner, *Rachel*. (Fortress: Minneapolis), 162.
[2]Dresner, 34.
[3]Sabina Teubel, *Sarah the Priestess*.
[4]For this information I am indebted to Samuel H. Dresner's *Rachel*.
[5]Lynn Gottlieb, Mother Chant from Jalala Bonheim, ed. *Goddess*. (Stewart Tabori & Chang: New York, 1997), 202.

PENELOPE, REGENERATION, AND a TURTLENECK WITH a HALO

Penelope, Queen of the island kingdom of Ithaka, can often be found at her loom in the private quarters of her husband Odysseus' seaside palace.

Today Thea and Ida, the two most loyal of her 50 serving women sit nearby. The laughter of many men flies up the stairs, followed by the sound of a wine cask shattering against the stone floor of the palace's open air great room, or metaron, below.

The Queen flinches. More laughter. The serving women cast down their eyes. Then bawdy songs start, three of them, all different, followed by the sound of men with wine-colored voices calling her name.

The characteristically smooth place between Penelope's brows collapses into a crease. Her light eyes, changeable as the color of the sea itself, shift decisively from their habitual gray green to the turquoise blue which they turn only when some string of her being has been plucked way too tight.

Her maids look away.

"Thea. Ida. Come. We are going downstairs."

Even now, Penelope's voice, well known in this island stronghold for its loveliness, is as supple as the sea on a day with gentle winds. There was a time when her voice was heard on the wind throughout the island. Shepherds heard it calming the breezes that played among the mountaintops and it helped the ewes to calf.

But those were the days before Odysseus went to fight the Trojan War. It was when Penelope spoke to Odysseus that her voice carried as it did. It was said

that she spoke reason to her husband when his own had left him, which was hard to believe, because even the gods knew that Odysseus was the most sturdily brilliant of leaders. But those who knew Penelope knew that her wit surpassed even his. It was, literally, the voice of clarity that had rolled through those hills, and the clarity that had given its volume part of its magical power, and made it more than a match for that wily, stocky, sturdy man who was also so incomparably beloved of the gods.

For a while, after Odysseus had gone to war, Penelope's voice could still be heard at large, like an echo. But now many seasons have passed since Penelope's voice has been heard anywhere but in her own quarters. Unlike others, Odysseus survived the dusty, bloody, brutal sack of Troy. But he has never returned home. His boat and crew set out across the seas with the others, and no one has seen it, or them, since.

The queen stands. Even for a mortal woman, she is not large. The sea of her own dark hair is bound tightly in gold. Her arms, pure white from years lived gladly in the lavender shadows of a noblewoman's quarters, are supple from weaving royal cloaks, and her face, without having any single outstanding feature, is astonishingly but almost inexplicably lovely. Queen Penelope lacks the violet and ebony magnetism of Troy's Helen or the peachy succulence of a priestess of Aphrodite. But her sum effect is still one of astonishing beauty. To look upon her is to enter a beautiful chamber lit by indirect light after a long, burning day on the waters. The fact that no one can put a finger on the exact source of the queen's allure only heightens it. Something about her promises that on each subsequent day you spend in her presence not only she, but also life itself, will subtly increase in serenity. She will take your hand and lead you there without your even knowing.

A loosely woven shawl that glows barely and inexplicably gold hangs on a knob made of ivory and horn near the door of her chamber. The Queen picks up the shawl and puts it over her head, frowning, and deep in thought. Thea and Ida exchange discreet glances. This particular shawl, which shines a little more brightly as she moves it, then settles, is a topic of conversation throughout the palace. What is of such inexplicable interest is the origin of that glow. Perhaps

PENELOPE,
REGENERATION,
AND A
TURTLENECK
WITH A HALO
140

the thing glows with the honey that is harvested from bees kept by the nymphs that live in a grotto somewhere below the island, and which is rumored to be the elixir that brings human souls to life. Then again, perhaps the thing is fashioned with some other substance entirely. Its magic is perceptible yet imperceptible, just like Penelope's.

"Let us go," she says firmly to the two serving women, and drawing the shawl over her face, where it glows even more complexly.

The three stop two steps before the bottom of the stairs, which is exactly where the stench of burned oxen fat and spoiled sweet wine becomes overpowering.

Are there six young men sprawled over the floor and tables of Odysseus' great room? Are there ten? Or are there sixty? These men have been eating and drinking their way through her husband's stores for month. Day and night, Odysseus' goats roast on spits that turn in freshly cut gashes in his smooth stone floor. Roasted legs of oxen are piled up in the corners and wineskins, both full and flaccid, are strewn everywhere. So are abandoned harps, scattered dice and partially completed woodcarvings which, subjected to this particular blend of small attention and lavish abandonment, look more chewed than honed.

Her tiny son, Telemachus, looking, as usual, both shocked and furious, sits in one corner.

A man who looks slightly taller and more bored than the rest raises his head, stands, and bows. As he does, his head of beautiful dark hair, worn very long in the Ithakan fashion, deliberately cascades over his head.

It does not escape either Penelope or her women that despite the chaos that has swept over the metaron, this hair is freshly and lavishly perfumed.

"Ah, lovely one," says Antínoüs, for that is his name. Antínoüs is perhaps the most clever of the queen's suitors and certainly the most vocal. "Have you relented? Do you crave our good company and our heat, our wit and our good sense? Come in. Take a seat. You can take as along as you like to decide which of all the heirs to the realm gathered here you would wed. You may even try each of us out. We are all very agreeable."

He eyes her up and down.

Her small son stands, glowering, in the corner. Too small to be on his own, but too large to hover within her protection, and without either a father or a grandfather to guide him. Laertes, Odysseus' father, is alive, but has withdrawn to grieve, or wait, or both, in a distant grove. There is not much that Penelope can do right now for Telemachus. Without its king, the order of all of Ithaka is unraveling.

But she can do this.

"Hear me," she says sharply and quietly from behind her veil, where she has begun silently to weep. The Queen veils herself out of sadness, as well as circumspection. Even now, no one knows that she is silently crying. "Once again I will have to decline your fine offer."

Her voice stops on the word fine like a mother resting her hand on a child's brow. Antínoüs catches the irony, which is not favorable to him, and smiles.

"Laertes, my father-in-law, is quite old now. You probably know that he never leaves the grove that gives him peace, so grieved is he by the loss of his son. I cannot possibly have discharged my wifely duties unless I weave him a proper burial shroud. Inscribed with the proper offering to the gods. When I am finished, well, then. But none of you would want a wife who did not honor your father in this way."

Beyond the end of the hall the violet sea flickers like the back of a gigantic animal. A wave seems to crest in its center.

Antínoüs, looking both surly and abstracted, looks for support to the other men lounging in the hall, who, in that moment, are all sucking on bones and pouring honeyed wine into their mouths, and seem entirely agreeable toward spending another season so in precisely this fashion. Penelope can't understand how it is that they don't grow as fat as cattle, these suitors, but as much as they eat they remain forever lean and alert.

Antínoüs shrugs.

"Well then your highness. We shall wait."

Upstairs, Penelope bids the serving women close the door behind them.

"Go and find the blind man and bring him here," she says quietly.

PENELOPE,
REGENERATION,
AND A
TURTLENECK
WITH A HALO
142

Ida nods and leaves the room.

The Queen sits on her low stool, and places one hand on the warp of her loom, as if to stroke it, or to steady it while dusk falls over the violet sea and as the carousing continues downstairs. No one in the royal family has the strength to wrest the suitors from the hall except Odysseus. It cannot be done. The power of his house is unraveling around her. She summons his warmth and deep heart and strength. Yes, it is still there. She can still feel it. It matches her own, equal, and different strength. Reassured, she lets the feeling of Odysseus go. And then she picks a plan out of her mind. One layer of it, and then another, and then another more. It is a brilliant plan and a subtle one. As she formulates it, she weeps.

Presently there is a quiet knock on the door.

"Enter."

A young man with the gaze of an old one and carrying a harp better matched to a god pulls up a stool and sits beside her. The Queen makes no effort to stanch her tears. Together, they silently watch the sea: He uses his ears and nose and tongue and mind, and she uses her eyes.

"They set you free," she says.

"You mean the sea nymphs?"

"Yes."

"But they took my eyes."

"Yes."

"Perhaps they have taken my husband."

From her tone it is clear that to Penelope the "perhaps" is a formality.

The blind man nods. "That could be. There is no way of knowing."

"Either they have taken him or he is dead."

The blind man pauses for a second.

"If they have him I do not think he is in the cave here."

She turns to him. The turquoise has gone out of her eyes and they are now the exact slate gray of a cloudy dawn sea. Not the gray of shining Athena's eyes. This is a gray of depth and substance. Not luminescent; creamy.

"No? I had hoped, although did not hope too much. He went there once."

The young man nods. "All the kings of the realm must closely approach those gates. It is part of their initiation. My understanding is that my lord withstood it better than most. So much that they wanted to keep him. Even more than they usually do, I mean."

"All nymphs want to keep all mortal men. And make them immortal."

"Yes. That is what I mean."

"They wanted to keep you."

The young man shrugs. "They kept my eyes."

"Was it worth it?"

He frowns.

"There is no way of saying. I think it was worth it. Nymphs are not permitted to keep mortal men. It is a longing without possibility of fulfillment; yet they long nonetheless. Nymphs are nothing if not ambitious. Poseidon retaliated. Against me, of course, since the nymphs are his. I believe he gave my eyes to two of his cyclops sons."

The young man's tone is level, almost impartial.

"I wonder what your eyes offered," murmurs Penelope, "that theirs didn't."

He shrugs again.

"There they weave their complex violet webs about looms of stone," she says crisply.

He looks surprised. "How do you know that? In that cave, yes. That is a nymph's secret not known to mortal women."

Penelope smiles. "Nymphs and men's secrets, more accurately, wouldn't you say? My mother had a few thimblefuls of nymph blood in her veins. When my sister and I were small, our father sacrificed to Athena and then she came to us and smote that blood out of us with a bit of wool. She then cast it back upon the waves and from that bit of fleece a small island was formed. You can see it sometimes." She points out the window. "Right there."

A wave flies up in the same place it had flown as Penelope spoke to the suitors. And sure enough, a tiny bit of land is visible beneath it. It is gray, like her own eyes, and there is something magical about the lines of vision that surrounds it that allows them to see, even from this distance, she with her eyes and

PENELOPE,
REGENERATION,
AND A
TURTLENECK
WITH A HALO
144

he with his mind, how it is dusted with small fields of violets and parsley. "Right there. That is the nymph part of my body and my sister's body grown fat with salt."

"I've never felt that isle before."

"Few do. It reminds me of what I am not and of what ability I do not have." Her face darkens. "Strong enough to retrieve my beloved." She pauses. "If he lives."

"They may have him."

"But it also gives me connection with their world," she continues firmly. "No woman can weave as finely as a nymph. But for a woman I weave tolerably. And so I am going to draw him home with their own thread. I was also hoping he might be in the cavern beneath our island. But since you tell me he is not. Perhaps you have some bit of thread to contribute. From your stay there."

He looks down.

"Oh," he said softly and sadly. "That's why you called for me."

The Queen is silent, and for a moment her hand rests a bit too heavily on the edge of her wooden stool at her side. It is clear what his answer will be. Her knuckles grow sharp against her skin.

They both watch the little island, no bigger than a pincushion, and apparently uninhabited, disappear and appear beneath the ocean spray. For a moment, a tendril of golden hair as tall as a man seems to rise above it in the air. But then it subsides.

"I have none of that," he said.

They sit silently for several minutes more.

"But here perhaps is something."

The blind man reaches into his robe and opens a locket pinned to its underside. From it he takes what looks like a tiny spindle wound tight, while leaving several other small items inside. From the tiny spindle, he unwinds what looks like a bit of fine golden thread mixed with silver.

The Queen lifts the stuff between her thumb and forefinger. The line of her mouth is both fascinated and repulsed.

"It is a bit of the nymph Ato's hair," he says patiently. "She plucked it from

her head and gave it to me after as I left her. She told me that some day I would use it to bewitch men's hearts with my tongue. There is a bit more of it elsewhere."

The crease returns to Penelope's brow. She rolls the bit of thread again and again between her fingers.

"No doubt you will," she says crisply. "And I shall put it in my cloth, perhaps to attract him home."

"And to keep the suitors at bay at the same time," murmurs the young blind man. "Clever."

The Queen smiles for a second and then her smile is gone as quickly as the tiny island disappears again beneath the waves.

After the blind man leaves Penelope watches two men bring the quarters of a freshly slaughtered pig into the hall below.

Then she turns and opens the olive wood chest that stands in a darkened corner. Its beautiful soft wood, sacred to Athena, will not last much longer than her lifetime in this salt air. Inside the chest lies a golden spindle, and many cones of shining thread dyed in shades of both intense and subtle shades of violet, white, and gold.

When she was a child, with no mother, for even with her small bit of nymph blood this island had proved too dry for Penelope's mother who had returned to the sea, her father Icarius had summoned an old, nameless woman to their home. She taught certain noblewomen the art of magical weaving. Through the conduit of Icarius, she had agreed to teach Penelope.

This woman had arrived on Ithaka with a golden spindle. She had also arrived with a skin filled with fine, deep violet fleece from a particular ewe that was particularly sacred to Athena and lived in the pastures beyond one of her most secluded temples. The nameless woman taught Penelope how to render the violet dye from creatures of the sea in every detail, down to which fishermen knew the most rich and secret of mollusk beds, and how to pay them, and what the signs were of a son who would reap the stuff as purely and deeply as his

PENELOPE,
REGENERATION,
AND A
TURTLENECK
WITH A HALO
146

father had. She also showed Penelope how and when to use the finished dyed skeins, and how to keep them properly, for this stuff was only to be used for the most magical of purposes. As a noblewoman, and potential queen, Penelope would hold the responsibility of knowing when it was to be used, which was for the good of the realm only.

Penelope summons Thea and Ida.

"Let's warp the loom," she says quietly. "Please take your time."

With each score of white threads they warp, the din in the room below seems to lessen. As the days pass, the flow of proposals lessens to a trickle. The men drink more and eat less, and soon begin to slip into a honeyed stupor.

Once the warp is strung, Penelope sits to weave.

Slowly, slowly, the Queen of Ithaka begins to render the multilayered weaving pattern she has chosen. Over this, she shapes the words of a story in a sacred violet lettering as carefully as she shapes each of the sacred letters. Whether or not this is a ruse, it is a thing that must be done with care. And so she commits the life of Laertes to eternity.

And each night she rips some of it out again.

And each morning she weaves.

And by torchlight she unweaves.

And Laertes lives and dies and lives and dies under her skilled hands.

The shuttle begins to sing. Its song is penetrating and deep. And because it is a love song, which cannot be helped, because it is also designed to attract Odysseus if he is indeed alive, it also slowly awakens the suitors from their slumber. Below her, as the months pass, Penelope hears the crackling fires start up once again, and with them the songs. And Penelope herself begins to weep deeply, and long, in accompaniment to her own work.

Soon the song of the loom stretches out across the waters, and softly penetrates the secret grottos of nymphs, whose looms are singing songs even more tantalizing than hers, and weaving violet threads whose import is even more powerful, and whose raveling webs are even more complex and fine.

The nymphs hear the song of Penelope's weaving, and she feels them set a

spell against her. In the night, bits of the far songs of other, underwater looms begin to reach the edges of the queen's ears. Sad songs, siren songs, brazen songs, merry songs, snips of songs. The nymphs play with the edges of her consciousness while on their stone looms and with their violet thread they weave the bodies that will be born as mortal women's children and, possibly, hold the man whose touch would make that life grow once he was at home. For hastening souls into life in this way is part of the nymphs' work. And so it is with women and nymphs. They are rivals and also they need each other.

The Queen's fingers find her life with Odysseus as wool and silk spun when he was home pass through her hands once again as these same threads are now woven, rereleasing her marriage into the nerve endings in the pads of her fingers. As the wool and silk pass through her fingers the events of their lives held within its fibers also pass through her hands. Ah, here is Odysseus requesting her hand in marriage. And here was the day they first lay together in their marriage bed. Here is the scent of honeyed wine in her hair and her hands spreading unguent on his hands, which were black from the sun, and callused by the ropes on the sail of the great hollow black ship he pilots. As she tended to the sore hands he had told her a story of a faraway tribe, and the odd and intricate system they used to keep accounts and track the movements of the stars. And as he told her, she found a flaw in it, and told him, and he clapped his hands together in delight, saying, "I knew there was something!" But Odysseus was a man, and all men have a weakness for the salty scent, lavish hair, and pillowy breasts of nymphkind.

A year passes in this manner.

For a second year Penelope weaves and unweaves as the story of Laertes continually draws to an end, then unwrites itself, then draws to a slightly different conclusion.

Whenever she descends from her private quarters, armfuls of violets or flowering olive branches are thrown at her feet, along with trinkets saturated with intoxicating scents known to be spells of Aphrodite. The men's faces, once as similar to each other as those in a pack of unknown dogs, begin to resolve into uneasy and foreboding clarity. With that one, who has the eyes of a leopard, she

PENELOPE,
REGENERATION,
AND A
TURTLENECK
WITH A HALO
148

can foresee a life requiring constant erotic responsibility and the tolerance of a perpetual mirthful superficiality. With this one, whose father owned all the low land on the western side of Ithaka, she can envision a life of toil, patience, the careful hoarding of resources, and the mothering of many wonderful daughters whose sex is an increasing disappointment to their father. This one, whose father owned the hills, and had a bit of the face of a jackal to him, would always be off to war, which would be convenient for her, excepting that she would have to acquire a further knowledge of herbs to prevent the acquisition of venereal diseases upon his return. The pictures simply come to her.

Meanwhile, Telemachus grows in stature, anger, and in the ability to access his own grief. She still cannot be a father to him and his own grandfather is secluded in the grove.

Whenever she descends into the great hall, the songs of her suitors' desire follow her like curses.

What she cannot know, because the gods have hidden the knowledge from her, is that as she weaves, and weeps, mighty Odysseus also sits outside the lip of a magical grotto, watching the sea, and weeps. He has done so for days, months, seasons. His great hollow ship is gone. His companions are lost to him. He is imprisoned where he stands. And a blond nymph named Calypso, who has the most beautiful of hair, holds him there. She loves him. Each night they sleep side by side, the willing and the unwilling, and each morning Odysseus returns to the point at the edge of the grotto and weeps for home, with eyes unveiled to Calypso's curiosity, and with perhaps an even deeper register of grief than Penelope's own.

As Penelope weaves, his grief grows deeper.

They do not know it, but soon they are weeping together.

"I'm sure I'm not inferior to her in form or stature; it's not right for mortal women to contend or vie with goddesses in loveliness or height,"[1] says Calypso.

"I, too," replies Odysseus, *"know that Penelope, however wise, cannot compete with you in grace or stature . . . nevertheless, each day, I hope and hunger for my house."*[2]

. . .

For a second year, Penelope weaves and unweaves. Her quarters become a place of peace for her, and time flows by quickly, as time spent knitting or weaving can do.

And this neither of them could know, but, soon, at the temple of Olympus, Athena asks her father Zeus to set Odysseus free. Odysseus was imprisoned with Calypso as punishment for blinding Polyphemus the Cyclops, one of Poseidon's sons. Zeus turns Athena down. According to Zeus, Odysseus did not respect the power of the sea to create life, thus he must stew in it a bit further.

A new serving woman comes to the Ithakan palace. She is quite young, with a blue gleam to her eye, and strange hair. It was rumored to be light underneath, but dyed dark with resins and wine. The hair becomes quite the talk of the palace.

As she hears this story at her loom, the Queen smiles as no one has seen her smile in years.

"Bring that one to be my chambermaid," she says to Thea and Ida, who are mystified.

"They have him," the Queen says exultantly to the blind man some days after as they sit together in a small, private room. "They have infiltrated my staff with one of their own."

"Dismiss her immediately," says the young man. "Find another maid."

"Absolutely not," says Penelope. And the word *absolutely* carries through the wind, and soars around the land, as her voice always had in the old times. And all the island's people look up in wonder, and then imagine they have imagined this.

Ida comes with news that the new serving woman and Antínoüs can be found together in a small, dry, and softly sanded cave at the water's edge in the heat of the afternoon. Penelope smiles and weaves.

When six more months have passed, to make a total of three and one half years, the suitors march upstairs as a group and fling her door open.

"You are not weaving this shroud," said Antínoüs. "You are ripping it out at night. We demand that you complete this item and marry one of us."

PENELOPE,
REGENERATION,
AND A
TURTLENECK
WITH A HALO

150

They smell of grease, lust, and anticipation.

"And how do you know this?" asks Penelope calmly.

"A maid of yours has told us."

"Very well my lord," says the Queen. "I shall complete this shroud."

And quickly, she does.

"Now what will you do?" asks the blind man, who himself was beginning to sing the most extraordinary of verses.

Penelope smiles to herself.

Even he looks puzzled.

She opens her olive wood chest and lifts out the shroud.

"Feel. Nymph hair. And here." She places his hand on a small dark spot that was both warmer and cooler than the rest of the shroud.

"Soiled?" But he already knows.

"Marked and blessed with nymph blood. The blood I lost from my own veins. In its own way. Mixed with a bit of sea water, I suppose."

"And where did you get this."

"Thea collected it for me. From the lovemaking of Antínoüs and the nymph."

His face sets. He is listening to something inside. "Ah. So in finishing the shroud . . ."

"I have finished my work of enchantment to tame the nymphs themselves. The first weaving held an attractor for the nymphs. I now know they have him. In obliging me to finish, the suitors have sealed their own failure. The spell is set. He is not dead. Some day he may come home. The figures on the shroud will hold me safe until then."

"And so this was always planned. All three levels."

Wise Penelope says, "Yes."

Fifteen more years go by and Odysseus does not return during any of them. Penelope tells no one, but at night, she often dreams of nymphs. They comb her hair and pluck bits of it from her head and eat it, laughing, as if it is a morsel of the sweetest bread. In their mouths, it becomes bread, then blossoms into giant

webs, which they blow from their lips to veil men who stand near by. But once in a while the hair they pluck is the long, dark, curling, Ithakan hair of her husband and they toss this to Penelope, saying, "weave with this, weave." As she begins to warp her loom with it, it dissolves as if it were strands of the very dawn.

She had not anticipated that it would take this long to see him again. Everyone notices how, even as she continues to evade suitors, perhaps out of sheer will, she grows increasingly sleepless, pale-eyed, and faded. In the fifteenth year after she finishes the shroud, Penelope wakes up one morning and mounts the tower where Odysseus kept his great smooth bow and his gray axheads, brings them downstairs, and makes an announcement to the suitors.

"I will marry whomever can string my lord's bow and shoot it straight down the sockets of this dozen axheads, as Odysseus used to."

That very day, a beggar arrives in her hall, a stooped man with deep kind eyes. As she washes his feet, as one always does for a traveler, something about his eyes urges her to tell him her plan. The man's eyes seem both to relax and sharpen as she reveals the decision that surprises even her.

"Do not worry," the traveler says calmly. "Because before you finish this contest your husband will be home."

She looks at him with clear gray eyes. Was he naïve, could he be party to a spell conjured by the nymphs, or could he possibly be telling the truth? There were so many currents underfoot in her husband's palace. The thought that he could be speaking truth is the one on which her heart settles.

She bows her head and weeps on his knees and he comforts her with gentle hands.

The contest occurs and not a single suitor can string Odysseus' bow. The suitors decide to eat yet another meal, then repeat the contest in the morning.

Before they can do so, the beggar himself picks up the bow and wins.

This is the one ending she has not anticipated, and it shocks her into a kind of transcendent silence.

Amazed, the Queen goes upstairs and falls into a very deep sleep. It is so deep she feels as though she had entered the underworld itself.

PENELOPE,
REGENERATION,
AND A
TURTLENECK
WITH A HALO
152

When she awakens, Eurycleia, her husband's trusted childhood nurse, is kneeling before her.

"Hurry. He is home. Odysseus! He has been here!"

"Oh," moans Penelope, "why do you tell me these things when finally I was resting so sweetly?"

Colors are different this morning, and her own skin feels different against the sheets, and a circumspect voice inside is telling her *beware,* this is a trick of the nymphs.

"*Hurry.*" Eurycleia is shaking her.

The Queen descends the stairway to the metaron to find the hall empty of suitors. The smells of sulfur and fire fill her nostrils. The hall is lit by firelight, and against the fire by the far wall of the great room sits her husband. She keeps walking toward him. Toward this man who looks exactly like her husband, but is younger, taller, and stronger. His hands and face are black with sun. His torso is as thick as a bull's. His dark blue eyes are clear and sharp. His hair cascades about his shoulders, more thickly than she remembered. He is dressed in beggar's tatters.

She looks at her own skin. It is younger, rosier, and more soft than it was when she fell asleep in grief the night before. She stops before a polished surface and looks at her own eyes. Young and bright. No sign of grief anywhere. She has been reborn. She walks forward, gracefully, but inside she is stumbling.

What even wary Penelope does not see is gray-eyed Pallas Athene standing behind her, and how it was she who gave the Queen deep sleep and this new form.

Penelope takes a seat before Odysseus, and sits in silent wonder.

He leans against a pillar and gazes back at her.

"Please! My lady! Speak to him!" Behind her, Telemachus sounds as if he has been smitten with a knife.

"I've no words," replies the Queen. "If it is he I shall know. We have secret signs that are known to us two only."

Hours later, emerging from baths and dressed in his own fine clothing, he has taken on the appearance of an immortal.

"Perplexing woman," he tells her, *"what other woman has a heart so stubborn as to deny herself her own dear husband."*[3]

"Wild man!" she replies. *"I am not proud and I do not taunt."*[4]

Inside, part of her is steely and part of her is waiting for her own clear voice to break, for it looks exactly as though it is he. Odysseus is here, at home. Is he himself or just another nymphine subterfuge? The gods were as strong in that part of the world as the suitors' desire, no, much stronger, and any sort of delusion was possible, especially after a night that has made her young again, slain the suitors, whose bodies are piled outside the hall, and wiped the grief from her eyes.

And then wise Penelope says the most difficult thing she has ever had to say, and one that she has planned and prayed to say for 18 years. There were other delusions abroad aside from nymphs. She was a queen and she had a queen's responsibilities.

"Eurycleia," she says imperiously, "please move the marriage bed outside his own chambers and make it up to my lord's taste. Make it soft, of course, with cloaks, blankets, and fleece."

The man who looks like Odysseus and sounds like Odysseus freezes.

"How can this be?" the man cries, and his voice is filled with the unmistakable sound of a breaking heart. 'Who tore my marriage bed from its base? It was built around the olive tree that grew in this place before this shining palace was even built by my hands! I planed and sanded it. The one that was our secret?" Tears fill his eyes.

Penelope finds herself throwing her arms around her husband's neck and weeping.

Kissing his head, she says, "Don't be angry, please do not be angry. I was afraid someone had sent a stranger to trick me. But no one knows about the bed but me, and you, and a single servant from long ago and far away." And now Odysseus weeps and the two hold each other, white arms intertwined with blackened ones, like shipwrecked sailors each grasping the land after years of being tossed and roughened by the ever moving sea.

And as they lie together in that bed, they trace white hands and brown

PENELOPE,
REGENERATION,
AND A
TURTLENECK
WITH A HALO
154

hands around each other and he tells her the story of his long journey, which is entirely too complicated to be related here, but included being Calypso's captive for eight years, being blown off course, encountering man-eating beings, spending time in the clutches of a siren named Circe who turned men into swine, visiting the underworld, meeting lotus eaters, being bound to the mast of his own ship, passing through the narrow passage between the watery vortex of Charybdis and the voracious cliff Scylla, and being shipwrecked while watching the sea claim each member of his crew after they ate sacred cattle.

After all of this and more, Athena had disguised him as the beggar, and he had arrived upon the shores of his own domain.

And Penelope tells him the story of her life, showing him how she has written the story of every year of the last eighteen into the cloth she has been weaving. Perhaps nymphs weave the bodies that are born through women. But only women weave the stories of all life.

Why Rippiing Out Rows (or Postponing Your Heart's Desire) Can Regenerate Your Life

In conversations among knitters, the topic of Penelope occasionally bubbles to the surface. It's kind of like admitting to a secret pleasure. In its own way, bringing up the topic of Odysseus' beloved is like speaking of any secret love or the sort of movie we like to watch when we are alone. So many of us also like to knit, rip rows out, and start them over, until they are perfect. We also like her blend of heroism, strategy, and perversity; the way she manages to stonewall an entire culture with this simple, serene maneuver. It seems only natural to us, given the liberties offered by the innate responsiveness of mythological time, that Penelope could keep a fleet of suitors at bay for almost two decades.

Did I say lots of us routinely rip out rows of knitting and enjoy it? Well, yes. I know how this might sound. Nonetheless as far as I can tell, this pastime is not a manifestation of obsessive-compulsive disorder, nor is it some kind of voodoo substitute for self-mutilation. Quite to the contrary. It's actually a deeply creative act; and, in its own way, an expression of liberation. We knitters love how knit-

ting allows us to experiment. We can try things and we can untry them if they don't turn out exactly the way we like them to, and with no great detriment to our materials. Yarn isn't like film, which can only be exposed once, or paint that can only be applied once, or houses that require a judicious application of the well-intentioned violence of carpenters to augment or transform them once you close up their walls.

As one of my teachers told me, you can't hurt fiber. If you cut it, or break it, you can tie it back together again. If it's gotten itself into a crimp from holding itself into the shape of a sweater, well, you just wind it up in a ball again and with a little time it'll relax and straighten itself out.

Lots of us knitters love the fluidity knitting gives, the way we can "doodle" with yarn and then erase that first doodle in merino or alpaca or tencel and try another one, the way this allows us to experiment with beautiful materials and without any cost but time. And time itself seems to melt away when we are at work at this thing that we do with two smooth sticks with knobs on the ends. We love the process as much as we enjoy the result. And so we claim Penelope as our own.

I once bonded with a new acquaintance over Penelope in exactly this way. She was telling me about a sister-in-law, who knit beautifully and amazed my friend Miriam by calmly unraveling the most beautiful of creations and starting over again. She hardly ever finished anything.

"But it wasn't perfect," the sister-in-law would say calmly, and begin from scratch, noticing, and this is sheer speculation on my part, that some tiny stitch pattern somewhere was out of skew. Or that she found a small obscure run of bias-leaning fabric, or a slight lapse in even tension, or that a half size smaller in needles would have rendered a more ideal drape. Of course, no one else would notice any of this.

"Penelope," Miriam and I said to each other then, and smiled, each delighted that the other had caught the reference.

Ergo, we love her discipline and control, her mastery of the delicious desire to finish, in some ways as delectable and temporary as the taste and texture of a champagne truffle. Penelope weaves in order to make that precious interior life

PENELOPE,
REGENERATION,
AND A
TURTLENECK
WITH A HALO
156

nigh near eternal. The clock of lesser desire, symbolized by the urgency of her suitors, literally stops ticking as she works.

Here in the place and time whose common denominator is grudgingly agreed to be instant gratification (the Vajrayana Buddhists call it "degenerate") we find this ability impressive. We love the way all the layers of desire, sacrifice, and fulfillment, personal, social, and mythic stack up in this story, and, specifically, they way they layer so complexly and deliciously within this act, like some incredible mille-feuille pastry. We may not be able to articulate them, or even count them, as we read. But, instinctively we know that they are there. Along with the evocation of the physical pleasures and nuances of weaving, and by modern association knitting, that this story brings, there is also this.

On to the life of the emotions. Non-knitters are equally appreciative of and inspired by Penelope. She was a favorite subject of Renaissance and Pre-Raphaelite painters (along with Greek Attic vase painters, of course). John Price Waterhouse, Frederick Leighton, and John Roddam Spencer-Stanhope all tried their hand at her. They lovingly dressed her in their signature flaming russet tones. And they portrayed her heroically: with her head averted from proffering bouquets as she wove, or kneeling between the loom strung with an extraordinary tapestry, her handmaiden, and weeping with grief. They were inspired by the heroic and emotional qualities of this woman, because, as she awaits the husband who may never return, she capitalizes on the shelter and privacy afforded by her weaving to grieve. These painters, who loved mythological subjects and dramatic coloration, were drawn to the emotional resonance of this moment, and the visual possibilities that the scene implied, all based on these same subtle, rich, and clear layers of fulfilled and unfulfilled dreams. Which held in solution the activity of weaving and ripping out again, of stopping time.

In his book *Ritual*, the African shaman Malidoma Somé observes, "Speed is a way to prevent ourselves from having to deal with something we don't want to face."[5] As an archetype, Penelope shows us the potential fruit awaiting us if we have the courage to slow way down. She spent years in her divinely inspired

limbo, and she also discovered the depth of her own love and grief. These are two emotions that sometimes seem to have but a vexsome hair's breadth of difference from each other: if we love deeply, so may we also grieve. And knitting slows us way down so we can reach all the dimensions of this essential inner world which is filled, like Poseidon's ocean, with our own emotions, whatever these may be. And, which, like the mind of Penelope, is also filled with our own wisdom.

The message is this: if you have the courage to notice what is behind the usual speed of desire, you will eventually receive your heart's desire. Slowing down is also a regenerative activity.

Perhaps this is why Britain's Elizabeth the First knit so avidly. It is not difficult to imagine her clearing her mind with the discipline and grace of stitch making, while all the decisions she needed to make began to line up and even solve themselves in her mind, and also while the suitorish tugs of politics and intrigue reassumed their proper place. Many problems solve themselves while one knits.

A Turtleneck with a Halo

I offer you a Penelope-like knitting experience in a beautiful, classic, cream colored mohair sweater (with another choice of the same yarn in deep Aegean blue;

Penelope,
Regeneration,
and a
Turtleneck
with a Halo
158

as per the instructions of the nameless weaver, as far as magical nymph violet is concerned, I leave you to your own devices).

It is a one-size-fits-all, squared-off cowl neck which is delicious and soothing to knit but requires awareness and patience to complete. This is an intermediate level pattern. The pattern and shaping are easy. The skill level designation is earned by the mohair yarn, which is not easy to rip out if you make a mistake, and so requires a Penelope-like patience if you haven't worked with it before, or are just learning the stitch. This yarn has the classic mohair halo, clouds of fiber that extend past the core yarn giving a halo effect. But if you found a non–halo mohair yarn in more or less the same gauge, it would probably work fine and also surrender the intermediate designation in exchange for advanced beginner. I 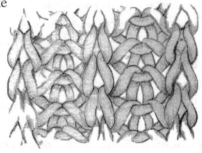 have some handspun from a small producer fitting this description that swatches up beautifully. In this case, you just want to make sure that your gauge gives you an airy fabric that doesn't weigh too much, since this is a lot of sweater and excess weight might cause it to lose its considerable grace and Penelope-like cloudy lightness.

As given, it makes a beautiful classic confection with a lot of textural interest, with a combination of aesthetic and textural appeal that will hold up over time. I wore the sample over the better part of the hump of a Northwest winter (it is heavy enough and provides enough coverage to take the place of a coat on some days, and light enough to go under an open coat on most of the rest, in part because the airy stitch makes for a garment that is both light and quite warm) and am fairly certain that not one of those days passed by without my receiving a heartfelt compliment on it from a complete stranger.

The stitch is Brioche Stitch (above), the foundation stitch of a classic family of stitches which uses extremely simple knitting stitches in an unusual combination to create sophisticated little half x's throughout your garment. It does so with nothing more than a knit stitch, a purlwise slipstitch, and a yarn over.

Even though this sweater looks ribbed, you will actually never purl once the whole time unless you opt to knit the sleeves in the round. It's a kind of knitting pun and quite worthy, in my mind, to be associated with the subtle cleverness of Penelope.

The finished product also combines a Penelope-like circumspection with a Penelope-like ability to fulfill desire in that it looks very classic but is a sensual treat to wear. In the mohair and wool yarn given here, it feels like a cloud when you put it on because the exuberant, soft halo of the yarn both softly kisses the skin and gives the sweater buoyancy, so it seems almost to "lift" off your skin. Also, it's so soft you really don't have to wear anything underneath it if you don't want to. No kidding. The first two women to try it on at my house both lifted their arms in spontaneous dance gestures. I have photos and everything.

If you choose a classic color and make it in this mohair or another yarn that displays a similar combination of loft and textural interest, I do not need to read a magical tapestry to predict you or someone you love will wear this sweater for years.

PENELOPE SWEATER INSTRUCTIONS

Start by learning Brioche Stitch on a non-mohair yarn, if you haven't used the stitch or the yarn before.

BRIOCHE STITCH

FIRST STEP: Cast on an even number of stitches.

SECOND STEP: Knit your foundation row. *Yarnover (YO), slip one purlwise, K1* repeat until end of row.

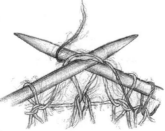

THIRD STEP: Knit your pattern row. *YO, slip one purlwise, K2TOG* The K2TOG will consist of the slipped stitch from the previous row and the yarn

PENELOPE,
REGENERATION,
AND A
TURTLENECK
WITH A HALO
160

over from the previous row. The only trick here is to pick up the front strand of the yarn over, not the back one, and to remember to release both the slipped stitch and the bar of the previous row's yarn over off of your non-working needle to complete the stitch. Otherwise you'll end up with an extra yarn over strand or stitch on your needle.

Fourth Step: Repeat pattern row.

Conceptual hint: After the foundation row, if you see a purl stitch slip it purlwise with the yarn in front and if you see a knit stitch, knit it together with the front strand of the yarn over loop that follows it.

PENELOPE SWEATER PATTERN

Ingredients:

- 13 50g (90 m) skeins of Filatura Di Crosi Mohair Lungo in cream Color 401 or deep blue Color 561 (mohair/wool)
- 1 pair of size 9 or 10 needles (depending on your gauge), circular or straight, your choice
- 1 pair of needles in a smaller size, to pick up collar stitches, circular if you like
- 6 stitch holders (small to medium size)
- And one pair of 12-inch size 9 or 10 circular needles to knit collar

Gauge: 3 stitches to the inch and four rows to the inch (16 rows of twelve stitches will equal four inch × four inch gauge swatch).

First Step: Make Back

❶ Cast on 90 stitches very loosely (you may want to cast on over two needles). Knit 13 inches in Brioche Stitch. (And of course, this is where you want to cut or add inches to make the sweater longer or shorter.)

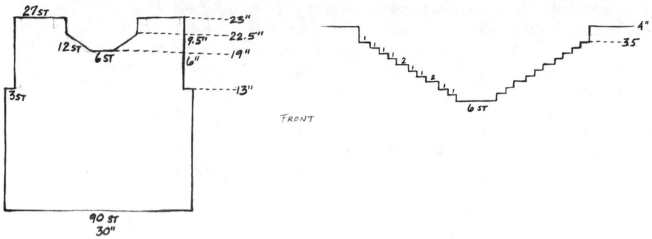

27ST

12ST   23" -- -- 23"
        9.5" -- -- 22.5"
6 ST   6" -- -- 19"

3ST   -- -- 13"

90 ST
30"

FRONT

4"
3.5

2

6 ST

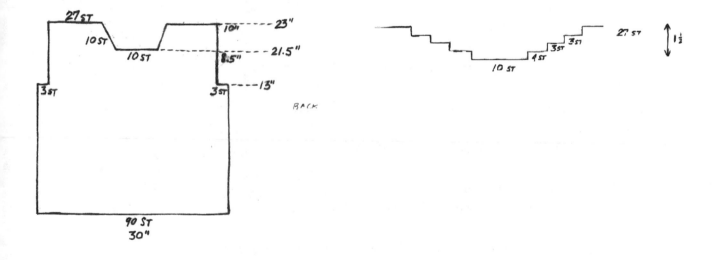

27 ST

10 ST   10" -- -- 23"
10 ST   8.5" -- -- 21.5"

3ST   3ST -- -- 13"

90 ST
30"

BACK

27 ST   1½
3ST
3ST
4ST
10 ST

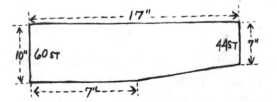

17"

10" 60 ST   44ST 7"

7"

2 Make armhole: Put 3 stitches on a stitch holder at each outer edge for a total of six stitches.

3 Work remaining 84 stitches another 8½ inches.

4 Shape back of neck. In next row, bind off center 10 stitches.

5 From here on, work each shoulder separately. Put one shoulder on needles and, starting at the inside neck edge, then bind off four, three, and three stitches every other row to shape neck slope. Repeat on other shoulder. Put last row of stitches on each side on stitch holders or leave on needles. You will have 27 stitches on each shoulder.

SECOND STEP: Make Front

1 Cast on 90 stitches very loosely. Knit 13 inches in pattern. (Or match the custom measurement you chose for the back.)

2 Shape armhole. Put 3 stitches on stitch holders at each outer edge to start armhole shaping.

3 Work remaining 84 stitches for 6 inches in Pattern Stitch, Brioche Stitch.

4 Start neck shaping. On your next row, bind off center 6 stitches.

5 Make neck. Work each side separately. Put one shoulder on needles (and the other on needles or a stitch holder) and bind off 1, 1, 2, 1, 1, 2, 1, 1, 1, and 1 stitch during every other row at the neck edge. Work 4 more inches (i.e., until the armhole opening from bottom to shoulder measure 10 inches).

6 Repeat on other side. You will have 27 stitches on each shoulder.

7 Bind off shoulders together. (See directions in Chapter Four if needed.)

Third Step: Pick up and Knit Collar

 Pick up 62 stitches evenly around neck with a needle in a size smaller than the one you are using.

2 Then switch to the needle you are using and knit approximately 6½ inches in pattern stitch Brioche Stitch, beginning with foundation row. (Measure your own neck to choose optimal collar height.)

3 Bind off loosely.

Fourth Step: Make Sleeves

Arms can be worked back and forth or in the round.
If you are working flat:

 Pick up 60 stitches (including the 6 stitches on holders) with a smaller needle around one of the armholes.

2 Work pattern stitch for 7 inches. If you want to make sleeves shorter or longer, make adjustment here. Follow the pattern, knitting knit stitches and purling purls, while also slipping stitches according to the pattern.

 Decrease 2 stitches, one on each side of the sleeve, for every inch of length until 44 stitches are left on your needle. Make your decrease either 1 or 2 stitches in from the seam.

4 Knit until sleeve measures 17 inches.

5 Bind off loosely.

6 Repeat on other side.

7 Sew up sleeves and side seams and weave in ends.

If knitting sleeves in the round:

PENELOPE,
REGENERATION,
AND A
TURTLENECK
WITH A HALO
164

Sew up side seams.

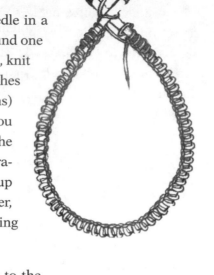

2 Pick up 58 stitches with a circular needle in a size smaller than the one you are using around one sleeve. Switch to your regular needles. Then, knit a couple of the loose, live underarm stitches (left over after you sewed the side seams) together with the stitches next to them so you have picked up a total of 4 stitches under the arm. Join yarn. To knit in round, see illustration. Join stitches in the cast on or picked up row by knitting first and last stitches together, placing marker as shown to mark beginning of round.

3 Decrease as above per round, keeping to the pattern. Bind off loosely.

More on Halos: If you are a new knitter, as you work on this project, you will discover exactly why it is that yarns like mohair are said to have "halos." The mohair fibers extend in a soft cloud all around the sweater. You can call it a halo or you can call it a mist. I go for halo, myself. In this case, while you do get the mohair halo, softness, and strength, you also get the strong tactile "base line" and elasticity of the wool to balance it with a bit of weight and definition.

Here is where you also get to see how small nuances in needle choice can make a big difference. In working with mohair, and, in this pattern, especially when you slip your stitches, you will probably find that a metal or plastic needle with a relatively sharper point makes a big difference to your knitting. Wood, and especially bamboo, with a relatively rounder point may hamper and slow your knitting a little. This is because mohair's distinctive texture doesn't slide over needles as easily as smoother yarns and thus does better with a "faster" (i.e., not

wood or bamboo) needle. Also, it can be difficult to pick up a fuzzy mohair stitch with rounder pointed needles, while with sharper needles this small but potentially annoying stumbling block basically vanishes.

Also, if you are a new knitter and suspect you might be pulling out stitches here is one last bit of advice in the spirit of Grandmother Spider: don't go with the off white, which will get dirty fairly easily. Give yourself a break and try the blue or another medium color.

New Knitter's Workshop

Slip Stitch

This is just question of slipping a stitch from the non-working needle to the working needle without knitting or purling it. When we slip a stitch knitwise, we put the yarn in back as if to knit, insert the needle as if to knit and just slip the stitch from one needle to the other instead. When we slip a stitch purlwise, we slip the needle in the front of the loop as if to purl. In this pattern we slip purlwise.

---

[1] Allen Mandelbaum, trans. *The Odyssey of Homer*. (Bantam: New York, 1990), 99–100.
[2] Mandelbaum, 101–102.
[3] Mandelbaum, 462.
[4] Mandelbaum, 462
[5] Malidoma Somé, *Ritual*. (Arkana: New York, 1997), 18.

PENELOPE,
REGENERATION,
AND A
TURTLENECK
WITH A HALO
166

Arachne, Body Love, and a Lively Shrug

A girl named Arachne sat at a loom strung in her yard, under the soft morning sun. Her shuttle moved so quickly that her warp sang.

This in itself was not such an unusual sight. Arachne sat in that spot almost every morning, and many Lydian girls wove all day. Arachne's father made his living dying wool crimson. She had no mother. Left to her own devices, and steeped in the perpetual magic of raw wool and silk, she had become an astonishing weaver. Even the most experienced artisans in the region gasped at the grace and fineness with which Arachne filled her spindle whorl with brilliantly colored thread. Some reported that the beauty and strength of the tapestries that came from Arachne's loom had temporarily blinded them. Others had been lost in their landscapes for hours, or perhaps even days. Even the local nymphs would abandon the vineyards and streams and come to marvel at the magic that flowed from her arms.

Arachne was a comely, sturdy girl but she was no beauty. Her parentage was not only common, but incomplete. No king would come and fight for her, and no god would take her in passion.

Yet, on this particular morning, the unearthly, disturbing, and completely arresting light of the gods was painted in the air and along the ground all about her father's house and well into the rest of the town. Most of the other villagers had awoken before dawn with that distinctive uneasy yet excited feeling that the elders among them knew was associated with the descent of an Olympian and which the younger ones had never felt before. And after the morning chores they

had all followed their feelings and their eyes to Arachne's father's house, to find Athena, the patroness of weaving, sitting directly across from the girl.

Athena was unmistakable as always. She was also guiding a shuttle through the warp of her loom with an impossible speed and grace, and wore a brilliant silver helmet that was so tall it scraped the sky. Her face was bright, cool, fearless, and fraught with a perfectly engineered beauty that made one want to weep or smash an urn upon the stones. Her robes flowed with their own perfect, irreproducible logic, like a river whose existence had been universally suspected but had never before been seen. Her own eyes were as silvery cool as sunlight on a river in shadow. And the eyes of the owl that perched on her shoulder were as black as the recesses of her own temple high on a hill in the city that bore her name. The aegis that covered Athena's chest writhed with snakes.

Arachne looked as she always looked. Utterly focused, small, sturdy, close to the ground, ruthless, and vulnerable.

Arachne's shuttle flew through the warp of her own loom, keening like a musical instrument, and whorls of brilliant color seemed to fly around her quickly and cunningly, like clouds. The sharp and implacable light of Athena further enlivened this sight.

"Contest, contest," whispered the vineyard and water nymphs who had been listening as they did every morning, for they loved Arachne's work enough to leave their own to watch. And then they laughed among themselves. "Weaving contest. The goddess and the mortal. Who shall win?"

The villagers gasped and crowded in. So this motherless girl had attracted attention after all.

From her post amid the cloud of divine color, Arachne heard them, and smiled. Yes, it was a contest. Athena had challenged her. And Arachne was not at all concerned with the outcome. Because, within, ever since she had started weaving, she had cultivated a rich and awesome inner relationship with this great being. The secret she had told no one, not the nymphs, not the local women, and certainly not her father, was that this owl-eyed, bright-faced, and helmeted warrior had been giving her inner instruction for years.

The patron of weaving and of Athens did inspire the shrouds, table linens,

marriage tunics and everything else good wives and daughters wove. But through Athena Arachne had discovered something a little different. The inner instruction had begun when, as a child, Arachne had eyed the creations inspired by Athena and found them technically perfect, but somewhat dull. In contemporary vernacular, one might say, they had no soul. Indeed, as she sat by her father's knee as he sold his wares, Arachne had watched as the village women admired Athena's creations and she had been perplexed.

Inspired by a goddess, Arachne would have expected something better. Something totally astonishing. Something no one had ever seen. But all of these items were utterly predictable. She couldn't understand it. She was both dumbfounded and fascinated, and this was an utterly seductive combination. Arachne just had that kind of mind.

Athena had begun to come to her at night to teach her. Arachne had summoned her with the power of her own desire, or Athena had recognized Arachne's aptitude, the whys of divine visitations are never clear, nor the gifts they bestow logical. For instance, she not been able to understand why Athena was using the same old patterns when she herself gave the young weaver brand new stitches to weave. Soon, Arachne glimpsed ways to weave that Athena hadn't seen herself—or just wasn't using. She saw patterns that were far more lustrous, strong, shimmering, and alive. Arachne discovered new ways to weave shapes. These were round shapes. The shape of a fig. The shape of a limb. The way a face looked when it was about to laugh.

The other village women would just sigh when Arachne talked about her visions. Dishcloths and shrouds and table linens were more than enough, really. Who had time to think about the sorts of plans that Arachne had? And who cared? Why wouldn't this girl rest her brain, which would never win her a husband, and, even more importantly, when was she going to get over herself?

Arachne had paid no attention. Because as her shuttle snaked around her fine warp in new permutations, her vision literally changed. She began to see not only her work, but also the world itself as if it were a tapestry in progress curving around a great loom. There were ways in which the world also could be woven more skillfully, astonishingly, and more beautifully.

And so, as she wove her tapestries, Arachne also began to repattern the world she lived in, and also the world of the gods. She saw things about them that they were trying to hide from each other. She saw things about them that they were trying to hide from the humans they alternately protected and tortured. She saw how the people of Athens were also blind to these things, and how, because gods were alternately kind and cruel, the people accepted their misery.

The sensuality of creation filled Arachne's body as she dreamed, wove, saw, and understood. This is a very particular form of sensuality. It has certainty and sharpness and gladness and courage, its only object is the wholeness of a complete and perfect creation, and it fills the body and soul with confidence and acuity. The rhythms soothed the currents running through her blood and nerves and her hands ran over the finished lengths of brilliant fabric, and, at the same time, the wool and silk caressed the palms of her hands. She held it just slack enough so it did not cut them, but also taut enough so it flew through the warp with perfectly even tension. As Arachne sat at her loom and was transformed from a young girl into a young woman, Athena spoke and Athena's owl spoke and, as they rustled, the folds of her gown spoke, and Arachne wove to the rhythms they gave her. With her very desire, and willingness to serve, Arachne had summoned the source of the wisdom of weaving to her.

This very morning, as Arachne had immersed herself in the patterns and curves and colors of this inner world, a crippled old woman happened by her loom.

"You silly little fool," the old woman had said. "No one dares to weave like the goddess Athena. You are sorely trying the ribbon that lies between the realms, and it was placed there for a reason. If you do this, you must honor her. Give her praises."

And here, exactly right here, Arachne committed a most egregious error, or an act of extreme arrogance, or a very deliberate and conscious gesture of freedom. Hard to say. Perhaps she was so absorbed in her work and with the feelings in her body and the complex stitch she was executing at exactly that point that she forgot principle 8A of the Audubon guide to interpreting the behavior of

divine beings, which clearly and unequivocally states—no, warns—no, admonishes, that if an old, crippled, and physically repugnant or outcast person crosses your path and gives you a piece of their mind, you are hereby rubbing up against the oldest trick in the book. Watch out! Pay attention! Heads up! This is a test! You are undergoing an initiation.

This would cover the first two possible motivations. That is, the one where she goofed. Or was just plain arrogant. Then again, maybe she had read the manual. And this particular eventuality would cover the third possibility. In any event, this is what Arachne said next: "Oh, get out here you silly old fool. You aren't going to change my mind. And I don't see Athena complaining."

Ouch.

In other words, she did not respect the old beggar woman's request at all.

In one instant the gnarled old woman transformed into the great shining helmeted one and said, with her eyes, her body, and her gray eyes as cool as Einstein's theorems, as cool as all of space, "I am she."

And then she drew herself up to her true warrior height.

"Let's see who is the better weaver, shall we?"

And this was how the stringing of looms, and the high, keening sound that accompanied it, had begun.

And now, with the great, cool light and flowing of robes, the instructress of her dreams becomes the rival of her daylight hours. Arachne wove, oblivious to everything but her work, and breathing deeply but lightly with anticipation. Everything she had learned from the patroness of her art, about weaving and about everything else, was written in wool and silk within this tapestry.

As suddenly as they began, and in exactly the same moment, the two were done. Both weavers pulled their tapestries from their looms.

"Let us see yours first," said Athena. And then she sat back on her stool and waited. But first she paused, and took one look around.

And for years afterward all the assembled would recall how she looked— filmy, shiny, there yet not there; indolent yet quite alert, astonishingly yet almost too beautiful, easily taking in the whole village in one glance. To be seen by Zeus'

favored daughter and the patroness of Athens, by the one who carried the olive branch, was to be beheld down to one's secret core, and to change as a result. After that, all the villagers recalled, and also the nymphs, that no one of them ever again felt quite exactly the same.

Despite all of this, and more, Athena changed her mind. She first threw down and then displayed her own tapestry, as, in later centuries, a man would throw down a glove while challenging another to a duel.

On it, she had woven a picture of good girls and bad girls. In the tapestry's center, she herself stood on the hill in Athens where she and Poseidon had entered a contest to see whose name would preside over this fertile land. He had produced a salt water spring in the center of the city, and that was pretty good. Meanwhile, she had produced the olive tree and the gods had looked on in wonder. Needless to say, she had won. What a good girl.

Each of the four corners of Athena's creation were quite cunningly festooned with bad girls. On one corner, she had immortalized Haemus and Rhodophe, that daughter of the river gods and her companion, who had come across the wonderful idea of calling themselves Zeus and Hera and developed a following. They had expediently been turned into immortal mountains by the gods as a reward for the breadth of their imagination. A second corner featured a Pygmy queen whom Hera had turned into a crane in a fit of jealousy. The third showed Antigone, whom Hera had turned into a stork after this princess had dared compete with her. The fourth featured devastated Cinyras embracing his daughter Smyrna who had been tranformed into a myrrh tree because her mother boasted that her daughter's beauty topped Aphrodite's. The whole was bordered very peacefully with a motif of olive wreath. The composition was quite beautifully balanced; tasteful, linear, with the central motif of Athena herself and the four corners stretching out into a perfect triumphant and utterly classical and serene x-shaped composition. You could almost hear Athena laugh and shout as she unfurled the thing. What a bad girl.

And then Arachne's turn came.

She smiled her small, quick, private smile, unfurled her glittering tapestry,

and stepped back. To reveal an astonishing, original canvas of Zeus, Poseidon, Cronus, Apollo, and Dionysus all disguised in animal forms and entwined with goddesses and mortal women in very compromising positions.

Arachne's tapestry canvas undulated in the astonishing curves and rounds she had found behind Athena's perfect symmetry during all those years of dreaming, seeing, understanding, feeling, and weaving. The curves spoke a language, and the language both hypnotized and clarified. No one had seen anything like it before, certainly not Athena, who had never woven with such originality. And not only was it brilliant, but it was also impertinent. There was Leda, being taken by Zeus in the form of a swan, and Europa being taken by Zeus once again in his disguise as the magic bull from the sea. There was Cronus fathering Chiron the centaur with the nymph Phylira; the erotic partners were disguised as horses. And there, in another corner, Poseidon in the form of stallion taking the grain goddess Demeter. And many more. The secret life of the gods lay exposed there in all its living color, with Athena's father as the center of the show. Flowers and ivy bordered the tapestry, affording it their own living curves, and slyly celebrating the absolutely flawless execution.

All around the lane, murmurs came to a halt and the thickness that particular sound gave to the air melted into a thin, keening silence. This was followed by a collective intake of breath.

They were all thinking *hubris*. Which, of course, is the ancient Greek version of chutzpah. In this world, to dare to best the gods was the most dangerous of offenses. Somewhat like high seniors being ruffled by a talented freshman. But with powers beyond superpower powers. Quite the potent combination. And as the warrior Achilles had discovered, the punishment could be fatal. Warriors who had hubris, even the greatest ones, fell on the battlefield, inexplicably wounded in their most vulnerable spot. In Achilles' case this spot was the place on the back of his heel where his mother, the sea goddess Thetis, had held him when she bathed him in protective water.

But for women, the punishment was different.

Athena's eyes glittered as silver as her helmet. She rose to her full and considerable stature. On her shoulder, the owl faded to a hole of pure black.

It was then that Arachne remembered that while Athena's father, Zeus, predominated in her mural, Athena herself, the true virgin goddess (if a few stray rumors were to be avoided), was absent from it altogether.

"Your stitch patterns are perfect," said the goddess. "Why, you have devised some that I have not even thought of or revealed. How did you accomplish such a thing? Which god has given you favors? And where are you within this?" She pointed to the mural.

"I—I—You taught me," said Arachne.

"I? I did no such thing! Such colors are not permitted to mortals. Where did you find them? On Olympus? Are they my father's?"

"Why, you . . . you showed them to me!"

"I did *no such thing*!"

The light coming from the goddess suddenly flashed cold and filled with an awful vibration. Everyone present covered his or her ears.

Towering Athena reached down, and rent a tear through the center of Arachne's tapestry with her spear.

Then she picked up her shuttle and began to strike the small young woman on the side of her head. She struck her again and again and again.

At this point the brilliant and spunky Arachne was so overcome by shame and pain, that she knelt, made a noose of fiber, put her head inside, and made preparations to hang herself.

Then the noble Athena took pity on her. And rather than allowing the girl to die, as punishment for her huge, unforgivable, apparently disrespectful glitch, she shrunk Arachne's head, bloated her belly, gave her eight arms, threw her into the shadows, and named her spider.

This is how the wily and powerful species was born. And, as punishment for weaving the most beautiful tapestry in the land, Arachne spent the rest of her days spinning endless, disintegrating, insubstantial webs in the dark.

Hmm.

Like Arachne, we knitters naturally learn to see other pieces to a pattern or how to adapt an existing pattern more truthfully or usefully to our needs. That's

just one module of the gift of knitting. So it's not too much of a stretch to squint our eyes, stand back, and observe how, by defying Athena, and metaphorically leaving the realm, Arachne gained immortality, power, and almost unimaginable influence. She did so by embodying spider magic, which, as we have already seen, is a great source of power. Not only is the arachnid the representative of Spider Grandmother, a.k.a. the source of the universe and the sacred and life giving process of emergence itself, it but lays seven hundred eggs a year, and in Arachne's case, inhabits a world that is no longer subject to the whim of capricious Olympians. Her new body mimics the infinity symbols and also the figure eight wrap that is traditionally used to tie a skein of newly spun and cut yarn so it will not tangle. Eight is also a sacred number of Isis in her aspect as Kwan Yin who protects travelers on the seas. And the multiple of feet, × 4, that each of the magical bamboo seeds grew to reach the sky in order to rescue Grandmother Spider's people.

In her own way, by besting Athena, Arachne, like her kindred spirit Ariadne, figured out, by reinventing the magical patterns of the loom, how to transform and reweave the pattern of her life to such an extent that she jettisoned the restrictions—and also the securities and comforts—of her life altogether. This story is also a metaphor for personal liberation. Arachne's tapestry, with its metamorphic theme, was also a sort of magical invocation of liberation, or the ability to change forms or states and in so doing achieve a goal that would have not been possible otherwise. What kind of liberation? Social? Spiritual? Creative? Who knows? Perhaps any or all of them. I like to think that others alive at that time would have recognized the same code at work in that story, and applied it to their own personal dream of liberation, and understand what the clue of spider might have meant when Arachne was transformed.

I also like to think that they understood this because spiders themselves always speak in a very specific, brilliant, and layered code. Certainly Wilbur the pig understood the spider Charlotte's code when, in E. B. White's *Charlotte's Web*, he was liberated by the messages Charlotte wove in her web concerning his amazing qualities. And certainly Charles Dickens's Madame Defarge understood

this when she incorporated the names of aristocrats targeted for the guillotine into her knitting in Dickens's novel, *A Tale of Two Cities*. Spiders themselves are equally canny. Dragline spider silk is five times stronger than steel, and tougher than Kevlar. Today, scientists study it, hoping to reproduce the arachnid's miracle in the lab.[1] Once again, arachnids are demonstrating the long term power of the disturbing innovation that is expressed by their namesake, Arachne.

Not to be glossed over is the competition between the two women, the divine and the human wanting to be acknowledged by each other, and each totally unable to do so. In a way they are mirror images; Athena, with her amazing godly appearance and perfectly limned tapestry represents the shining, classical orderly surface while Arachne brings in the yummy, luscious shadow that surrounds it. They are order and disorder; foreground and background; and the feminine versions of those two artistic paragons and ancient super-celebrities known as Apollo and Dionysus.

Both are motherless, and both are born from creative, life-giving fathers. Ovid's version of the myth states Arachne had no mother. Red thread is the thread of life, and this is the color that Ovid reports that Arachne's father dyed his wool. Athena literally was born from the head of Zeus. Neither of these women was ever mentored by a domesticated woman. In their own ways, they each explore what it means to be an exceptional woman who has never had to conform.

They are also equally competitive. As Athena and Arachne duel it out with their looms, without seeing how similar they really are, I think of criticism among women concerning women who seem different from themselves, of the longing for the comfort of seamless uniformity without the sometimes uncomfortable surrender to inclusion.

So let's bring this one to the present. Knitters seem to rally to one of two camps. Some of us like the appeal of geometric stitch patterns rendered in crisp, monotone yarns (using the combination of color variety and stitch pattern undercuts the stitch definition) or we are attracted to the appeal of soft shapes in simple stitches and colored yarn. I'm thinking of a knitting teacher who whipped

up fabulous entrelac (a diamond shaped pattern that looks great in different colors and has to be knitted backwards in part) creations but frankly admitted she was perturbed by novelty yarns and bright colors. She would be an Athena in my book. A sky knitter.

And then I think of another master knitter who hardly ever works with a pattern at all. Almost entirely intuitive, she works as she goes, thinks with her hands, rips out stuff she doesn't like and redoes it the way she does like it, and does beautiful work that wins prizes all the time. She would be more of an Arachne. An earth knitter.

I'm just a novice, but I myself started off as an Arachne knitter. But then one day I out-Arachned myself, and innovated and rebelled my way into experimenting with part of a lace weight shawl, the type you pull through a wedding ring, knitted up on size zero needles. I did it just to be contrary, and to find out if I could. And as I discovered that I loved knitting lace—the concentration required was like the concentration required to do a complex, classic Eastern meditation practice, and gave similar results—a clear, focused mind, serenity, and, consequently, the ability to learn and assimilate new ways of being through the cleared inner platform I had created. The flow of stitches also had a kind of musical or linguistic quality to it. When I knit lace, I feel like I am speaking a wonderful new language, or playing a beautiful song. And, in each case, I feel like I am writing a kind of universal code understood by women all over the world. And then, after a while, it is time to go back to luscious Arachne-type yarn choices and undulating patterns again. So, in my own way, I travel my own figure eight or infinity symbol, moving from one style of knitting to the other and back again. Many knitters do.

In a way, this myth points out what happens when we don't let that flow take place—a war within the self ensues. In its darkest, campiest, funniest form, the bright side literally destroys the identity of the dark side, so intensely is she disturbed by its power.

This story also reminds us that working with fiber can be a very sensual experience. In part, Athena punished Arachne to repress Arachne's sexuality. As a wildcrafted woman, not a domesticated one, and left to her own devices, Arachne

becomes an original and daring weaver. Allowed to grow freely, and focused on creation of beauty for others, Arachne's sensuality and creativity attracted the attention of all the nature and fertility spirits in the area—the vineyard nymphs were friends of Dionysus', and the water nymphs who were purveyors of emotion and healing and, as we have already seen, had their own deep connection to weaving.

As the story ends, and the encounter is finished, each side of the mirror departs for her own, extra-human world: Athena back to the brilliant sky, and the realm of the gods, and Arachne to the womb of the goddess. From their respective strongholds each of them, one highlighting theme and the other the brilliant potential for variation, will, in her own way mutually continue to succor weavers, knitters, and spinners throughout the generations.

KNITTING AND BODIES

Arachne's tapestry was filled with creatures fulfilling sensual needs. Knitting has this odd, backdoor kind of way of promoting body awareness. It's not just the touch of the fiber, although there is that. Nor is it or the steady, insistent rhythm of the moving needles. (In ancient times, it would have been the spin of the fluffy, diffuse fleece growing agile, firm, and smooth as it dropped towards the spindle, or the song of the shuttle. And, to classical women this shuttle song was said to weave a love spell.)

You knit and you just naturally get to know more about bodies. You're forever measuring your sleeve length or the length from your hipbone to your collarbone, or noticing whether your shoulders are wide, or narrow, or sloped, and whether your bra size has changed. When you knit for other people, you get to discover and savor all the quirks and differences in a variety of bodies, not just your own. Here I always find *hozho*, the Navajo ideal of harmony, to be the most descriptive of this particular aesthetic that settles into the heart and spirit and is enhanced as we knit. We learn that there is always variation in the world, and certainly in art. Through our eyes and hands, we are reminded of the Navajo carpet where you might find slight variations in the size of pattern elements, or the

color of yarns, and always a small hole here or there to show that no one but God is perfect. I discover the *hozho* in the world when I knit and design, and other knitters do, too. I love wrapping the Isis stole around different women, because it looks different on each one and I get to learn something new about them. I do the same with the Penelope sweater—even though it is a simple one size, it hits everyone a little differently. You learn to appreciate the shape of a neck or the slope of a shoulder as it is highlighted by the same flowing shape of yarn. And each nuance in fit and enhancement to the basic shapes you favor are enlightening and aesthetically interesting.

What's both fun and liberating about this in knitting is that there is no physical size template to which you need to subscribe, and variations in body size give birth to all sorts of creative designs. I'm thinking particularly of a friend, whom I happened upon about a week ago, finishing up a gorgeous, dramatic cardigan sweater in mitered squares and stripes of different colors of natural alpaca: dark brown, off-white, cognac, and cream. It turned out that some of the arresting striping and mix of fibers and colors had been inspired by a need to alter the fit of the sweater pattern. The sleeves had been too tight, so she had cast on and knit additional bands of color on each side of the sleeve, then continued the pattern around the sweater as she went. The result was spectacular and, in my opinion, much more interesting than the original design.

As you design for yourself, you get to know and appreciate your own body. There is no need to "squeeze into" or to "fill out." You just alter the dimensions, some of which, like my friend adding extra inches to the sleeves, consists of nothing more than common sense and doesn't necessarily need any book to figure out. I remember walking through a knitting class in progress, where the students were calculating the yarn they would need and the dimensions they would knit to make a sweater done in a specific advanced technique. I heard them rattle off the length of sweater and sleeve they preferred, down to the half inch. The recitation was totally un-self conscious, like knowing the color of their eyes, or how many children they had, and, in my opinion, the expression of a very particular, unexpected, and tangible variety of self-love.

As we knit for ourselves, we also inherently and instinctively express appreciation for our own bodies. We choose yarns that feel good against our skin, and colors we like, and shapes that we carry well or flatter our own form. This isn't a narcissistic activity, it is a practical one—knitting teaches you to find what works. It's also creatively stimulating. You begin to have a good time looking for variations on patterns even as you instinctively look for variations of things that have worked well in the past. Regardless of your body type, when you knit for yourself or someone else for a while you naturally develop an organic sense of how to ornament your own, and others' unique bodies. As you do, you also naturally develop delight in the process. And since this concerns the sacredness of ornamentation, it becomes a particularly Isis-inspired enterprise.

As an exemplary weaver, Arachne naturally would have developed a delight in all the variations in the human body. This delight and intelligence, so like an artist's rendition of the variation in individual flowers or stones on the beach, would bubble up into the motifs that filled the only tapestry that ever bested its divine equivalent. In this sense it is telling, and even predictable, that the perfect, classically proportioned Athena would be incensed by this artistic celebration of the unique, the organic, the varied, and the unrepeatable—a feat she herself could never perform.

Speed in Knitting

Knitting slowly is a pleasure. But sometimes we just want to get something knitted up on a deadline, my favorite examples being gift giving, keeping little shoulders warm on the playground when the season turns, or discovering the pressing need to throw something wickedly clever around your shoulders as soon as possible.

If you want to knit more quickly, here are a few tricks culled from the oral tradition of knitters.

Use or create patterns that knit in the round. When you don't have to turn your knitting around to start the next row (even when you are knitting back

and forth on circular needles) it goes faster.

Change to metal needles. If you are a new knitter, this may not save you time at first, because you may end up losing stitches, which at first may spend the time you've gained. And if you knit loosely, you will knit even more loosely on metal. But you will knit faster. Cotton is considered by some to always work better on wood or bamboo, as are socks.

Learn Continental. Continental is a different style of knitting (developed on continental Europe as opposed to England) which, among other things, feeds the yarn differently, enhancing knitting speed.

Switch to a larger needle size. You will knit more quickly with larger needles. If you're making an afghan or a shawl or scarf, or another project where gauge doesn't matter that much, it may not make that much of a difference to the finished garment. Exceptions are projects knitted with single ply yarn. On larger needles the yarn is more likely to break, so double ply and multi-stranded yarns are more suitable for this tactic. Also, sometimes, even one larger needle size will add enough additional drape to result in a finished project that is too "droopy" for your taste, or more transparent and airy than you would prefer. So try a few rows and check it out.

Choose a project that is knitted on large needles to begin with. This is the strategy behind many of the projects in this book. Sweaters and shawls and hats and anything knitted up in bulky yarns on large needles will be finished more quickly with a beautiful result. However, not everyone wants to wear this kind of sweater. Either a very small person or a larger person might find the bulk overwhelming and prefer a less "juicy" knitted fabric.

Arachne Shrug

Black for Athena's owl's eyes, the Arachne shrug can be worn with all sorts of things. Wildly yet judiciously striped for Arachne's combination of boldness and cleverness, this shrug is an homage to her divine skepticism. Subtle stripes of soft strawberry, pale yellow, and violet wrap around your wrists. Tiny, precise blocks of many soft and vivid colors float on the black background. It contains

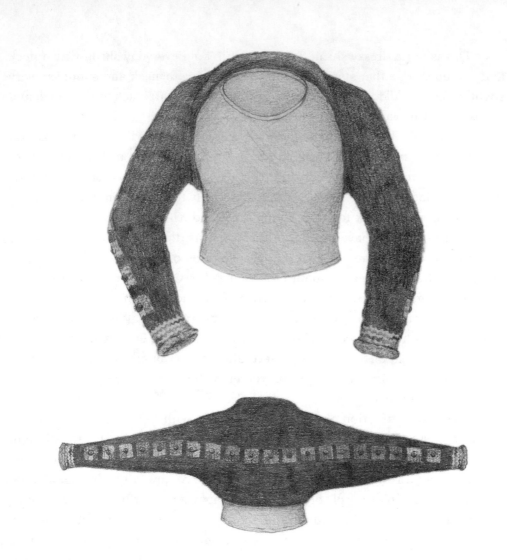

tiny surprise ornaments.

Made of bits of wool, a blending of silk, and a very healthy dose of viscose in the sweater's main body, this shrug can be worn for three seasons.

Because it is a shrug (therefore nothing more than two sleeves and a back that covers your shoulders), you can have the satisfaction of making a whole garment in about half the time and at half the expense of a full sweater.

This is not a dressy shrug. It's a cheerful, bold everyday shrug with a neck and shoulder edge that stand up a little to frame your neck and shoulders very slightly. Very useful for travel, since it rolls up small, has a black background, and keeps you fairly warm.

Technically, this sweater takes advantage of the different variegation rhythms in the two-colored yarns to play a simple trick that makes two balls of yarn look like four or five. As a result, you get variety in your color without having to use a lot of different yarns, which is not only fun, but economical, to boot.

This is a neat trick to know, if you don't know it already. Both the colored yarns in this chapter have repeats in them, that is, the color changes from one shade and tone to the next in a regular pattern, kind of like a laser show. For Colors B1 and B2, the repeat is about four inches. For Color A, the wool silk blend, it's rather longer, approximately 6–7 yards in fact, and the transition between colors is more harmonious. (More analogous colors are pulled along from change to change.) Yarns like this seem musical to me, because they explore more than one rhythm of color at once, sometimes several, and the rhythms harmonize, creating a pleasing, musical sensation that you enjoy but can't quite figure out unless you stop to analyze it.

Part of the attraction of working with a yarn with a color repeat is figuring out how to let the repeat work for you. For instance, if you swatch yarn B1 up at the usual twenty stitches or so, you'll find you have pretty even color stripes, they are just about a row each—the first row might be yellow, and the second pink, and the third green or purple or blue, depending where your hank of yarn begins in the pattern or dye lot. If you knit the longer rows you typically knit to make a garment, you'll create a somewhat more blended, multicolored field, because there will be more than one color to a row, perhaps several, and each additional row will add several more colors. Still, because this is a soft but medium grade wool, it has a lot of definition to its stitches, and the colors will stand out. Certain patterns, such as entrelac, take advantage of color repeats to create a pattern, in this case, small colored diamond-shaped sections in your fabric.

Here I just created a common sense variation based on a much less techni-

cally complicated version of the same principle. I figured out how many stitches would make a block that used only one of the pattern repeat colors, so I could put individual blocks of color into the same motif without using different yarns. Then, for fun, and because the whole thing was getting a little too geometric for Arachne, I added a round bobble made with novelty yarn from my stash smack dab in the middle. Bobbles look neat and are easy to make.

Yarns like this will naturally give you this kind of variety as you use them, but knowing what the possibilities are just gives you more opportunities to play.

Arachne Shrug Pattern Instructions

- One set size ten needles, straight or circular (Pattern is knit back and forth).
- Four 100g 90m skeins of Horstia Mogador in black, color 8 (wool/viscose)

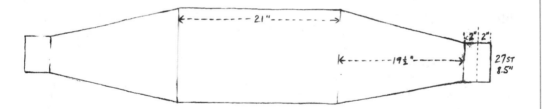

(MC)
- One 100g (110 yd) skein of Noro Iro, in pink, violet, orange, green, Color 14 (wool/silk) (Color A)
- One 100g (110 yd) skein of Naturewolle Black Forrest Yarn in Farbenzauber, color 30 (wool) separated into two equal size balls. These will be colors B1 and B2
- Little scraps of ribbon, bouclé, metallic, and other novelty yarns from your yarn stash, leftover ribbon yarn from the Red Isis stole, or a skein of Trendsetter ¼-inch Bon Bon ribbon in Tapestry, or any variegated ¼-inch ribbon yarn
- Tapestry needle for finishing, and bobbin holders

Gauge: three to three and a half stitches to an inch in a twisted stockinette stitch in MC. Take time to check your gauge.

The sweater is knit in a single piece. The stitches used are twisted stockinette, stockinette, and small bobble. To learn the very simple twisted stockinette, which adds a bit of additional interest to a smooth, solid yarn, see New Knitter's Workshop.

To make a small bobble:

K1 P1 K1 into the same stitch, turn your knitting, K3, turn your knitting, slip one knitwise, K2TOG, PSSO (See New Knitter's Workshop for directions for PSSO, or pass slip stitch over). If you are a new knitter, know that all of this is pretty straightforward, if you just follow the instruction, the three stitches you make from one turn into their own little row, which you then "pop" with the PSSO decrease. If you've never seen a bobble, it looks like a piece of popcorn. By knitting "in place" for a minute, then fixing your stitches down, you get volume, and your "knitting in place" "pops."

INSTRUCTIONS FOR ARACHNE COLOR BLOCK CHART (see facing page)

dark squares = MC
A = color A
B = color B1
b = color B2
Small dot = bobble

Chart begins at 31 stitch increase in MC. After row 92, continue across the back according to instructions to complete back and second sleeve and alternating the colors in square in the same frequency of four: B1 and A, B1 and B2, A, and A and B, maintaining the same placement throughout and using novelty yarn of your choice to make bobbles. I alternated metallic, ribbon, bouclé, and a little handspun silk and merino in mine.

Smaller and more narrow-shouldered women may want to delete one (or even more) of the squares and its attendant surrounding MC rows on the back section for a tighter fit. Measure to find out, or even knit and test the fit and rip out a square if needed. Fit along the back bottom edge is a shrug fit: slightly loose with an even edge. Depending on what body is wearing it, it may drape slightly.

Chart courtesy of Stitch and Motif Maker.

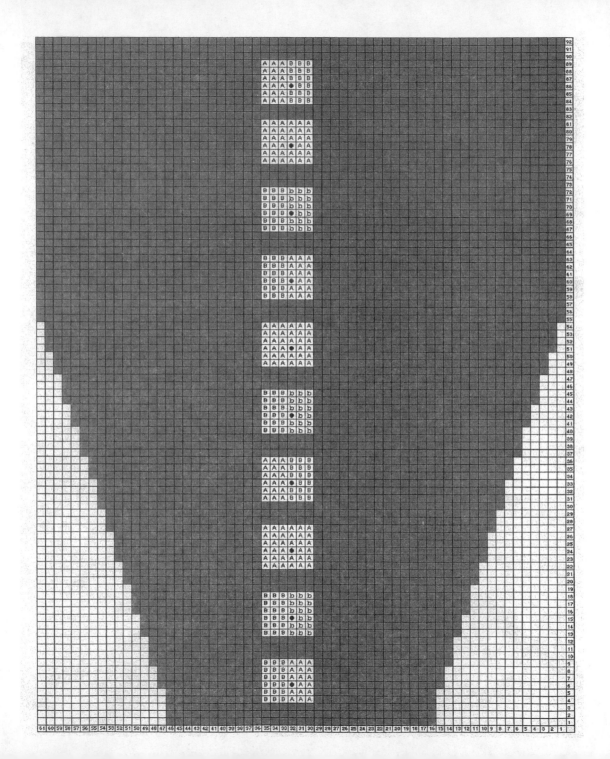

First Step: Make cuff. Cast on 27 stitches in Color A. Knit two inches in stockinette. The edge will curl. Then change to Color B1 or B2 (Use either ball.) and knit seven rows in twisted stockinette, ending on a purl row. Change to MC and continue in twisted stockinette until you have knit four inches total (including the sections in yarns A and B). Increasing four stitches evenly across your last row (every six stitches, with four left over on the end) to make 31 stitches.

Second Step: Make sleeve. Knit two more rows. (Anywhere through this point you can add or subtract sleeve length.) Then, increase one stitch per side on every third and fourth row alternating, increasing one or two stitches in from the edge, until you reach 19½ inches in length total. AT THE SAME TIME follow Chart to create the following design, winding all yarns but MC and bobble scraps on bobbins (see New Knitter's Workshop), twisting your yarns in back at the change a couple

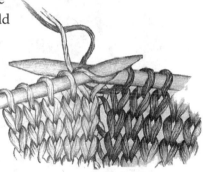

Color Block Knitting

of times to avoid making holes in your fabric, and stranding your MC through your contrast yarn a couple of times each row so it ends up unobtrusively on the far side of each square where you need it.

This simple trick will create squares that look like they are made up of either many different multicolored blocks, or small, interesting color field patterns but are actually only made up from two skeins of yarn. All you have to do is make sure that Color B2 starts at a different point in the variegated pattern than Color B1 when you knit them together in the same block. The half block is about the same size as the yarn repeat size so you will get discrete colors in each of them. If you want, you can do the same thing with Color A, however the repeat is longer, so you'll have to wind off and put aside intermediary lengths of yarn for a different purpose to get to the next color.

If this effect doesn't interest you that much: A) just use your single skein of

Color B and you will end up with tiny blocks that will approximately match the second cuff color in pattern or B) if the blocks don't interest you, eliminate both A and B and knit the whole thing in MC. You should have just enough black yarn to complete your project with four skeins, but it'll be close and will depend on your own personal knitting gauge and whether you add length in the sleeves. I'd get five just in case, or do the cuffs with a bit of cheerful contrasting yarn from your stash.

THIRD STEP: Knit the back.

After you have placed a sleeve marker, work even across the back, following the chart to continue the square motif, until you reach 21 inches from first marker. Place two more markers to mark beginning of second sleeve.

FOURTH STEP: Knit second sleeve. Reversing directions of first sleeve to decrease instead of increase, that is, decreasing one stitch each side every third and fourth row alternating until you reach 12 inches and 31 stitches. Knit two more rows. On the following row, decrease four stitches evenly throughout to get 27 stitches. Knit one more inch or the number of rows necessary to match the final length of the MC color portion of the sleeve on the first sleeve (probably three rows). Change to Color B1 or B2 and knit seven rows, beginning with a purl row. (I recommend choosing the color repeat you started with mindfully, and to choose a paler or brighter color repeat of this yarn that will contrast sharply with the black.) Change to Color A and knit two inches in regular stockinette. Bind off loosely.

CUFF OPTION: You can choose the color of your second cuff by choosing what point in the skein of Color A you begin to knit your cuff. You can use the repeat of color that presents itself, or another farther along in the skein of your choice, to make two matching but slightly different colored cuffs. Or you can find the beginning of exactly the repeat you made the first cuff with and having two identical cuffs. My sample has one lightish violet cuff with some rosy pink in it and one rosy pink cuff with some lightish violet in it.

Fifth Step: Sew up each arm seam from cuff to marker. Weave in ends, taking special care to weave in the bobble's ends securely.

Option: Adjust finishing of sleeve edge to your personal style. If you want it to roll only very slightly, or not at all, seam normally, one stitch in from the edge to make a cuff that fits snugly around your wrist. If you want more of a curl, leave the first quarter inch or so of each sleeve unseamed.

Variation: As knitted, neck and back edges will curl slightly, giving you a slight "stand up" effect. To get a colored edge here, and the subtly different line of a smoother shoulder and a slightly "stand up" neck, finish neck edge or neck and lower edge of sweater in single crochet, using either Color A or B or both doublestranded. Or knit approximately 28 inches of I-cord in one or both of these yarns (see Chapter Two) and sew to neck edge (approximately 56 inches to trim neck and back edge).

New Knitter's Workshop

Twisted Stockinette Stitch

Knit your stitch through the back of the loop on your non-working needle instead of through the front of the loop. Purl normally.

Bobbins

Plastic bobbins are available for purchase at knitting stores and through mail order. You simply wind your colored yarn around them, and let them hang from the back of your fabric once attached and knit as needed, replenishing as necessary.

PSSO

Pass Slipped Stitch Over. Insert tip of non-working needle into the stitch that has just been slipped. Then draw the slipped stitch over the stitch that has just been knitted, over the tip of the working needle, and off the needle.

---

[1]Janine M. Benyus, *Biomimicry: Innovation Inspired by Nature*. (Quill: New York, 1997), 132.

Gretchen, the Miller's Daughter, and Ez Instructions for Knitting Dross Into Gold

*I*magine you are a young, pious girl and you live in the Germany of the eighteenth century. You live with your mother; your father is dead. Your brother is in the army and you took care of your baby sister for most of her life (she died young) because when your father died, your mother changed. Your mother loves her priest and treats you more or less like a favored maid—you do all of her sewing, her cleaning, and her cooking, even though your father left enough money for you to be at leisure. Sometimes, when you are not working, you spend time with a neighbor, also lonely, and a little older, her name is Martha. You are somewhat lovely, but a little hesitant; even meek; and who can blame you. You have no dowry or social position; your future prospects are as soothingly grim as certain winter days in Paris; your life is routine and boxy; only prayer gives it the oomph and luster you can just barely yet anxiously imagine might come from the advent of a great love.

One day, an ordinary day in the midst of all of this orderly oppression, you are on the verge of opening your locked bureau when you suddenly feel frightened.

In fact, just as you go to the drawer, you shiver.

And when you do open it, you gasp. Inside, there is something that you did not put there: a burnished gold jewel casket. A love token meant for a wealthy woman. Just sitting there. Entirely physical and real. It is nestled among your own modest, handspun, hand woven and knitted things.

You touch it. It is cold and, as you move it with your hands, it catches the weak afternoon light.

You open the latch and find the box is filled to the brim with gems as juicy and brilliant as grapes: brooch, necklace, rings. You gasp, and show Martha, who also gasps. Your mother promptly gives the jewels over to the priest, for she recognizes them immediately as the devil's work. He consecrates the jewels to the Holy Mother.

You felt their touch once.

You will never see them again.

What of the man who left them there?

It must have been a man.

He is nowhere to be seen.

You sigh. Inside you are devastated, for this one mystifying miracle moment has been the high point of your life so far. But there is nothing to do. Day and night you long for the jewels and wonder about their provenance. You receive no answer. You hear nothing but the silence of sewing, spinning, sweeping, your own footsteps, and prayer, endless, predictable, soothing prayer.

Then, miracle of miracles, a few weeks later, it happens again. You open your chest and this time another treasure waits.

He has come back.

He has come back!

Who is he?

Somehow, this unknown man who has inexplicably gained access to your locked bureau and vanished like the night, and for whom you nonetheless feel a strange affinity, has left a casket made of finest ebony among your knitted cotton stockings. Inside, a second nest of brilliant jewels awaits, can this be possible. It is, even more extravagant and deeply luminescent than the first.

Oh, luck, oh grace.

The world brightens a little.

You run to Martha's house and show her, putting on one piece, and then the next. You both admire the way they show off your form: the hollow of your throat, the curve of your wrist.

GRETCHEN,
THE MILLER'S
DAUGHTER,
AND EZ
INSTRUCTIONS
FOR KNITTING
DROSS INTO
GOLD

194

As you do so, you take your own soft delight in these body parts.

And then the two of you decide that you will leave the jewels there with her. Because your mother would just dispatch these jewels in the same manner as she dispatched the first. Praise be to the Holy Mother.

Ah, you poor girl.

What you don't know, and will never know, but might rest better if you did know, is that this dashing feat of the jewel casket actually *is*—no kidding, straight shooting—the work of the honest-to-gosh, original, no substitutions permitted, Devil himself. Not Prince Charming, not a good fairy, the real live devil, the real deal, the fellow named Mephistopheles. Your mother, your tyrannical, demanding, stultifying mother, horror of horrors, was absolutely right.

Oh, what a terrible joke.

Why you? Why has he chosen you?

Well, the clever rake has got a shill in tow. His name is Heinrich Faust, and he is a too-smart-for-his-own-good type who has puttered around in all the great arts—literature, music, theology, etc.—committed to none of them, unintentionally but definitely deluded his heart with the discarded by-products of his mind, and generally made a cynical muddle of his soul. ("I fear neither hell nor its devils—but I get no joy from anything, either," he mused.[1]) He has encountered a dead end inside and can't get himself out. So he's hooked up with the devil, who offered him a deal. Mephistopheles would be his servant in this life, make his failed dreams come true, and renew his power. And then, in the next life, Faust would serve him.

It's all because of this Heinrich Faust. Or, actually, because of the two of them. Soon after they made their arrangement this Faust wanted to meet the ideal woman, and, as part of their agreement, Mephistopheles was required, in a manner of speaking, to deliver her, that is, deliver you.

Mephistopheles has given Faust a love potion, so Faust thinks, a potion that will allow him to first find, and then win, the ideal woman. In fact, it is a potion, not unlike the one Puck was dispatched to give to Titania by her fairy king husband Oberon, that makes one fall in love with whomever one sees. Because fairy

folk are mischievous, the first being she saw upon awakening was an actor, turned ass, named Bottom. And the woman who walked by Mephistopheles' magic mirror just after Faust swigged the potion happened to be you.

You are not an ass.

But then again, a potion has chosen you, in a manner of sorts.

Why you? Why were you walking by this mirror? Were you chosen by the witches who brewed the potion, or was your selection random? Or, perhaps, are you really his ideal woman after all but receiving a love tainted with the unnecessary doubt and false security cast by the additional prop of devil's magic? All of the above? Was it random, was it fate? The answer is unclear.

What we do know is that the origin of Faust's love for you, the perfect woman, is as genuine and yet as deluded as yours for him is about to be. And both of your right, loving minds have been sullied by the same source. That Meph. Your predicament is blackly, hilariously human. His love potion is so crazily recognizable. Like the media image that suggests to a man what type of woman is most desirable. Once the image has been installed in him like a software program, and induces him to love her based in part (how much of a part?) on this illusion. It also persuades her, in turn, to believe she is loved for herself, while she is also drinking the potion of illusion because part of her secretly knows the truth. Neither of them ever knows consciously what has actually occurred. Noble choices, ignoble motivations, some people are able to live their lives seamlessly under such conditions while for others, permission is simply not given. What is certain is that the whole affair was a luscious farce from the start. And also so achingly real. Hard to avoid falling for that one. So romantic. So magical. So pure. So blackly comedic. So erotic. So confused.

Why, exactly, is delusion so sexy?

You are not a goddess but you ought to be because your trials are just as momentous, and the insights you stand to gain are equally empowering and would become prodigious gifts. You have vaulted from your mild, if constricted existence, to supernatural realms. You have been chosen.

A short time later two gentlemen inexplicably come calling for you and Martha. One is disturbingly ugly and misshapen, but Martha loves him, his man-

GRETCHEN,
THE MILLER'S
DAUGHTER,
AND EZ
INSTRUCTIONS
FOR KNITTING
DROSS INTO
GOLD
196

ners are so courtly, upper-class, genteel. The other one waits upon you. You are sure he must be of noble class—his brow is so strong, his eyes so clear. You do not question where he comes from. You simply walk together through the village. He is a man who spoke to you on the street, adulating, just a few days before as you left the cathedral. An admirer. And when he walked through your garden gate, you recognized him right away. He calls you angel, and before he leaves you pluck the petals of the flower that bears your full name, Marguerite, which is another name for Daisy, and the last petal says, he loves you.

His name is Heinrich Faust

Your mother doesn't know.

The two of you make love in the summerhouse.

You were a virgin, of course.

You were.

The curve of your wrist; the hollow of your throat.

And after he leaves, you carry his touch carefully, on the center of your tongue, inside you, like another heart, its life-giving elixir flowing everywhere. You can no longer live without its taste, its beat. But like a hard candy hoarded in the center of the tongue, like a heart whose oxygen source is weak, it is growing smaller and more featureless every day.

You cannot live without this sensation, and it is fading.

When will he return?

He will return. He will.

This sensation. This slowly receding sensation that seems to brighten even as it subsides. It is as vibrant as the jewels. It vitiates the stolid grayness of your emotional life with a deep, bright, almost narcotic burst of color. It turns your world into a cache of garnet stars, your very breath into something silver.

You spend all of your time alone to hoard the feeling.

When will he return?

He has not returned.

He will not return. He must.

Your mother does not notice the change, at least not consciously. Perhaps this is why she seems to be ordering you around even more assiduously than

usual. Cooking, cleaning, sewing, spinning, you have always excelled at order and detail but now it is all too much.

You retreat to your spinning wheel. Every day you spend more time spinning; alone. There is plenty of wool to spin. The treadle rhythm comforts you; the whir of the bobbin mimics the whir of your heart, no one bothers you when you situate yourself productively behind its protective and hypnotic rotation. When you spin you can leave this stultifying world that is gradually losing its precious enrichment. You can twist the yarn around your passion the way you twist it around your bobbin.

You love the feeling of the quiescent wool passing through your hands and then standing up sleek and strong as you and the wheel coax the twist into it. You feel like you are making something, who knows what, but something, as everything else about you falls apart. You shut yourself up and spin and think of him and hoard that delicious mass of crushed garnets that is slowly, inevitably seeping out of your soul.

When will he come back?

What if he doesn't come back?

You might be pregnant.

You are pregnant.

As you spin you begin to sing about a little bird, a little bird becoming free. You forget you feel like you are making something and instead just let the rhythm and the feel of the wool comfort you.

As you spin now the wheel loosens something within and you begin to sob. Gradually you slip over the line, the point in the skein that divides spinning for comfort from spinning to stir up your distress. Your head bends over your wheel, your heart whirls even faster, your fingers draft more furiously.

Next you slip past the point in the skein that marks your exit from distress from your entrance into insanity.

Your brother comes home from the military and calls you a slut. Then he is murdered in the street. You and your mother are entirely alone.

And what of your lover? The man who made a deal with the devil and then looked for the perfect wife? Ah Faust.

GRETCHEN,
THE MILLER'S
DAUGHTER,
AND EZ
INSTRUCTIONS
FOR KNITTING
DROSS INTO
GOLD
198

For a while after your erotic encounter, Faust sits in a cave, penitent, refusing to see you, because he really does love you deeply and knows he has ruined you by introducing the bewitchment and chaos of the dastardly Mephistopheles into your life. To see you further would be to corrupt you further; to cause more suffering. He loves you; he hurts you. Familiar story. So he drops the relationship, which hurts both of you.

Of course, no one bothers to tell you any of this. I can't help wondering; if you knew the truth, would it help? I tend to think the answer is yes. Either Faust thinks he is protecting you, or he is an emotional coward. And just about now if we did not know a man wrote this story, we would become certain. A knitter certainly did not write it.

The juice is in the yarn, the feel of the fiber as it slips through your hand and turns from fluff into something substantial.

Any knitter would want to know what it was, exactly, you were spinning as you held on to the thread you hoped would keep you from madness but led you there instead. We would be curious about the exact nature of the yarn. We would know that was a sort of prayer.

Was it a coarse rug wool, spun slow and thick, chosen to slightly flagellate your hands? Silk spun as fine as Grandmother Spider's web, intended, perhaps, for your trousseau? Or, perhaps, it was ordinary domestic wool. A sort of fuzzy slipper fiber meant to coddle you as no one ever did, and which, for a short time, served its purpose. To us, it remains a mystery. Made of your unrequited desires, but so much more enduring. A fabulous, unique hoard whose eventual disposition is unknown.

The next time we see you, you are in a prison cell. It is late at night and Mephistopheles and Faust observe, undetected (What can a madwoman detect anyway?) out the window. You are entirely disheveled and recognize nothing. You, who raised your baby sister from infancy as if she were your own, spent countless hours with her upon your knee, and mourned her greatly, have been convicted of murdering your mother and your own newborn child. Your mother was poisoned and your baby was drowned.

You will be executed in the morning.

As dawn breaks, Faust comes to visit you. Outside the window, the helpless lover watches you, and the destruction he has helped create; and feels the destruction in his own heart. And as this heart of his is destroyed, it is also opened. The heart that called in the Devil because it could not feel is cracked devastatingly wide. For this is why you were really chosen. You, and your life, and your fate, were uniquely designed as a surgical instrument to open Faust's heart. And eventually, much much later, and after Faust meets his own death and wanders through a legion of confusing and purifying worlds the two of you will be reunited in his mad, alchemical, literary heaven.

First, you yourself will be forgiven by the Holy Mother. Next, you will beg for him to be forgiven, and your wish will be granted.

I still like to think, that in that cell, you are still spinning, spinning, an invisible thread on an invisible wheel. An incredibly soft thread, a fine thread, one that caressed your hands the way your absent lover did no more than once; this time over and over and over again.

I suspect that what you were trying to do was spin dross into gold.

This, of course, is the impossible task assigned a Miller's Daughter, in fairy tale Germany, some time before. The miller had no money, but he did have a beautiful daughter. To get the king's attention, he told the king his daughter would spin straw into gold. The king expressed great interest in this feat. So he locked the girl up in a room full of straw, gave her a wheel, and told her if the room wasn't full of gold in the morning, he would put her to death.

That was when the little man showed up. A manikin, to be exact. He said to her, give me your necklace and I will spin this straw into gold and he did.

The king arrived at daybreak and he was surprised and pleased. But he was not finished. He took the girl to another, larger room also full of straw and commanded her to do a repeat performance. When the door closed, the manikin came back, and the beautiful girl paid for the magic with her ring.

In the morning, the king took the beautiful girl to an even more enormous room stuffed with straw. This time, he told her, if she succeeded in turning the stuff into gold, he would make her his wife.

GRETCHEN,
THE MILLER'S
DAUGHTER,
AND EZ
INSTRUCTIONS
FOR KNITTING
DROSS INTO
GOLD
200

And this time the manikin wanted her firstborn child as payment.

Not having much of a choice in the matter, and not knowing whether she would ever bear such a child, she said yes. And in the morning the beautiful but poor Miller's Daughter became the queen of the realm.

A year later she gave birth to a child, and the little man returned. She cried, panic-stricken, when he demanded his payment. He took pity on her and told her that if she could guess his name within three days, she could keep her child.

She sent a messenger out into the realm, and on the third day, he found a ridiculous-looking little man jumping around a fire in front of a cottage at the top of a mountain at the end of a forest. As he jumped, he said a rhyme about the queen's child.

"And Rumpelstiltskin I am named!" the manikin exclaimed at the rhyme's end.

When the little man returned for the infant the queen told him what his name was. In a fit of rage, he plunged his right foot so deep into the ground that his whole leg went into the ground and then he pulled his left leg so hard that he tore himself in two.

So, what I can't help wondering, Gretchen and Marguerite, is whether what you wanted to do as you sat and spun was to make life out of death and harmony from despair, or whether you wanted to rescue yourself from the dissolution of your heart with healing somehow spun from the tangible creation of your yarn. I can't help wondering if, like Faust and Mephistopheles, and like the beautiful Miller's Daughter and that puny little demon with the similarly multisyllabic name of Rumpelstiltskin, you were instinctively performing alchemy.

Alchemy, of course, is the art of transmuting one substance into another. Lead into gold. Straw into gold. Faust was a practitioner; that's part of what got him into trouble. So was the Miller's Daughter in her own way. And, of course, so was Isis. The Great of Magic was a great healer, and alchemy was part of the basis of her healing.

I suspect this was what you were doing as you spun. You were instinctively clutching the magic of Isis, all those years later, after it seeped through the fairy

kingdom where countless little people sat in the fields, spinning, and summoning power by name. You were instinctively summoning and creating the red sash and knot of Isis. ("I am the knot where two worlds meet . . .") You hoped to turn sorrow into joy. You were grabbing and grasping the magical umbilical cord you hoped you could follow out of death and into life and which was the source of Isis' alchemy.

You were also instinctively trying to climb the ladder of Grandmother Spider, hoping it will take you out of this world and into the next. And this ladder is another type of umbilical cord, and another type of alchemy—far more etheric, and far more difficult to grasp. It alchemizes that which is impossible to that which is eminently doable.

So, when your instincts were so good, why were you unsuccessful?

A few reasons, I think.

The Miller's Daughter was a practical girl; not a romantic, as far as we know. This was one of the circumstances that just made her more circumstantially fortunate than you were. She was also fortunate because her adversary was miniature; no more than a mere homunculus who destroyed himself with his own boastfulness and ire. The two of them were rather evenly matched. The Miller's Daughter with the ambitious father had to work hard, but with help of the manikin, whom she eventually outsmarted, her alchemized golden thread took her both to new life and a new world. She started out as Arachne, a motherless, lower-class girl who spun admirably. And, she was able to use the assistance proffered by what could also be construed as a very odd version of Daedalus, the technical man on the sidelines in matters of yarn, to spin her way safely to becoming a Penelope: a tactical queen, and mother of a son.

However, finally after Faust's death, you and your love, Faust, are reunited in heaven, as promised. And his harsh lessons at the knee of the Devil have inspired his heart to deeply open. He has not only had to die, but voyage through layer after layer of gods, heroes, heroines, and sages to find the place where you await him. You are both thrilled, tender, forgiving. And as you reunite, a chorus sings that woman, eternal will show us the way.

GRETCHEN,
THE MILLER'S
DAUGHTER,
AND EZ
INSTRUCTIONS
FOR KNITTING
DROSS INTO
GOLD
202

THE FASCINATION OF YARN

It is easy to become transfixed by yarns because they are such sources of curiosity and pleasure. I asked Elizabeth, a proficient knitter who loves to knit fine lace, whether she found yarn addictive. She immediately told me about her favorite yarn of the moment, a cone of incredibly fine and soft cashmere. She had just finished a Shetland lace shawl on size two needles made out of the stuff. It was addictive because, even after knitting an entire shawl, it was so fine that it didn't really look like her cone of precious yarn was any smaller than it had been before she started. It was also addictive because it was so soft and fine, that as she worked on it, it caught in the invisible little rough spots on her hands. The quality it had was both fairy-tale and entirely practical: a precious, sensuous substance that was at once almost self-replenishing and somehow, conscious, observant, a helper, in that it gave her an additional awarenesss of her body.

The fascination of yarn, a wonderful phrase, is not my own. I was bantering with several knitters last year, total strangers, brought together for a few hours with our need to think up projects, finish projects, work on projects, looking for more in the busy week before Thanksgiving. Meanwhile, some of us were bantering about the extraneous things we could excise from our lives because we couldn't do everything. Other people, for instance, were doing the cooking during the following week for family meals.

One woman, a passionate, lifelong knitter, mentioned how she no longer read as much as she used to, because yarn was so fascinating. She just couldn't do everything. As she said this, the two of us happened to be admiring the chunky, multicolored yarns—one a pure, soft wool with mixed pale and bright shades and the other a chunky, nubby wool silk blend in lavenders and oranges and greens—that are part of the Arachne sweater. I had never seen yarns exactly like these. They were wonderfully, arrestingly contradictory: thick and intensely colored, dramatically spun, in their different ways, so light and dark colors spiraled gleefully up the core of the yarn and intermingled. But at the same time, they were light in weight and incredibly soft and subtle in texture. Placing them

next to each other was, very roughly, like placing two colors of paint next to each other, pointillist style, and watching them vibrate into a third spectrum and effect entirely.

They were in many ways beyond my experience range with color—too bold and bulky for what I usually do—but, well, absolutely fascinating. Looking at them was like looking at the first page of a great novel—a visual and tactile beginning that hooked me right in. How would I combine them? What would the shape be? And the stitch patterns? How would it feel to knit, and, once I started to knit, how would the repeats in color work into the overall pattern? Would the effect in the fabric be a unified field of color, or stripes of different lengths that wove into each other? I wouldn't know until I started experimenting with them. These were "chapters" of the sweater that I would read through, flipping through them, following the story that the yarn itself told me.

Her odd comment was absolutely accurate. Yarn is fascinating, and it does draw us in the way a good book draws us in—one more row, one more page, one more chapter, one more section—how will it turn out? Another in the list of synergies between knitting and words. It's not surprising that reading would be eschewed for knitting, because, in some ways, they satisfy the same itch.

Variation in yarn is also part of its fascination. This brings us back to *hozho*, or the principle of harmony that includes natural variation in size and form. On a very basic level, anything but the most perfectly milled strand of commercial yarn itself displays *hozho*—variations in color and size, always changing and yet always the same, not unlike the sky from horizon to horizon that inspired the Navajo. Even if our yarn is completely uniform we give it *hozho* when we use it and make a garment. The slight variations in tension, our choice of colors, our gauge, the nuances that unique bodies give yarn as they stitch—all of these will combine to create a uniquely precious, irreproducible garment and blend of colors.

Yarn itself displays *hozho*. It is straight, and its ply (the way the strands are twisted around each other if there is more than one strand to the finished yarn) is predictable. The yarn may be a single ply, or a double ply, or have up to twelve or more different strands incorporated into it. (This is not uncommon for a com-

GRETCHEN,
THE MILLER'S
DAUGHTER,
AND EZ
INSTRUCTIONS
FOR KNITTING
DROSS INTO
GOLD
204

mercially produced yarn such as cashmere, where the fiber is very soft and fine and warm but not necessarily strong—the many additional plies add strength, much as they did to Grandmother Spider's ladder.) But somehow or other, it is going to twist around itself like a candy cane or DNA. But even the most regular, commercially milled and technically even yarn usually displays some irregularity somewhere—a fractionally thicker or thinner diameter in a certain spot, a slightly thicker millimeter of fiber for a cross section of an inch. And even if it doesn't you'll give it some as you knit. Because you are a human being and not a machine, your stitches will display at least some subtle variation. Together, one way or another, you and your yarn will create *hozho*, and *hozho* is fascinating.

The way this somewhat irregular material will make a garment that may be almost entirely regular, and in any case whose pattern and construction will suggest regularity due to evenness of stitches and the straight lines of knitting, but will have display variations throughout that will please our eye and our soul.

Marketers and lovers also know about *hozho*. Ice cream with mix-ins displays *hozho*. We keep eating the ice cream, in part, to experience the next slight variation in taste, color, texture and size mixed in the predictable substance. Successful long term relationships display *hozho*. They combine consistency with constant, slight variation. Sunlight also provides *hozho*—at any given moment of the day, our familiar world will look slightly different due to variations of light and placement of shadow. And so forth. Yarn naturally falls into this category, and this is also why yarn is fascinating.

Sometimes yarns become *too* fascinating and we have to take a break. You know it's time to stop knitting when your hands, elbows, shoulders, or back begin to hurt. Some superknitters eventually suffer from RSI, repetitive stress injury. To do what you can to avoid this, if something in your body hurts: (1) stop for a while; (2) vary needle size and yarn—change to small needles and a skinny yarn if you are working big, change to chunky yarn and big needles if you are working small; or (3) stop regularly to stretch and shake out your hands.

And once in a while, we have to give it up. Sharon, a therapist, knit for years and years. One day she stopped knitting. She still had many unfinished projects around the house, which plagued her—what to do with them? They were beauti-

ful, but she felt as though she had knit in a stressful part of her life, and when she looked at the unfinished garments and imagined herself completing them, her body crinkled up in the tension patterns she had felt during that time. Finally, she combined them all into one piece and displayed them formally on an empty wall as an art installation. When the exhibit was over, she disposed of it.

So many of us can relate to this one. As another knitter told me when she heard this story, honoring the projects as art in themselves prior to purging them can be a therapeutic, liberating experience. Why do some projects go unfinished? Usually because something about them didn't feel right. Our body didn't feel right while we were making them, or the yarn didn't feel good to work with, or we suddenly couldn't stand the color, or we broke up with the guy we were making it for at the time and we can feel the distress in the fabric. Or we just plain grew out of this project and found another one that was more exciting and better conceived.

On the one hand, working through a challenge can be a rewarding experience. Joan, a knitter who finds learning new things and solving creative problems to be relaxing and enjoyable, recalled how she once spent so many pleasant hours by a sunlit pool deciphering a new lace pattern (lace knitting, so light and portable, is great for traveling, the Palm Pilot of the knitting world) that she ended up with a patch of slightly blistering sunburn. The combination of the beautiful weather and the engrossing challenge was so sweet, Joan literally didn't have the willpower to reach up and put on more sunscreen.

On the other hand, not everyone has exactly these preferences, or is interested in paying this particular price. (Even Joan says she won't do that again.) Knitting cultivates innovation and flexibility, and one form of flexibility is the ability to change our minds. Not every last strand of life needs to be tied up. Some are best left to curl provocatively in the breeze.

And, perhaps more importantly, sometimes, there is nothing more creatively and spiritually compelling, and appropriate, than giving oneself the gift of an entirely clean slate. This is a highly charged, creative state—not unlike looking at a clean kitchen and dreaming up what you will cook next. When we dispense with loose ends of yarn, this may also be a sign that we are ready to

GRETCHEN,
THE MILLER'S
DAUGHTER,
AND EZ
INSTRUCTIONS
FOR KNITTING
DROSS INTO
GOLD

206

dispense with other loose ends in our lives. For instance, several months after Sharon told me this story she began to knit again, after her break of many years. Soon afterward, we ran into each other in a knitting store, where she was looking lovingly through celadon yarns. Recently, I got a note from her, in which she blithely mentioned she'd whipped through the new project in a month.

While she was working on it in a doctor's office, another woman, who was also a knitter, came up to her and they began talking. The other woman began to wonder what to do with her incomplete projects. When Sharon told her about the art installation, her new acquaintance burst into a smile of relief.

ADDING SHINE TO YOUR GARMENTS

Here is another reason that yarn is fascinating. One of the most frequent questions I, and I suspect any handspinner, is asked is, do you spin straw into gold?

I can spin *gold* into gold (or into any other color) and so can most spinners. But straw into gold? I still haven't figured that one out.

However, *knitting* straw into gold is extremely easy to do and risks significantly fewer hazards to your health. For this reason, and, more importantly, because this is a simple little trick that creates a very handsome garment with a minimum of fuss and will also impress your friends, I recommend this trick highly. You may not snag a king, but you probably will make something you like to wear and other people like to see you wear.

Metallic yarns usually consist of synthetic fibers blended into natural ones or one hundred percent synthetic fibers. They are often the nylon or other synthetic content in an otherwise natural fiber yarn. They often appear in slubby, eyelashy novelty yarns, and silk or nylon ribbon yarns, and they also come blended with mohair. This combination is particularly masterful because the dull mohair texture frames the metallic glint, and the metallic glint plays up the texture of the mohair—the way an amber lantern plays up a magical evergreen park or grove.

These yarns add a wonderfully distinctive (and even sometimes *subtle, yes subtle)* element to many different kinds of garments, and they aren't that hard to

use. You can choose almost any of the projects in this book (I would only eliminate the Brigit baby blanket in the following chapter from the list, for obvious reasons—you don't want an infant or toddler tangling with something synthetic, and, metallic yarns are almost always hand washable if not dry clean only) and add (doublestrand) a metallic strand judiciously, or even throughout, and create an entirely different project.

Here are basic principles to keep in mind when using metallic yarn as a transformational tool:

Depending on the thickness of the yarn, you may have to move up a needle size; do a gauge swatch and check.

If you doublestrand metallic yarn throughout, or create a project entirely from metallic yarn, it will probably make your project more dressy so factor this in. But a touch of glitz here and there doesn't always create a formal garment.

Here are some ideas for knitting the projects in this book into gold:

Isis Shawl: Substitute a copper or cool (pinky) gold metallic ribbon of the same diameter for the Bon Bon ribbon in hot pink.

Ariadne's Scarf: Doublestrand a softer metallic with some natural content (like Jaeger Venus) in gold or copper through the red parts of the corrugated rib border pattern. Or substititue it entirely for the gold/yellow parts of the corrugated rib pattern. For a more dressy or extroverted scarf, doublestrand the black with a thin gold metallic or a thin multi-color and gold metallic.

Moirae Pullover: Doublestrand with something silver through the Color A sections. Or, through whatever section you like. Substitute a metallic or metallic multi-color yarn for any of the three yarns. If you use a novelty yarn with just touches of gold, the effect will probably be subtle and magical.

Penelope Turleneck: Doublestrand with gold throughout. In mohair, this makes for a more technically difficult project due to the interest of working with an additional texture as you knit. This will make a dressy, gorgeous sweater. Use a more delicate metallic (gauged for a size six needle or smaller); this will give a delicate look. Check your gauge. You may need to move up a needle size.

Rachel Pillow Cover and Bag: This project already uses a metallic yarn. It's a dark yarn, which creates the simultaneous effect of shine and depth, like a

GRETCHEN,
THE MILLER'S
DAUGHTER,
AND EZ
INSTRUCTIONS
FOR KNITTING
DROSS INTO
GOLD
208

darkly colored precious stone. If you substitute a brighter metallic, the effect of the pillow will change accordingly.

Arachne Shrug: Knit all or many of the bobbles in metallic ribbon. You can also double strand some or all of the squares or halves of the squares in gold. Personally, I would leave the black alone. You may have to move up a needle size if you doublestrand the squares.

Athena Smoke Ring: I wouldn't add a metallic to this pattern as made in this yarn. However, Athena's black-eyed owl is reminding me to tell you that black doublestranded with metallic is always interesting because black makes other colors stand out. This pattern done in black and a brightly colored metallic would give an effect that is almost neon like, but could also retain some elegance, depending on your yarn choices.

Yarn is fascinating because it behaves almost alchemically when you add an additional element, even a small, simple, or even obvious one, to what you are doing. Adding a bit of shine to your sweater can be like adding just a bit of sunshine to a cloudy day—and not in the spirit of Pollyanna. It's a subtle small change that changes everything, and whose exact effect you can't really predict in advance. Also experiment with doublestranding a smooth or more familiar yarn with silk, chenille, slubbed yarns, and other unusual yarn textures. In this way, it is probably also like a first kiss, which brings us around full circle to the original meeting of the Sun Spirit and Grandmother Spider, which led to the discovery of her original magic, and there I'll leave you.

No project for this chapter—go out and take a walk, give addiction the slip, and immerse yourself in the *hozho* of your own footsteps.

And, by the way, this probably goes without saying, but if you happen to trip over a hammered gold jewelry box as you skip out the door, just pick it up and drop it in the cosmic recycling bin.

---

[1] Stuart Atkins, ed. and trans. *Goethe: The Collected Works Vol. I and II*. (Princeton: Princeton University Press, 1984), 13.

Brigit, Her Fire, and a Round Baby Afghan

A gentle, thoughtful woman who artfully manages an apartment building for senior citizens had been hearing about the knitting goddesses from me for about a year before she slipped into my breakfast nook to tell me about the special lamb who had once been her companion.

In the years when Naomi traveled between being a child and a woman, her family lived on a farm whose pasture land was nestled against forested hills. Her family raised sheep, among other animals, and in that year many lambs were born. As she matured into an adolescent, she often became upset with her parents. After they fought, Naomi began to take refuge in the barn. In this particular spring, she craved the comforting, sweet smell of hay, and the warmth and breath of the paddocks of the fleecy babies. The lambs themselves had a dark, sweet scent from the earth and the lanolin that glistened in their coats.

She would go into the barn, inhale it deeply, pet and feed the animals, and soon feel better.

Soon, one lamb in particular began to await her arrival, respond to her touch, and put her head in Naomi's lap. Naomi fed the lamb carrots, which she took gently from her hands, looking up at her with elongated brown eyes. Within a short period of time, she had named the lamb Sunshine Isabella Elizabeth.

Soon, Naomi was visiting Sunshine Isabella Elizabeth often. They started to leave the barn and take long walks together. It wasn't even clear whose idea of the two of them it had been. Regardless, Sunshine Isabella Elizabeth always kept

close to Naomi's side, and Naomi was especially charmed by the way the lamb, like so many lambs, did not run. Instead, she bounced.

Summer came, and the awkwardness among family members that can come with rites of passage intensified with it. Naomi began to sneak out of the house late at night to meet her friend and they began to venture farther. Girl and lamb would run up the wooded hill above the farmhouse to their retreat in a world made of trees, fog, and glimpses of the brilliant, silvery moonlight, which, in remote mountains seems to come alive. Their goal was a special clearing in the woods at the very top of the hill. There they would twirl and spin around side by side in the mist and under the glow of the moon.

In this way, running and dancing and spinning together, Naomi and Sunshine Isabella Elizabeth spent the entire year.

When it had passed, Naomi's awkwardness had passed with it, and she had settled into the feelings and sensations of being a young woman. Her fury with her parents had passed with it, as had their irritation with her.

Her playful yet magical connection with this creature had been her sanctuary, and also her form of healing. The lamb was both a mystical and earthy companion, showing Naomi her soul while simultaneously comforting her with the sensations and scents of the Earth. Thirty years later, Naomi could still find refuge in her special companionship. The relationship between girl and lamb had felt so special and miraculous, that she had told hardly anyone. There was a certain special quality there, an essence of Naomi, that was so familiar it had rested silently there to this day. It was the kind of experience that lodges in the soul and nests there almost invisible, so close is it to one's spirit, that, sometimes, only a certain kind of reminder can bring it out.

Many centuries ago, in another time, flocks of special lambs were fostered in County Kildare of Ireland by a being who is forever linked with them. Her name is Brigit. Her day, which is the first day of early spring in the old Celtic ways, is also the day on which the lambing season begins. Part of Brigit's gift is to alleviate creative anxiety of any kind, by helping to give it the reassurance of inner clarity and a strong physical form. This would include physical birth of any

kind, the ultimate disposition of creative inspiration, and also the impulse to heal and be healed. Another part of her job is to protect and foster children. As a goddess of battle and ironworking she both accepts and brings together conflicting views of the world and also lends the much needed bite and grit to the processes of creativity. In all three of these areas, she is able to take advantage of her very unique contribution to the heart and soul as knitting goddess.

I like to think Sunshine Isabella Elizabeth was a descendant of Brigit's fleecy charges. The name, which was this lamb's true name, is particularly apt.

A Tale of Brigit

The morning sun drifted through the arched windows of the Kildare Abbey and cast its weak winter ray on the floor, just between the place where Patrick, the man who has just rid the country of snakes, stood at the lectern, and the rough stone pews filled with the town's newly converted flock of warriors, shepherds, smiths, poets, gentry, maidens, mothers, and healers. The women's braided hair, all gold and auburn, shone like gold and copper work in the stone chapel.

At the moment, the idea of resurrection was particularly appealing. It had been a cold and scratchy winter in Kildare. The snakes may have been gone from the land, but nothing in Kildare was yet going quite smoothly. Some of the neighbors had embraced the faith of the risen man whose high cross, embellished with stories of his life drawn in the old way and painted in the most brilliant array of color, marked the boundary of the property outside. But the rest still preferred the old ways. Some of the smiths were decorating their bridles with the traditional knot work. While, at the next bench, their neighbors had taken up the cross and the fish. Some of the maids planned to come out as usual on Beltane to lie with the sacred beloveds of one night only, to participate in the sacred pleasures that enrich the growing season. Others had recused themselves in this very abbey with a white veil. What was certain last year, last season, for the last five hundred, one thousand, even five thousand years was certain no more. Even now, the abbey was fragrant with the cakes that were being baked outside it on

that very day, which was February first, Imbolc, and the day of the Feast of the Queen of Heaven. But here there was no bread at all.

The calm handsome face of this beautiful and brave man Patrick veiled a force of transformation that was by no means tranquil. While the villagers continued to think it over, they had settled on an uneasy harmony as the provisional, if fragile, order of the day.

Except, that is, for the matter of the local chieftain, who was of the pagan persuasion.

"He has our share of the plains," a couple on a back bench whispered to another in front of them while Patrick spoke.

"Ours too."

"Almost everyone's."

The green place was rid of snakes, but what good was the liberation of their land if this two-bit bully held it?

"It is easier for a camel to go through the eye of a needle than it is for a rich man to get into heaven," Patrick observed.

None of them had never seen a camel, but they supposed it was something about the size of a large horse. The chieftain had a large horse, but he also, as far as they were concerned, had filched heaven.

The gathered shuddered. And it was true that on that particular morning the mossy rocks of the unheated sanctuary were giving off a distinct chill. But today the topic was a particularly bitter one for another reason. Imbolc, the name of the old spring festival, which marked the beginning of the year's quickening of green growth within the bowels of the earth, meant "in the belly," and also "ewe's milk." Imbolc marked the first day of the lambing season. And, the newborns would not be able to graze and prance on the choicest land of the county this year, as they had not been able to during the last and the year before. Settling into their shared perception of promise laced with uneasiness, and the theft of their land by a bully no Christian could roust, the gathered surrendered into the comfort of a kind of shared pessimism.

Just then, the weak ray of sun poking at the floor turned a brilliant gold.

Then, as if a finger was pointing, the ray in question rested on a golden girlish head in the front pew.

If it must be known, the blond head in question was snoring.

Patrick, courteously nodding to the sun itself, rolled his eyes, and leaned toward it.

"Don't you get enough rest in your own soft bed, Brigit?"

"I was talking to God, Patrick." The voice that belonged to the head responded instantly. The voice in question was like a flute, penetrating, clear, sweet, and laced with just a flutter of humor. "In fact, he was in the middle of an important sentence when you called me now."

The faithful sat up in their seats, blinked, and looked expectantly at the man in the pulpit. He in turn raised one eyebrow, first opened and then shut his finely shaped mouth. Few present had missed the fact that the tone of his voice, while clearly cross, was as loving as the touch of this sun.

Brigit sat up, raised two long white-clad arms over her head, and stretched. She had Celtic knots on her sleeves and a golden rosary wrapped around one arm.

No one had really expected this figure of the old ways to become a Christian abbess. Even less had they expected her to be listening to a sermon on her own day, and, least of all, to have fallen asleep in the middle of Patrick's sermon.

"Sit down then, Brigit," Patrick ventured sweetly then. "So we may continue."

She turned back to him from the window and gazed at him. Her green eyes, unusually penetrating and also matter of fact, were still dreamy. And the shadows of an oak branch caressed her cheek. Many great oak trees bordered the abbey lawn outside, and now their majestic bare branches swayed to and fro, playing over her face through the suddenly buttery sun.

"Not just now, Patrick."

Even before she stopped speaking, another bright sunbeam slid down from an angle through the window and hardened into something resembling a plank. A shining blue mantle was neatly hung upon the end of it.

Brigit picked up the mantle, and the sunbeam retracted back into the sky.

"Thank you," Brigit called out the window.

Then she flung the cloak around her shoulders, turned to Patrick, and fell into a deep and charming curtsy.

"Please excuse me," said Brigit.

Patrick could do nothing but nod.

"Good day then." Brigit walked out the door.

No one but Patrick, who had been here for a while but still held the status of just passing through, was actually surprised. Brigit was abbess of this unusual place where monks and nuns were both lodged. She was also the one for whom the cakes were being baked, and the one these fires were being set to welcome. She had been young and beautiful for so long no one could remember when she had gotten that way, or why she never got old, like everyone else. Her beauty came from the old rocks, and the leprechauns, and the fairy folk, and was nurtured in part from the old wise crone Cerridwen who stirred their cauldron of life. By now, they took Brigit's eternal flowering as matter-of-factly in stride as they did the green of the hills and the gray of the sky.

"Breed," a pair of waiting villagers called after her as she walked down the stone path to the abbey's entrance, because that is how Brigit is pronounced. "Breed, would you come and bless our water? Two of our daughters are ill."

"I need not come. From here I will do it." And she spread her arms and blessed the well where she stood. Later, one of the two girls said she had seen a beautiful woman with a white dress and veil and a blue cloak out near the well in the hour just after the sun brightened.

"Breed," said another who was waiting, "will you come and help my wife? She is having a terrible time delivering this fifth child."

"Oh," said Brigit. She paused in a way that looked absentminded. But everyone knew better. And then she picked some reeds that grew around a little bit of a stream that grew at the side of the abbey and twisted and plaited them into a magnificent cross, using a pattern that no one had ever seen. "Here," said she. "It is the power of the sun. Have the midwife hold this over her during her time. It will help with this, and also with protecting your house from fire."

"And remember," said two women to the father-to-be, "no other spinning or twining in your house today. It is Brigit's day."

"I thought today was the spring festival and tomorrow was Brigit's day," he replied.

"They blend together now, don't they?" one of the two women said mysteriously, and the pair moved on.

When the midwife held the cross over the woman, the new mother reported later how the birth gradually eased. And soon after that women all over the land were weaving Brigit's crosses, and they still do.

Meanwhile, Brigit had come to a fire that burned within the abbey's inner courtyard, for, after all, it was her day and other fires were being burnt in kind, to celebrate the change from the pure white light of the winter solstice to this earthy, amber light that marked the transition from inspiration to birth. She stopped a second and looked it over from a chink in the stone wall.

And what a fire that was. A maiden dressed all in white sat before it. It was as clear and rich as the brightest amber, dappled with the hues of dark sunlit honey and enriched with orange and red glints deep in its core. At certain sacred moments impossible to predict, it also softly turned into nothing but the palest and most clear hues of the rainbow.

Nineteen maidens tended to that constant flame, a different one everyday. And in those days the air was so clear and as of yet only so sparsely filled with people's thoughts (today it is quite saturated with them) that if you watched these maidens walk around the abbey you could see those rainbow colors emanate from the edges of their bodies.

Those who saw the rainbow light emanate from them said it reminded them of the shape of the robes worn by Jesus' Mother, Mary. And those same folks lovingly called Brigit the Mary of Gael.

It was rumored that under certain undivulged circumstances these maidens would celebrate the old ways in the abbey with specially chosen men, not choosing to wait for Beltane, where they could receive their sacred lover in the soft and fertile fields. When anyone mentioned the subject of their hypothetical sexual availability, Brigit's maidens just smiled.

They did wear all white, though, just as she usually did. And when marriage ceremonies were instituted in Gael, each young woman was called her name and wore her dress in order to call in the deepest, most joyful blessings for her union. And today brides still do this exactly.

Every twentieth day Brigit herself oversaw the fire. Sometimes the children of the village would peek through the chinks in the walls to watch her. This was not officially permitted, however, it was generally accepted that she had made those chinks herself. The curious children would often see the abbess crooning to that fire as if it were a baby, one of them being sung to by its mother. It would burn higher and more brightly at her words. They would watch that fire begin to emanate from her hair, which grew burnished with the earthy tones of whiskey and butter and honey, and also yet fire's glow. They would admire the fire's glow in her white skin grown warm and flickering all over, and how it flamed out of her sparkling eyes. And they would also hear it in her voice, because when she tended to her flame Brigit was sometimes silent as a deer, but just as often she laughed or spoke to it. And even in the grayest, most dank part of winter, when Brigit's fire rose up like that, and the children carried the story of it, the people in the village came to feel how life was, even at that moment, beginning all over again.

Sometimes Brigit's fire also emanated through the world, where it surfaced in the shops of the smiths, who saw it struck off the end of their irons. Whether they adorned their bridles with crosses or knots they all became dear to her and also to each other. Brigit also gave her fire to the spinners, who saw it whirling around their spindles, and, in later centuries, in the light that still reflects off their metal knitting needles as they work in the sun. And, back at the abbey, on a particularly lucky day, the children were able to tell their parents and their friends that they had seen her wear a twelve-spoked, fiery spinning wheel that whirled above her head.

No one knew this back in that century, but Brigit and the fire were conspiring to seed the dream of the spinning wheel that would be invented many centuries later on her continent, and which would make women's work go faster, and more easily. When the spinning wheel was invented, women knew it was Brigit's

doing and exactly what that flaming spoked thing above her head was. And then they understood that she had once used it to rescue the baby Jesus from Herod's soldiers by putting it above her head just long enough to scare and distract the centurions, and to whisk the child away.

It is said, two angels flew the baby Jesus over the water to Ireland, where she herself fostered him and kept him safe and showered him with golden light, even as he did the same for her. No one had actually ever seen him on the green isle, however. This was a detail that attested either to Brigit's superior powers of fosterage or the superior storytelling skills of the Celts.

But this day was not Brigit's to tend her fire, and she stopped there only briefly. Instead, blue cloak flying, she sped over hills and through green bogs, and skirting a few of the leprechauns who scampered at her heels, and only just flying by the sun wells scattered here and there to catch light in her honor, to a beautiful stand of land high up in the precious velvet green Curragh, or plains, to a grand castle.

"Good day to you, my lord," she said to the chieftain she found there, after being led to him by one of his men. He received her in front of his stand, which had a good view of the Curragh. Even though he wore the skins of a pagan, she found him praying beneath an oak tree with the help of a shining ruby rosary. Since this was a man who had seen many battles, some of which had been against the Christians, the sight was odd. But the abbess had recently cured him of a fever in his kidneys and the man was properly grateful.

He greeted her with a hand decorated with rough but brilliant red and green gems as he dismissed the fighting man who had brought her to him.

"You are looking well," she said gaily.

"I am well," he said. "Thanks to you."

"Herbs and fire," she said. "They will do the trick."

"And your hands," he said drily.

"Ah yes, the hands."

"Have you come then for your reward, Brigit?"

"Yes, I have."

The chieftain had offered Brigit her heart's desire in gratitude for saving his

life. He might have been grateful, but he wasn't dumb, either. He was the leader of all of this part of Gael, and if you were the leader, this white clad Brigit was definitely one you preferred to have on your side. She was, among other things, rumored to make the results of war go in one direction or another. He himself had prayed to her as he fought. Now he looked up at her with gratitude and also a bit of pique.

She sat down cross legged in a bed of shamrocks at his feet.

"See that plain there," she said. And she pointed to the loamy, incredibly green shelf of land that surrounded them, which was also as moist and inviting as the moistest and most inviting of cakes. This county is named for Brigit herself, Kildare being a version of Cell Dara, which means the church of the oak tree, which is probably what they called it back then.

"Yes," he said placidly. "The chieftain's treasure. The Curragh. Thank you for helping me gain it in battle, my dear."

"Well, sire. It occurred to me that I would like just a wee morsel of it to myself. In order to properly graze my sheep."

Among her other talents, Brigit was a shepherdess. To lambs as well as to infant saviors and other simply divine children. He looked at her incredulously.

"I was thinking, oh, just enough of a crumb to wet with a bit of strong tea. Not more than the amount, for instance, that would lie beneath under this blue cloak I wear here. That would do nicely."

She seemed to grow smaller and more docile and even more girlish as she spoke. Maybe it was something about the shamrocks she sat in, maybe not.

The convalescent chieftain's face broke into a smile.

"Why, wish granted, Brigit! Like your cake! Come on then!"

Together the two of them walked out to the Curragh.

Brigit smiled distantly and the chieftain thought, at the time, stretching his ringed fingers, a bit of romance. She took off her blue cloak and placed it on the resilient emerald turf, where it seemed to ripple.

"Ay, look at that," said the king. "Fairies and leprechauns teeming under

those blades. Maybe they'll stretch this cloak and give you a bit more Brigit, I don't think there's enough there yet to graze a ewe and her kid."

"Well then," said she gaily. Later the chieftain recalled just then she seemed to grow tall again. As she spoke the blue cloak began to grow, as if it were not cloth but a small ocean of blue buttercream icing which had previously been confined to a teaspoon but was now finally in the process of coating the chocolate mint ganache of its dreams. Within a minute it covered all the land visible as far as the eye could see.

Why, way, way over there, over those rocks, past that small berm and in the lee of that particular tree, you could see something that looked like the woven frog closure that snapped around a golden button at her throat. Except now it was oh, maybe three feet high and flapped in the wind. Over there, maybe half a league to the right, you could see what ought to be the hemstitching, but looked more like a medley of finger fjords. Except there was no inland water, not exactly here.

Brigit knelt at the chieftain's feet.

"Thank you, sire," she spoke in grave, hushed, noble tones, perhaps a half an octave lower than usual. "For your generosity. For these are special, brave sheep, and they shall help secure the future of this land."

Speechless, he nodded.

Back at home in her abbey, Brigit sang. And everywhere in the realm on that night the ewes gave birth to lambs, because that is what happens on Brigit's day, or Imbolc, and why it is celebrated exactly right then. Because with lambs, comes spring. Two or three creamy ewes from each flock heard her song and, when they were ready, with their strong newborns following them, walked gently to the Curragh and began to graze.

In the morning, the people saw them there, jumping and dancing and bleating with a combination of brand new faces and mature ones that looked older than the hills. The whole green Curragh, for it was green again, as Brigit had taken her cloak with her, looked as though it was dancing with fluffy clouds.

And the word ran through the village, from pagan to Christian and back

again, that the Curragh was theirs again, all of theirs. And together all of them rejoiced, and in the weeks that followed Brigit would lead them and all of their flocks there.

In the morning the man who would become St. Patrick watched the one who had been on the Earth and beneath the sun for thousands of years come and sit beside him beneath one of the many fine oak and apple trees at her abbey.

"Catch up on your sleep?" he asked her.

She smiled, reached over, and scratched him under his chin.

"Dagda," she said, calling his secret old name.

He shrugged. "Sometimes the sun god can hide his light for a good cause."

"In the future," she said carefully, "they won't know that you were here now. They will think that a man from Canterbury brought the Christ to this land later."

"Well, I am both. As you are." He paused, then made a face—it was hard to tell whether he was frowning, or slightly amused. "I shall be going shortly," Patrick said then.

"Ah," said she.

And then Brigit did something she hardly ever does. She cast down her eyes.

"I know that you cannot do your work with me anymore," she said. "Nor would you want to."

"Nor I with you. Alas." As he spoke he still looked calm, but also slightly more pale than usual.

"They would say I had done it, or that you helped me. For it will be like that in this world for a while. And also, if they do not see me alone they will not think that they can be whole on their own."

"My path is not so different, you know," he said after a time.

"No. Let's visit," she said after a long pause of her own. In it, the sun began to stream through both of their hair, and into both of their eyes. "From time to time."

He nodded.

Peacefully, they intertwined their hands. The experience of each other's touch was as vast as a sun ray and as pointed and densely colored as a shamrock.

In this way they sat together quietly for a while, as fairies and angels flew about them like argumentative birds. For that was near the end of those times in which those two groups, one pagan and one Christian, had not yet made fast friends, which we know they have today, seeing as they so cozily share bookstore shelves.

Soon after that the goddess and the saint-to-be each rose from the green grass of Cell Dara Ireland and headed in their respective directions.

The Dream of the Golden Maiden

At the very beginning of February, in Celtic lands and those with similar climes, the energy of spring returns to the world. The first snowdrops and crocuses push their pointed green shoots above the ground. The wondrous but abstract luminescence of the solstice stars and the slanting, diffuse light of winter days gives way to a slightly warmer, more earthy golden glow that is promising of spring. The earth softens and things that were frozen thaw. The earth softens a little and starts to give imperceptibly beneath the feet. And the lambs are born. Both the light and the earth return to the world.

These are Brigit's sacred days.

Brigit's life details are mysterious—was she a pagan goddess? Was she a saint? Was she young or a widow with five children? Was she blind or did she see? Did she and St. Patrick work together and love together, or were they at cross-purposes? Since, as the historians would have it, Ireland did not convert to Christianity until the eighth century, was he really Dagda, the sun god? Brigit is the flower of a nation of storytellers after all, and there is as much truth in the tales as there is anywhere else. What I have done here is take a few stories about her and knit them together. She would like the mystery, I think, because she, and we, respond so well to the dream of her, and the beneficent presence she emanates. That slight uncertainty all this creates as we get to know her just impels us to follow her wherever she takes us. As a result, our individual journeys toward her will be creative, healing and

strengthening, and very much purely our own, which is one of the gifts of the maiden goddess.

Brigit does dispose of rich tradition as a triple goddess-maiden, mother, and crone—all three of whom respond to the same name. But the first is the most popular, and she is the symbol of our own ever renewable maiden state—courage, strong heart, feeling of safety, and stability and that feeling that all things are possible on earth. Her overriding story is the story of the return of light: how it comes back into the world, how it warms and reassures us with its inevitability, how it nourishes the young, and, also, how we come to experience our own embodiment as a bit of resplendent light incarnated into the wisdom of the earth.

Naomi and Sunshine Isabella Elizabeth may have roamed the world at night. But what they were celebrating and exploring was this doctrine of the sacred eternal, feeling and quality of life, which are central jewels of both Celtic mysteries and Christian ways. Since Brigit is also the goddess of spinning and woolwork, this gives us a knitting goddess who is aligned with the brilliance of the day. The golden, shining spinning wheel that is one of her emblems is a symbol of joyous, easy manifestation. It reminds us, after a long, comfortably, hibernating winter, that it's time to dust off our light and take it out from under its protective bushel. Her day, or any day on which it feels as though the golden light of life is re-entering our lives, is an auspicious one on which to begin a new project.

As she is also the patron of iron and smithing, she reminds us that the new is not always as ephemeral as fruit blossoms, and that we can endow it with the symbolic iron of endurance and reliability as we go and keep it around for a while. The combination of iron, sunlight, and new life will make something as durable as she is.

One traditional way to welcome Brigit, and the spring, into your life, is to place items that nurture and warm with her honeyed, ambered, warm golden light around the hearth. These include fire (clean out the hearth and lay a new fire on her day, which is celebrated on both February first and second of each year), butter, honey, beer, and Irish whiskey. You can also fill a cradle with a

beautiful blanket, and place it next to that clean hearth, to welcome the return of Brigit herself.

THE POWER of THE TANGIBLE

One summer day I went to a nearby lake with two friends and one of the other women's three-year-old son. Brigit would have approved of our goal: we had brought inflatable rafts, and were going to take turns floating on the lake while absorbing the sun which Northwesterners so much appreciate when it starts to makes its appearance in late spring after several seasons of mist and rain. For our purposes, the lake in question was also a sun well—a sun trap designed to lure the life-giving energies of the sun goddess, and also to infuse the water with Brigit's regenerating qualities. We took turns floating on the water and watching Kevin. Then, for a while, all three of us sat on the shore. I pulled out a knitting project—a long yoked sweater in a very big thick and thin yarn that was marbled with lavender, pink, peach, and gray. Quietly, Kevin came up in front of me and watched. Then he simply reached over and began to help. Working with the rhythm of the stitches, he waited for just the right moment, and began to slide the old loop off of my non-working needle for me on every stitch. It was fun, so we worked like that for a little while.

I'm sure that for him part of the lure was the thick, happy, peppermint-patty yarn, just perfect for a three-year-old. But, really, boys of all ages are liable to be attracted to knitting. When I ask why that is, I am sometimes told that it reminds them of time spent silently and happily with their mothers helping them to wind yarn into balls in this traditionally shared mother-and-child activity. The joy of the shared moment was expressed by the sight and feel of the beautiful colors passing through their hands, which perhaps also expressed the loving connection between mother and son. When a grown man asks to wind yarn for you, you can be fairly sure that a woman he loves or once loved knew how to knit. (Unless, of course, the woman in question is one he suspects he may love in the future, or in the next two seconds . . . oops, they've passed.) Also, some of the appeal may

arise from the love spells that may still emanate from the looms of ancient queens and nymphs. Between you and me, I wouldn't put it past them.

But a lot of the appeal is also the basic appeal of the physical or the tangible. Kevin couldn't talk much yet, but he could see how yarn was turning into fabric before his eyes, and he wanted to participate in the process. The excitement of something beautiful and fun and even playful turning into something more lasting clearly held a specific allure.

This is part of Brigit's gift. The powerful, radical, and wonderfully hilarious detail of a sunbeam becoming literally as hard as a board and a cloak hook offers, among other things, a cosmic reminder of the very real possibility of making feelings of exuberance and joy into tangible and lasting artifacts. (I have modified this story only slightly from the original. In it, the mantle was white, and she discovered its solid properties when, coming in on one rainy day after tending to her sheep, she found her hearth was cold. She turned around to hang her cloak on what she thought was a rafter, but was actually a sunbeam. The sunbeam grew hard as a board, and her mantle hung there until it dried.[1]) The sunbeam turns into a plank, mind you, not a rope or a silk scarf or a golden chain. It's something we could build a house out of—not something that we might lose on the subway, or use to futilely lasso, albeit temporarily at best, some other object of affection entirely.

So often, we assume that this kind of joy or creative life force is something that disintegrates or waits for us somewhere out in the future. Sure, the particulars of what gives us joy today may disintegrate, or evolve into something better, given time. But the experience of making happiness tangible can be constant. Under the auspices of a being—is she a goddess? Is she a saint?—who could exuberantly reclaim a vast green precinct with one little cloak, knitting provides an easy and accessible physical example of exactly this to us, and to those that we will certainly attract with our work.

Celtic poets were particularly aware of this aspect of Brigit in her power as creative muse. The aging, the consumptive, and the merely creatively anxious have all reached out to her.

Appreciated in another way, this gift of hers becomes a powerful gift of protection. This ancient genealogy was recited by ancient Celts:

Radiant flame of gold, foster-mother of Christ:

Bride daughter of Dugal the brown

Son of Aodh, son of Art, son of Conn

Son of Crear, son of Cis, son of Carmac, son of Carruin.

Every day and night that I sing the genealogy of Bride

Shall I not be killed, nor harried,

Nor shall I put in cell, nor wounded,

Neither shall Christ leave me in forgetfulness.

No fire, no sun, no moon shall burn me,

No lake, no water, no sea, shall drown me,

No arrow of fairy nor dart of fay shall wound me,

And I shall be under the protection of Holy Mary

And my gentle foster-mother my beloved Bride.

As they who said this prayer told the story of how Brigit herself became physical, her protection of their own physical bodies became real. The practice of reciting a genealogy for protection or assistance is ancient and widespread. The Old Testament genealogies or "begats" invoke the line of lineage for the Jewish people. Some Buddhist meditation practices begin with lineage prayers, in which the line of transmission from the first teacher of this practice down to the present, a lineage that has been recorded, is invoked. As I once heard an American-born Buddhist teacher advise students, reciting the lineage prayer is like summoning your team to help you. Brigit's genealogy has a similar purpose. Genealogies provide another case of the lure of the physical. As you recite or silently read them, the tangible development of something miraculous from theory to practice is reinforced and, by inference, becomes available to you in the same way.

In this case, even though the lineage or genealogy in question is composed mostly of men, it is the genealogy of a woman. Many lineage invocations go through the paternal line only. For those of us who have not heard such a prayer

before, it is wonderful indeed. Also wonderful is the cultural mixture of the prayer. Many genealogies prize pure cultural or genetic integrity. Here the mixture of Christian and Old Celtic is proclaimed proudly. This is another example of the power of the physical, and also of the process of knitting the many threads of life together.

Y𝔢LL𝔬W AS 𝔞 CR𝔢ATIV𝔢 ALLY

As knitters working under the auspices of this goddess or saint of craft, we add another element and further the genealogy with our work. Yellow and gold are associated with Christ's consciousness, and with the sacred miracle of incarnation—spirit become flesh. As sun goddess, Brigit carries the same message. Emanating from Ireland, one of the gray green lands, the sun, when it arrives, takes on a special, more supernatural force. It is more appreciated, perhaps, than in other areas. My two friends and Kevin and I were taking advantage of that same force here in the Pacific Northwest, with its similar climate, one in which meteorologists forecast sunbreaks (a word that is not found in dictionaries), and traffic reporters report slowed traffic due to their blinding characteristics, cautioning drivers to take other routes. Although many cultures have a sun goddess, perhaps this is part of why this particular form of appreciation has evolved here, and also in Northern European cultures.

More practically speaking, yellow has well known and very particular attributes. Painters, gardeners, and fiber artists use it judiciously, because it tends to stand out and separate colors and shapes and forms from each other. Therefore, you need less yellow than you do anything else. This makes it a particularly good ingredient for cultivating new and sweet beginnings, whether they be lives, projects, or growing seasons, because it shows off their unique and distinctive qualities and outlines and, by enveloping them, allows them to stand on their own.

In this regard, and in her bright goldenness, I often sense some of Brigit in the advice, good cheer, and clarity traditionally offered by knitting teachers and

women who work in knitting stores. Much of the knitting information in this book was given to me in such sanctuaries, either because I asked for it or because it was being given to someone else while I walked by. Knitting stores are the places where you will find out that it really doesn't matter if your needle size is eight and the pattern states nine; one size up or down probably won't make all that much difference, or that knitting is really a free form enterprise and you can do what you want, or that some of the exacting steps and flawless technical flourishes that are recommended for the finishing process aren't always strictly necessary or even visible, the whole thing is usually a lot more laid back than it seems. This is the noble and unsung oral tradition of knitting. All myths arise from oral traditions (Homer being a prime example) and in a way we pay homage to the knitting goddess by continuing this tradition and Brigit particularly, because she husbands creativity which is passed on by us through the medium of her beloved words.

I also feel that yellow quality when I go and put up a trial balloon on a new design to the women I know in these locations. They always instinctively examine my—and anyone's—ideas and choices using a creative eye and a "golden" heart. They always appreciate the distinctiveness of the idea (even if it isn't as distinctive as I think it is!), give it the attention it needs to stand out and flourish on its own, and provide just enough enlivening inspiration that is needed to make a beginning into a middle, and a middle into an ending. Like Brigit, they take the light of birth down to Earth.

Finally, part of Brigit's message is also about design—that we should feel as free as the poets she regularly inspires to experiment with knitting as a form of creative self expression and joy. When we knit, we can be adventurous, and play.

Brigit's Soft, Shiny, Round Baby Blanket

Here is a circular baby blanket, based on the Pi shawl, a modern innovation in knitting designed by the beloved master designer and knitter Elizabeth Zimmerman, that allows you to start in the center and work your way out into a circle. Traditional Shetland shawls also begin in the center, and then become squares.

Pi shawls turn into all sorts of marvelous creations, including tablecloths and doilies. They aren't the same as Shetlands, but are reminiscent of them and are made with a similar knitting method. And in her book *Traditional Lace Shawls*, Martha Waterman places the yarn over increases so they make spokes, which, before you know it, make the thing look suspiciously like a spinning wheel.

Symbolically speaking, the two shapes are related as well. When we "square" the circle, we bring the divine to earth. The circle is a mystical symbol of wholeness, and when we take the roundness off the thing and give it four equal sides we make mystical wholeness tangible and physical. (Providing another example of Brigit's more amber light tempering the inspiration and promise of the solstice, and of Grandmother Spider's magic-making prayers into physical reality through the invocation of four equal sides.) Here we knitters have returned the favor, and liberated the symbol back into the more limitless curves of its original dimensions.

This pattern adapts Waterman's variation on the Pi shawl to worsted weight yarn, takes the lace repeats out (you can reinstate lace patterns if you want; but it is very pleasant just to knit around in circles), adds color, and makes it into a 40" round baby afghan, so useful for very small fry who can tangle themselves up in something of even vaguely rectangular dimensions. Like Brigit's genealogy, the genealogy of this design honors previous departures from an even older tradition.

The afghan is knit in pastel yarns subtly highlighted with a narrow, luminescent second ply that reminds me of the pastel rainbow auras that Brigit's maidens emanated and, who knows, might even attract the blessings of good fairies. Because the yarn is worsted, not lace weight or even double knitting weight, the piece knits up fairly quickly and feels soft and comforting. Because it is baby-sized, it doesn't get too heavy, although it does have some soothing bulk and feels nice against mom's skin, too.

Many knitters like to make baby things out of grown up fibers like this one and don't mind hand washing. (These yarn choices require hand washing.) Others feel strongly that acrylic blends and washable wools are the only fibers of choice for baby wear. Plymouth Encore (an acrylic and wool blend) in worsted

weight looks good in this pattern. So does Jaeger washable baby merino in color 0211 (a variegated pink, gold, and off-white blend that brings in Brigit's golden tones). This is a DK weight yarn (works on size six needles or so), so you will either need to doublestrand it (buy double yardage) and use the same gauge and needle size or use as is and knit for twice as long.

If you wanted, in the worsted yarn given, you could get more yarn and keep knitting, and end up with a grown-up afghan, or a really luxurious throw for your chair back or your lap.

You could also, theoretically, make it out of something blue, keep going way past forty inches, and end up with a throw big enough to cover the entire Curragh.

Of course, this might take you a little longer than it took Brigit.

Last but not least, it also makes a really eccentric but beautiful covering for a small, round side table. A sweater for your furniture, so to speak.

This is an intermediate level pattern, without lace inserts, advanced intermediate if you decide to add them. (Use one of the stitch dictionaries, listed in the reading list, and use repeat lengths short enough to radiate out consistently along the spokes as the pie slices grow.) Because the pattern is worsted weight, instead of lace weight yarn, it gives you the vicarious experience of working the technique with a smaller commitment of time.

The center of the afghan is started on double pointed needles, and the whole is knitted in the round. Round knitting is different than knitting in the round or back and forth flat knitting. The pattern begins with a set of double pointed needles (dpns). Instructions for using dpns for new knitters come after the pattern. You can edge it in ribbing (easier) or make a lace border and add it on when you're done.

This afghan is going to grow and grow in size. The good news is, early rows will go quickly. Be advised, though, that the closer you get to the end, the longer it will take to finish a row. When I work with a pattern like this, I like to keep trading my work up to needles that best support its burgeoning circumference. The knitting in progress will soon look like a round bag (which, as Elizabeth Zimmerman has pointed out, gives you somewhere to store the yarn).[2] But if you like to see things the way they are, or get tired of explaining to your friends that the

thing's a circle, not a purse, the time will come when it gets too big for even a set of 40" needles or perhaps even a set of 60" needles. So, if you want, you can add a second or third pair of needles to your afghan to keep it properly circly. You just have to keep moving a foot or two of stitches off of the far end of your working needle every once in a while and onto the next set so all of them don't bunch up on a single set of needles. Perhaps a charming child of any age will offer to help.

The soft light emanating from the pastel and white yarns that circle around the wheel is lovely, quiet symbolism for swaddling a child. Or, for welcoming the inner Brigit into the cradle that traditionally sits at the hearth in honor of exactly this event on the nights of February 1 and 2 of every year.

Brigit Baby Blanket Pattern

Ingredients:

- 100g (94m) skein of Colinette Zanziba in Marble, Color 88 (wool/viscose/nylon) (Color A)
- 2 50g (48m) skeins of Lang Polar Silver in pale pink, Color 7919 (wool/nylon blend) (Color B)
- 3 50g (48m) skeins of Lang Polar Silver in pale blue, Color 7920 (wool/nylon blend) (Color C)
- 50g (48m) skeins of Lang Polar Silver in white, color 7902 (wool/nylon blend) (Color D)
- 1 set of double pointed needles (dpn) in size 8
- Circular needles in size 8 in a few successive lengths, starting at about 12 inches and ending at 40 inches or even 60 inches (with at least one incremental size in between, more according to taste, all depends on how you feel about knitting many stitches bunched up on your plastic on one hand, or about having them stretched as tight as a spider web on the other, at any given moment).
- Split stitch markers

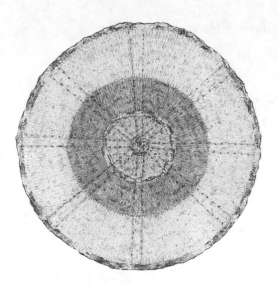

Gauge doesn't matter that much in this pattern. You will start in the center and continue until the diameter of your circle is 40 inches. In my pattern, the Zanziba center piece measures 4 inches in diameter. If you knit much more loosely, just get an extra skein or two of the white yarn (or whatever color you use for the outer circle). If you don't use it, you can probably return it. Stitch gauge is 3 stitches to the inch on size 8 needles.

Since the piece is a kind of "bull's eye" target, directions are split into steps reflecting each of the color rings.

TEP ONE: Knit Inner Circle

1 Cast on 6 stitches in Color A, on a dpn needle, leaving enough yarn at the tail of your cast on (about 6 inches) to finish later.

2 Row 1 (ws): Knit.

3 Row 2 (rs): K1 in the front and back of each stitch to make 12 stitches.

Rows 3–5: Knit.

 Row 6: same as row 2 to make a total of 24 stitches.

Divide your stitches evenly among 3 or 4 dpns, placing one of 8 split stitch markers after every 3 stitches to mark the lines of increase. Use a different color of marker to indicate the beginning of the round, and make sure to hang this marker *in* a stitch instead of on the needle. Join into a circle, being careful not to twist your stitches.

STEP TWO: Knit First Inner Ring

1 Change to Color B.

2 Rounds 7–9: Knit.

Round 10 change to color B, Knit.

3 Round 11: *[K1, YO] 2 times, K1, rep from* to make 40 stitches.

4 Rounds 12–14: Knit.

5 Round 15 *K2, YO, K1, YO, K2; repeat from* to make 56 stitches.

6 Rounds 16–18: Knit.

7 Round 19: *K2, YO, K3, YO, K2, repeat from* to make 72 stitches.

8 Rounds 20–22: Knit.

9 Round 23: Make one YO increase [YO] two stitches before each marker and one YO increase two stitches after each marker, or five stitches after the first YO, increasing 16 stitches total.

10 **Successive Rounds:** Repeat this pattern (K 3 rounds, YO 2 stitches before and after each marker for an increase of 16 stitches per round every fourth round) until radius of work from centerpoint to end is 5½ inches. Move to circular needles when you have enough stitches, which is probably now or at your pleasure.

Step Three: Knit Inner Stripe. Change to Color A on row 2 or 3 of pattern. Continue above 4 row pattern for one-inch, ending on the second or third K row.

Step Four: Knit Middle Ring. Change to Color C on row 2 or 3 of pattern. Continue same pattern for 6 inches, ending on the second or third K row.

Step Five: Knit Outer Ring. Change to Color D on row 2 or 3 of knit rows. Continue same pattern for 7 1/2 inches, ending on row 2 or 3 of pattern.

Step Six: Edge

1 **Choice One: Edge in Moss Seed Stitch (easier and faster)**

Change to Color A. Knit one row, then follow this pattern for the next 1–2 inches.

Round One: *K1, P1 repeat from*.

Round Two: K1, *P1, K3, rep from*, ending last rep K2, *P1, K3.

Bind off very loosely.

2 **Choice Two: Change to Color A, K one row, then edge in lace edging pattern of your choice.**

This is for more experienced knitters who are familiar with lace edging—a five to eight row pattern works fine—and would enjoy the perversity of knitting a lace edging in a thickish, wavy yarn. The result looks more like flower petals and not much like a distinct, crisp lace, but it can be worth the effort nonetheless.

You can either graft on your edging stitches "live" or bind off last row of afghan loosely and sew finished edging to circumference of afghan, easing for curve as you go, and attaching two short ends to each other.

Use short tail of yarn in center to sew together sides of central "slit."

Weave in ends.

On Row Markers: You have to slip the markers every 4 rows to keep visual track of your lines of increase. I've suggested split stitch markers (to hang in the stitches) because ring markers tend to slide off your needles when you are knitting in the round. Split stitch markers require a little more maintenance to move, but are more reliable. Nonetheless, as you knit your tendency is not to move them and to just go on to the next row. In case this happens to you, this is not the end of the world.

If you lose track of the markers in your fabric, your hands will eventually start to remind you where the yarn overs are supposed to be and you can begin to track the central stitch (the one you YO two stitches before and after) with your eyes. The one marker you don't really want to lose track of is the one that marks the beginning of rounds, but even here, this stitch is going to line up with the vertical slit in the center of the circle where you originally joined your stitches together. You'll be able to eyeball this pretty well until the afghan starts getting rather large.

Neat Lace Trick: Lacemaking is considered to be challenging. Actually, it is just a question of following a pattern that consists of all the basic stitches you already know: knit, purl, yarn over, slip, KTOG, and other increases and decreases. It's like learning dance. First you learn the basic moves, and then you put them together in choreography. As choreographies go, this one is pretty simple.

The trick lies in managing not to lose your place in your pattern, because tearing out lace or fixing dropped lace knitting stitches is a bit more inconvenient than doing the same in other kinds of knitting. A traditional method for keeping your place consists of enlarging a lace repeat pattern on a photocopying machine, carrying it around, and "bookmarking" each line with a Post-it as we go. This works well to a point. The problem is, no offense to Post-its, but they tend to fall off, especially if we have to shove our pattern into our knitting bag in a hurry and run to catch a bus or pick up a crying child. Also, if we are following a lace pattern without a marker, and happen to want to do something else at the same time, such as talk to someone we like or watch a video, we can get distracted from the pattern.

Elizabeth, a proficient lace knitter, offers the following suggestion: Blow up the lace pattern to a very large size, and put EACH LINE of it on a separate flash card (index card). Make holes in them with a hole puncher and bind them. As you work on each line, flip your cards so the lines match. Eventually, your hands get to know a lace pattern on themselves, but the visual reinforcement still helps, especially if you stop in the middle of a row to talk to that delightful person sitting next to you.

This way, you can knit lace and stop to kiss someone, knit lace and listen to music, knit lace, be visited by Brigit, and have a Eureka-type inspiration, or knit lace and go into the kitchen and turn the turkey when the timer goes off. In short, this way you can knit lace and have it be as powerfully interruptible a task as any other form of fiber work. You get the picture.

NEW KNITTER'S WORKSHOP

DOUBLE POINTED KNITTING (DPN)

To separate cast-on stitches among several double pointed needles, follow the illustration below. Be careful not to twist the stitches (A). Join them into a round by making your first stitch (placing a marker before this stitch to mark the beginning of the round) (B). Use an additional needle (the fourth if you've split the

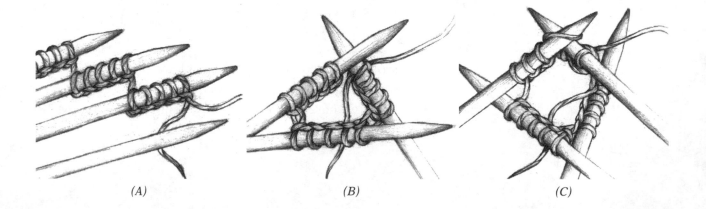

(A)   (B)   (C)

stitches across three needles; and the fifth if you've divided them among four) to knit the stitches on each needle; then use the newly "liberated" needle to knit the stitches on the next needle, and so on, around and around (C).

---

[1]Patricia Monaghan, *O Mother Sun!: A New View of the Cosmic Feminine* (Crossing Press, 1994), 67.
[2]Nancy J. Thomas, ed., *Shawls and Scarves: The Best of Knitter's Magazine* (XRX, 1999), 52.

THAT PARTICULAR HARMONY KNOWN AS PALLAS ATHENE, AND A SMOKE RING BLOWN FROM THE CAVE OF THE NYMPHS

One night, near the end of a talk I was giving on the knitting goddesses, I began to hand out tufts of Romney wool, dyed a deep, hot pink, but still in original curly lock formation as it had grown on the sheep, to each of the sixteen people sitting in the circle. Most of them weren't knitters yet, and my plan was to connect them practically to the material before we did a brief guided meditation.

As I finished handing the locks around I turned to discover a delightful surprise. Almost everyone had begun to separate the individual locks, tease the ends of the fiber from each other with their fingers, comb the wool with their fingers until it was even in density throughout, and elongate the tuft into something long and yarn-like enough to be wound into a very small ball.

Then, almost everyone had begun to twist her or his long string of airy fiber into yarn by rolling the fiber back and forth on a knee or twisting it, inch by inch, between his or her fingers.

In other words, they were spinning.

This, it has been speculated, is exactly how ancient humans may have begun to spin yarn. First they took the fibers of bast plants like nettle, and, then they took the coarse, kempy hairs of primitive sheep, and instinctively rolled and twisted them back and forth along their knees until they bound together into a yarn.[1] The mysterious human instinct to make things that are curly and fluffy and uneven and loose into things that are tight and wound and even and smooth is one of the instincts that allowed us to stay warm enough to survive.

Delighted, I explained to the group what was going on, while, entirely non-

plussed and totally engaged, they carried on. Within minutes one woman had chained a little pink necklace out of her yarn, and another had fashioned an abstract little stick figure with knots. Everyone else was twirling the fiber on her or his knee, discovering the strong, resilient character of the fleece of a Romney sheep.

Only fifteen minutes before the air had been almost tingling with everyone's different impressions and experiences with the archetype of the evening, which happened to be Brigit. Because it was her day, and Northwesterners have a particular passion for Brigit, some participants had shared stories, personal experiences, and pieces of her lore they felt were essential to the evening. Others were just excited to meet each other. As we all spun, apparent minor differences in experience and acquired knowledge fell away, and we all hung out in a concentrated but relaxed state. The excitement that had been hovering dropped to the floor and sunk into the ground. The room became calm and relaxed and focused and homogenized. There wasn't really any need to meditate, because we were already meditating. So we decided to do the visualization with our eyes open as we combed the fleece with our fingers.

This is a particular quality of harmony. It begins with the easy instinct to take something physical that is bumpy and diffuse and turn it into something that is long, even, uniform, durable, functional, and aesthetically pleasing. And then it skillfully and naturally overflows into harmonizing different kinds of people and ideas as well.

In a way, Athena's magic has been cast all over this book. One of the most ancient and influential of knitting goddesses, we have already met her officially in two chapters. As a shining, gray-eyed, helmeted ally, a sword in one hand, a dark-eyed owl on one shoulder, and a divine and fearless ability to weave the world together along straight lines, and she helped orchestrate the return of Odysseus. In this capacity, Walter F. Otto calls her the goddess who is "ever near."[2] And Jean Houston calls her "a friend in court."[3] We also saw her punish Arachne, when Arachne appeared to violate the social order of the land. Here, we saw her remorselessly punish the chaotic, rebellious, Dionysian force that appeared to threaten the foundations of her perfectly ordered society and, at the

same time harm the reputation of Athena's Olympian father, whose peccadilloes were being deliciously immortalized in the most enchanting of tapestry stitches.

It is often observed that some of Brigit originated in Athena, and carried across old Europe with the Romans, where she grew into a new form in the fertile green ground of Ireland. For instance, both are known as warriors, healers, and inspirers. Both are essentially maiden goddesses, although each brings her own cloud of erotic mystery. And both are associated with the sun and with snakes.

And, in a curious way, we also meet Athena, or the extent of the great brightness she exudes, when we meet Gretchen and the Miller's Daughter, Arachne herself, and many spinners from fairy tales, and even Penelope. These women, like Athena, are either motherless daughters or daughters who are only identified by their paternal parentage (as in the case of Penelope, whose father Laertes is mentioned in the Odyssey, but whose mother is not).

As a warrior, like the greatest of leaders, Athena has a way of not only uniting us by convincing us to partake in group tasks, but also by showing us the common, perhaps almost invisible thread that unites our apparently contradictory role models. As a master weaver and spinner (which, in present times, would translate into a master knitter), she has a way of uniting different strands of wool into a single tapestry, whether those strands be ideas, information, goals, or people.

When we call in Athena, she accesses our ability, demonstrated in our weaving, our knitting, and our simple, roll-fiber-on-the-knee spinning, to instinctively create evenness and strength, and the way we tune to each other when we do that.

There are many stories to be told about Athena. Each showcases one of her many abilities or the foresight, strategy, wisdom and heroism she uses to protect her beloved heroes from unnecessary anguish, for as a guide to heroes she is peerless. As we have seen, Athena helped Odysseus return home. She helped Jason retrieve the golden fleece. She beat Apollo a couple of times in battle, and she was victorious over Poseidon in the contest to become the patron of Athens,

THAT
PARTICULAR
HARMONY
KNOWN AS
PALLAS
ATHENE, AND
A SMOKE RING
BLOWN FROM
THE CAVE OF
THE NYMPHS
242

the mythical city that bears her name, when she produced an olive tree on a hill high above the city. (Her people found many more uses for this peaceful, nourishing tree than they did for the salty waters of the emotions which Poseidon produced in a sea water spring that appeared in the same place.)

But one of the most interesting stories that can be told about Athena is the underlying story of how she came to be all of herself: that is, how, during the many centuries of evolution into the classical Greek goddess we know her to be (for Athena was born when the triple goddess was born, which may have been in Libya many years before she literally burst onto the Olympian scene) she was able to hold on to all of herself, even as she moved on and also became someone else.

Within herself, Athena harmonizes many different aspects of the sacred feminine. And she does it so well, that, unless we look closely, we hardly even notice. That is the source and pedigree of her ability to balance others with a little piece of yarn while conveying a clear, brilliant, perfectly tempered and particularly warrior-like appearance. She's been there, and she's done that. Athena is a goddess who walks her talk.

Like many warriors, Pallas Athene carries her history, her strengths, and even her grief in her appearance, dress, weapons, and tools.

She was literally born armored. Her conception is well documented. She was conceived when Zeus, king of the Olympians, made love to Metis, the goddess of the sea. Zeus was told that Metis would first bear a daughter, but that she would subsequently bear a son who would become king of gods and men, usurping his own position. So he made Metis tiny and swallowed her whole. In time, he came down with a great headache. The pain was so profound and lasted so long that clever Hermes, or in other versions, the forge god Hephaistos, finally ran and got a double-headed axe, symbol of the goddess, and cleft Zeus' head open just in time to allow a beautiful, resplendent and fully armored and helmeted girl to jump out. The newborn but fully formed maiden goddess had arrestingly brilliant, cool, gray eyes and was carrying a drawn sword or spear. Some thought her armor was solid gold. But it was so bright that some others thought it was brilliant silver. And, by the way, she was shrieking.

First, about that resplendent quality. Her radiant overall coloring reminds us that, unlike most of the knitting goddesses, who are lunar, Athena, like Brigit, is instantly clothed in the heat and clarity of the sun, which represents her clear, brilliant mind and great courage, and ability to see strategically into the future. Unlike Brigit, who represents sun as pure undifferentiated life force, Athena falls more squarely into the identity of a patroness of the life-giving and saving powers of the mind. Athena is sometimes seen with the sun shining in the background—symbolizing her connection to the light of knowledge and the power of the discerning and strategic mind. Beginning with Grandmother Spider, we've seen how the ability to plan and create order in dark and even chaotic crevices is an essential component of knitting goddess power. But while Grandmother Spider plans in the dark, Athena thrives in the light of inner and outer illumination. She brings women's plans into the atrium, the square, the forum, and the plaza where they do their fiber work together.

Metaphorically, the armor in which Athena is born and which she characteristically wears thereafter (even when she wears flowing robes, the helmet usually sits upon her head) clues us in to how well defended Athena is by that cool, bright mind that also radiates from her brilliant silver eyes. As well armored as it is, that mind is impervious to the slings and arrows of emotion.

Since Zeus, Athena's father, is the god of the lightning bolt, all this brilliance that surrounds her lets us know that it exists partially thanks to her function of her appointed role as Daddy's protector. This "little" hint is backed up with the much broader clue of her parthenogenic birth. Many gods and goddesses and other divine beings are born or conceived parthenogenically—that is, with the physical participation of one parent only and, in mythology as opposed to flesh and blood creatures, through avenues other than the womb. The Buddha, for instance, was born from his mother's side. And Jesus was conceived through Mary's ear, with the help of the angel Gabriel. In religion and mythology, there is usually something very, very special or different about a being who is born this way. But the very particular avenue of Athena's parthenogenesis lets us know she is daddy's girl.

To help understand why, let's take a parenthetical jaunt back to ancient

THAT
PARTICULAR
HARMONY
KNOWN AS
PALLAS
ATHENE, AND
A SMOKE RING
BLOWN FROM
THE CAVE OF
THE NYMPHS
244

Libya, where there is some evidence that an ancient triple goddess, known as Neith, who was in each of her aspects, patron of battle, healing, and the arts, was born. Athena began her life here. Then she moved to Minoan Crete, where she was called Lady of Athana, protected the palace and city, and taught the women to spin, dye wool, and weave. In Crete her symbols were the serpent and the dove.[4] We have seen this goddess throughout this book: maiden, mother, and crone she represents the power and harmony of creation and the potential and wisdom of the natural world. She is present, in the Moirae, and in Penelope's weaving, and in Brigit's vastness, and in the Miller's Daughter's instinct for survival, in Rachel's endurance and fertility, Ariadne's complexity, Penelope's vision, and Arachne's exuberant virtuosity.

As she jumps out of her father's head many centuries later, Athena enters the forum of the Olympians as she simultaneously does them the favor of putting everyone on notice that the triple goddess has been officially assimilated and reborn through the unusual birth canal of a man's head and thrown off her familiar lunar world. Not patron of women, but helpmate of the father whose favorite she instantly becomes. Athena is able to persuade Zeus of things that others are not. In this incarnation, this ancient figure shows herself first in her aspect as warrior, ever ready to ably and heroically protect her father's supremacy: the classic man's woman and male fantasy of the ideal, autonomous, and emotionally low maintenance helpmate.

However, the same warrior aspect that signals her loyalty to Zeus begins to turn the corner into other Athenian possibilities. Coupled with the history of her conception, and her history as the dark goddess who presided over the arts, the armor also brings up the intriguing question of whether Athena did not decide to come forth fully armored in self-defense. After all, her father had first shrunken and then devoured Metis, her own mother, while Athena was in the womb. Her armor protected Zeus' world, but it may also have protected Athena from it. It is unclear whether her birth shriek, so loud it frightens the other gods, is a shriek of victory or outrage.

Zeus quickly assessed Athena's strengths and reliability. He must have decided that the shriek was one of triumph, since he summarily endowed his

specially born daughter with some of his own resplendent war implements. Athena is the only other god who is allowed to carry and wield Zeus' massive, fatal, and cosmically electric thunderbolt, which she does, upon occasion, with great skill. This shows that she is balanced and responsible enough to be discerning about the right use of great power. And Athena is also the only member of the pantheon allowed to carry Zeus' aegis, the goat's skin breastplate or shield that covers her heart, divinely and magically protecting her from harm with the power of the lightning-bright king of Olympus.

But the light of a brilliant mind does not hide; it illuminates. Traced and camouflaged in her own light and the light of Olympus, Athena also bears the powerful tools of the world of the dark goddess from which she came. Her lightning effulgence, which she comes by naturally, may distract us and cause us to turn away our eyes. But that light is etched all over with the signs of her inheritance.

Let's start with the aegis itself. Etched on this breastplate, which is usually made of goat skin but is sometimes portrayed as shining gold or silver, are the writhing snakes of the ever-renewing snake goddess we met in part through Ariadne (Brigit is also associated with snakes), and also an etching of the head of the Gorgon Medusa.

The Medusa is an ancient, snakey, pure and powerful symbol for feminine power. Like sexuality and life force, she can be fatal if ignored, and essential to life if honored. She may have begun her existence thousands of years before classical Greece, as an Amazon queen and purveyor of snake magic.[5] In her Greek incarnation, she was a very lovely woman who was desired by Poseidon, who raped her in Athena's temple. Medusa became impregnated with twins. And Athena, instead of punishing Poseidon, turned Medusa's beautiful hair to hissing snakes and caused Medusa's glance to turn men to stone. Later, Athena helped Perseus to sever her head, in order to save his true love Andromeda from a larger horror. In so doing, this ancient ally of the feminine became a magical tool in the service of the men gods of Olympus. The display on Athena's heart shows the part that Athena played in this change of hands for the Gorgon's power in the classical Greek mythology, and also warns of Athena's own invincibility, because the

THAT
PARTICULAR
HARMONY
KNOWN AS
PALLAS
ATHENE, AND
A SMOKE RING
BLOWN FROM
THE CAVE OF
THE NYMPHS
246

being who looks into the eyes of the Gorgon turns instantly to stone. But, as she carries the Medusa's head over her own heart on the aegis as a sign of victory, Athena also displays an unmistakable a sign of her own origins in the much more ancient power of the snake goddess, and perhaps even an ancient emotional connection. As she is the patroness of weaving, the spiraling snake head also affirms the connection to the ancient, life giving power, and protective of yarn.

The irony is wonderful. Even though she killed the snake goddess, Athena continues to disperse her power silently as fiber arts' patroness. Under Athena's Grecian reign, the regenerative serpent power was again transferred to the wool that twisted into snakelike spirals. Wool was considered to have healing powers by both the men and the women of the classical Greek world. Remember how before embarking on his search to retrieve the golden fleece, itself quite the testament to the magical power of wool, the hero Jason wrapped a piece of wool around an olive branch, another Athenian symbol, as he made a sacrifice at her temple while requesting her help and protection on his voyage. Wool was often hung at sacred sites as a symbol of purification.[6]

Wool was also associated with magical fertility. An old story relates how the god of smithcraft, Hephaestus, tried to take the beautiful Athena by force. First she defended herself against him, and then she took a bit of wool she found to wipe his ejaculate from her thigh. The wool fell into the earth near Athens, and was absorbed by Gaia, the earth mother, who subsequently bore Athena's child, Erichthonius. Erichthonius had a snake's body and a human head and was known as the bearer of wisdom. Athena raised him secretly in her temple, and he proclaimed the prophecies of the oracle, eventually becoming a king of Athens and establishing the temple of Athena.[7] Wool also had the power to thwart fertility. Women were prohibited from spinning near cultivated fields because the turning of the drop spindle could spoil the harvest. And before the onset of labor, it was customary to untie or loosen clothing and hair to open the body for the passage of the newborn child.[8]

The dark goddess is also present in Athena's name. Athena is often referred to as Pallas Athene. Her surname is Pallas. It is said that one day the young war-

rior Athena got into a contest with her foster sister, Pallas, daughter of the sea god Triton. Zeus intervened and placed his aegis between Athena and Pallas, distracting Athena and causing her to accidentally kill her sister.

In ancient Libya, Pallas was a maiden protectress of the Amazons, or matriarchal order. So in adding this name to her own, Athena adds another aspect of her own dark origins to her classical Greek identity and, through the death symbolism of the story, acknowledges the demise of that more ancient culture while also carrying it harmoniously along with her through her current and more masculine orientation.

And then there is the magical owl, the familiar whom Athena was never without. The owl is a very ancient symbol for the fertility goddess. Starting in the Neolithic age, Athena spread through Eastern Mediterranean, the Northern Aegean, Western and Northern Europe, and Greece, leaving behind a trail of owl-shaped burial urns, with wings, beaks, and occasionally a human vulva or snake-like umbilical cord, marking the owl as another bearer of the power of regeneration and fertility that is also found in wool. The owl's distinctively dark gaze matches the equally notable bright, neutral, and silvery gaze of Athena herself. Once again, the newest and most favored servant of the father is also endowed by the power of the mother. Athena's silver eyes suggest the power to edit, simplify, discern, and plan. The black eyes of her owl balance this power with its yin yang match, in this case, the power of ancient mysteries which cannot be deciphered with even the most brilliant mind. As a symbol for the eyes of the goddess, owl eyes are visually associated as a source of divine, life-sustaining liquids or supernatural powers. So not only do they answer the power of the light, but, by ancient association, give Athena's silvery gaze an additional dimension of power, while providing others with their even more ancient reminder of their origin. And, of course, the ability to balance light and shadow and all other opposites is basic to harmony and the ideal execution of statesmanship and all other peacekeeping and healing arts.

Also, in her Minoan life as Lady of Athana, Athena was associated with the serpent and the bird, in that case, the dove. By wearing the Gorgon's head and

That
Particular
Harmony
Known as
Pallas
Athene, and
a Smoke Ring
Blown from
the Cave of
the Nymphs
248

carrying the owl on her shoulder, Athena brings her ancient allies into the classical Greek present.

Finally, Athena is also often depicted holding a spindle, that most ancient symbol of the triple goddess and of fate, and the feminine counterpoint to the more masculine magical spear, which Athena also carries.

One of Athena's greatest and most harmonious achievements is to become marshal all of these conflicting powers within herself to one who bestows harmony to others. This may be the real source of her authority among the gods, and her skill in counseling heroes, and certainly what gives the wool that is in her dominion its deeply healing powers. Behind her silver façade, she manages the same complexities that humans do with divine poise, and without much ado, and without it wounding or diminishing her prodigious gifts. A warrior has guts and Ernest Hemingway rather famously defined guts as grace under pressure. This describes Pallas Athene as a warrior and as a knitting goddess. The dark and the light, the old and the new, the light and the brilliance of the sun and the snakelike regenerative powers of the Gorgon co-exist in her perfect, graceful form. Because the spear is not only a symbol of battle—it can also be the hallmark of the spiritual warrior, it lets is know that she is the one who can meet any set of circumstances with grace, joy, and equanimity. Perhaps this weapon is also intended as a gentle clue that even gods have their woes and that, aware of the contradictions inherent within, Athena chose to meet them with the brilliance, clarity, and balance that this weapon has always suggested. Meanwhile, the spindle she also often carries allows her to skilfully weave all her aspects together.

When we wield any of her tools, symbolically or literally, we can access this gift.

The Roman emperors, who knew this, used Athena to maintain compliance in the home. Women visited Minerva's temple in Rome (Minerva is the Roman Athena), where they could view a frieze of the punitive myth of Arachne on the walls, presided over by Minerva herself. Distaffs and spindles were also carried in wedding ceremonies as symbols of domestic harmony.[9] The principle of harmony underlying this tactic can be, and is, often employed in ways that are more

affirming to women. For instance, this scene is memorably and powerfully recast in Marion Zimmer Bradley's *The Mists of Avalon*, where the women of Camelot are often depicted spinning and speaking together.

And, these days, as my evening talk surprisingly and charmingly demonstrated, as we access the basic impulse to spin, to knit, to develop evenness and strength in natural fibers, and to create beautiful things, we simultaneously seem to balance and harmonize the differences among parts of ourselves, and among each other. Like Athena, we each comprise an inner community of diverse aspects even as we participate in even more diverse communities in the external world. As we work with wool, we also access the natural force that comes from the earth, like the snake, and like Athena's child, which heals our history as it may have healed Athena's own. With her sword, as she develops clarity for herself, Athena is able to apply that clarity to others. She implements it with the ancient power of the snake within her, the regenerative, healing force that heals the goddess herself along with mere mortals.

In this quality of profound complexity and need to constantly balance divergent and sometimes antithetical responsibilities, allegiances, and aspects of herself, she is, to my mind, also one of the most contemporary of knitting goddesses. She gives us a shining example of how we can meld all of our complexity into a single, beautiful, balanced sword-like awareness of how, and when, to act, create, and implement our power.

ATHENA SMOKE RING

In her aspect as the ever near, Athena often accompanied her heroes invisibly, at their shoulders.

This is a piece of clothing that has many names. Some people call it a cowl. Others call it a wimple, and others just call it a hood. Or you could put it on your head, pull the front over your face, close it, swing it around like an elephant trunk and call it a Snuffleupagus, which is what Rob did, delighted, after I brought the sample to a party and he snatched it out of my hands. (Just to complete the picture, Rob is a really big guy.)

THAT
PARTICULAR
HARMONY
KNOWN AS
PALLAS
ATHENE, AND
A SMOKE RING
BLOWN from
THE CAVE OF
THE NYMPHS
250

It is a drapey tube that you put around your shoulders, where you can wear it like a really wide cowlneck, or pull it over your head, where it makes a lovely, flattering hood. The native women of Alaska, who make it out of qiuviut, a fiber that is warmer than cashmere, call it a *nachaq*, which means hat or hood in Eskimo language and is also known as a smoke ring for its warmth and lightness and the way it frames the face in a soft knitted circle. This piece is more open and made out of a different fiber mix, so it might not keep you warm in the Arctic. I like the name because it also suggests invisibility. I've done this version in a rayon and mohair yarn called La Boheme, which you should know about whether or not you decide to make this project, because it knits up so beautifully into shawls, vests, and the like, with fascinating, subtle variation in colors and textures. This pale gray, violet, blue, and pinky cream colorway suggests Athena's eyes, and her invisibility. If you have light eyes, it's also particularly flattering. (You can always choose another colorway.) When you wear it you stand out, but you don't stand out from the crowd. Because of its color and its airy, shiny quality, it also reminds me of something that would wash up from the cave of the nymphs.

And, of course, the emphasis on the head is intentional.

This knits up quickly and is warm without being too warm. You can wear it either for fashion or for your ears. The stitch is Turkish—a simple form of vertical faggoting from Volume I of Barbara Walker's invaluable *A Treasury of Knitting Patterns*, which, in one of those mysterious quirks of knitting, goes diagonal when you knit it in the round. It is classic, useful, and also slightly unusual. Rather like Athena herself.

Athena Smoke Ring Pattern

Ingredients:

- 2 4 oz. skeins (145 yds) of Fiesta Yarns La Boheme in quince (kid mohair/rayon bouclé)
- 1 pair circular size 10 needles, or size required to duplicate gauge.

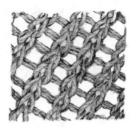

Pattern Stitch (Turkish Stitch)

Step One: CO even number of stitches.

Step Two: Knit one row.

Step Three: K1, *YO K2TOG*, end K1.

Repeat row 3 for pattern.

Athena Smoke Ring

Step One: CO 80 stitches and join, being careful not to twist the stitches.

Step Two: K 5 rows.

Step Three: Work 1 inch in pattern stitch

Step four: Work 1 inch in K1 P3 rib

Step five: Work 14 inches in pattern stitch.

Step six: Work another inch in K1 P3 rib

Step seven: Knit 5 rows.

Step eight: Bind off.

That's it!

The edges will curl backwards slightly, framing the face.

---

[1]Barber, *Prehistoric Textiles,* 50.
[2]Walter F. Otto, *The Homeric Gods* (Thames and Hudson: New York, 1979), via Shinoda Bolen.
[3]Jean Houston, *The Hero and the Goddess* (Harper and Row: New York, 1992), 61.
[4]Demetra George, *Asteroid Goddesses* (ACS: San Diego, 1986), 82.
[5]George, 81.
[6]D'Ambra, 101.
[7]George, 83.
[8]Marija Gimbutas, *The Language of the Goddess* (HarperSan Francisco, 1991), 194–195.
[9]D'Ambra, esp. 100–101.

Epilogue:
Maya

When Ed's mother died, she left behind an enormous knitting stash.

A stash is all that yarn you know you will use "someday." Almost everyone has one. They start out innocently—the half a skein that was left over from your first sweater or scarf; a ball of unusual ribbon yarn your friend brought over because she had to have it but didn't know what to do with it, and so she brought it to you. And then you enrich them with the irresistible (the handspun honey-colored alpaca that you found on vacation) or the untouchable (the pure white Shetland you decided to temporarily put aside after your four-year-old began to display inspired creativity in the area of hand-painted textiles). Well-mannered yarn stashes live in tightly closed bags, often under beds. More exuberant yarn stashes overflow into plastic buckets and garbage bags and become the rollicking tenants of your basement or spare closet, where they seem to start multiplying like the angora rabbits whose soft fur they may actually contain.

It is the destiny of most stashes to fall into the exuberant category sooner or later.

Ed's mother's stash was quite exuberant.

One day, Ed's friend Elizabeth helped him sort and unpack it. It contained many commercial yarns. But Ed's mother had spun and hand-dyed fiber as well, so unique handmade treasures tumbled from the open door along with the store-bought ones. As they worked, and as Elizabeth admired the contents and explained to Ed what they were, he told her how his mother had made many

sweaters for him, but that he had had never really worn them too much because they weren't his style.

Elizabeth naturally offered to knit him a sweater, made from his mother's yarn stash, in the style and colors of his choice.

Ed chose a soft wool in greens and browns. His mother had both spun and dyed this yarn herself. Together, Ed and Elizabeth decided on a simple turtleneck with a few cables in it, and lined the turtleneck with cashmerino, a blend of cashmere and merino wool, to make it especially soft and warm.

When Elizabeth gave Ed the finished piece, he was extremely moved. The reality of being able to wear something close to his skin that his mother had touched every part of—that he also was going to love to wear for a long time—brought them both to tears.

Knitting is, finally, like that—a hoarded treasure, both consistent and flexible, to be passed with love from one great being to the next, and to as many beneficiaries as possible.

But the instinct is probably less philosophical than heartfelt. Like any legacy, it's filled with wisdom and love and potential. If the stash is knit by another pair of hands it will gain life. As the mother hands it on to the daughter, it will acquire both expected and unexpected stitch patterns. It will become a kind of descendant, as one woman's creative hopes and plans and delights are superseded yet also fulfilled by another's. Like a new human being, this treasure's ultimate fate will be both predictable and unpredictable. Such is the price, and the promise, of longevity.

The Mother of the Universe, sometimes known as Maya, disposes of her own yarn stash. She is Hindu, and she is Tibetan, but as she partakes in her characteristic pastime of weaving webs, she is also one of us.

Maya weaves the entire world from her thread. In the East, they call this world illusion, but we might call it the mother of all yarn stashes. Maya's world is also the *lila*, or play, of the universe. Something that goes on endlessly, in different forms. When Maya is done with her creation, she rips it out, or dissolves it into a beautiful cloud that subsides into a mist, then clears to show a beautiful blue sky, which is what is behind all the illusion. And what is that blue sky?

Emptiness and fullness at once; a mystery. Then, once again, after this pause is over, she weaves or knits the universe into a new form.

This, so the story goes, is how lifetimes come and go and come again, and how nations rise and fall; how biospheres rise and decline.

In a way, each knitter takes part in Maya's work. We celebrate and grow as we partake in the play of reality as we knit up microworlds between our needles. As each yarn stash is disposed of, something else wonderful comes into being. Elizabeth can make Ed a sweater that he loves, and in its touch against his skin, his mother lives on, even if she never would have knitted him that one exactly.

Elizabeth's mother is also an expert knitter. When I met her, I naturally complimented her on her daughter's work.

An unexpected expression crossed Ellen's face—almost, but not quite, a shadow.

"I have three daughters," she said. "And one of them knits. It was the answer to my prayers—now I have someone to inherit my stash."

I hope you will come to find your own patterns and inspiration in your own yarn. (Get a stitch dictionary, see the Reading List for some suggestions or use your own favorites, and experiment.)

Whatever you do, make sure to play, the way Maya does. You are part of her lineage now.

Give the same gift to your daughters.

Give it to your mothers.

Give it to your friends.

Tell them it's courtesy of the knitting goddess.

Who, by the way, is you.

Bibliography

Knitting

Bliss, Debbie. *How to Knit*. Pomfret, VT: Trafalgar Square Publishing, 1999.

Don, Sarah. *The Art of Shetland Lace*. Berkeley, CA: Lacis, 1980.

Falick, Melanie D. *Knitting in America*. New York: Artisan, 1996.

Hiatt, June Hemmons. *The Principles of Knitting: Methods and Techniques of Hand Knitting*. New York: Simon and Schuster, 1988.

Raven, Lee. *Hands On Spinning*. Loveland, CO: Interweave Press, 1987.

Square, Vicki. *The Knitter's Companion*. Loveland, CO: Interweave Press, 1996.

The Editors of Vogue Knitting Magazine. *Vogue Knitting*. New York: Pantheon Books, 1989.

Thomas, Mary. *Mary Thomas' Book of Knitting Patterns*. New York: Dover Publications Inc., 1972.

Thomas, Nancy J., Editor. *Shawls and Scarves: The Best of Knitter's Magazine*. Sioux Falls, SD: XRX, 1999.

Walker, Barbara G. *A Second Treasury of Knitting Patterns*. Pittsville, WI: Schoolhouse Press, 1998.

———. *A Treasury of Knitting Patterns*. Pittsville, WI: Schoolhouse Press, 1998.

Waterman, Martha. *Traditional Knitted Lace Shawls*. Loveland, CO: Interweave Press, 1998.

Zimmerman, Elizabeth. *Knitting Without Tears*. New York: Fireside/Simon & Schuster, 1971.

Mythology/Literature/History/Spiritual Traditions

———, *The Holy Bible Revised Standard Version*. New York: New American Library, 1962.

Apuleius. *The Golden Ass: Being the Metamorphoses of Lucius Apuleius*. Harvard University Press, 1977.

Benyus, Janine M. *Biomimicry: Innovation Inspired by Nature*. New York: Quill, 1997.

Barber, E. J. W. *Prehistoric Textiles: The Development of Cloth in the Neolithic and Bronze Ages*. Princeton, N.J.: Princeton University Press, 1991.

Barber, Elizabeth Wayland. *Women's Work: The First 20,000 Years*. New York: W. W. Norton and Company, 1994.

Bennett, Noel; photographs by John Running. *Halo of the Sun*. Flagstaff: Northland, 1987.

Bonheim, Jalaja, ed. *Goddess: A Celebration in Art and Literature*. New York: Stewart, Tabori & Chang, 1997.

Budge, E. A. Wallis. *The Gods of the Egyptians Vols I and II*. New York: Dover Publications, Inc., 1969.

Calasso, Roberto. *The Marriage of Cadmus and Harmony*. Vintage International, 1993.

Dresner, Samuel H. *Rachel*. Minneapolis: Fortress Press, 1994.

D'Ambra, Eve. *Private Lives, Imperial Virtues: The Frieze of the Forum Transitorium in Rome*. Princeton, N.J.: Princeton University Press, 1993.

Ellis, Normandi. *Awakening Osiris: The Egyptian Book of the Dead*. Grand Rapids, MI: Phanes Press, 1988.

Fortune, Dion. *The Sea Priestess*. York Beach, Maine: Samuel Weiser, Inc., 1938.

———. *Moon Magic*. York Beach, Maine: Samuel Weiser, Inc., 1956.

Gimbutas, Marija. *The Language of the Goddess*. San Francisco: HarperSanFrancisco, 1989.

Grant, Michael. *The History of Ancient Israel*. New York: Charles Scribner's Sons, 1984.

Graves, Robert. *The Greek Myths*. Mt. Kisco, New York: Moyer Bell Limited, 1955.

Homer, translated by Allen Mandelbaum. *The Odyssey of Homer*. New York: Bantam, 1991.

Homer, translated by Richmond Lattimore. *The Odyssey of Homer*. New York: Harper & Row, 1965.

Houston, Jean. *The Hero and the Goddess: The Odyssey as Mystery and Initiation*. New York: Ballantine Books, 1992.

Hubbell, Sue. *Waiting for Aphrodite*. Boston: Houghton Mifflin, 1999.

Johnson Newcomb, Franc Johnson. *Navajo Folk Tales*. Albuquerque: University of New Mexico Press, 1967.

Moon, Sheila. *Changing Woman and Her Sisters*. San Francisco: Guide for Psychological Studies, 1984.

Mullett, G. M. *Spider Woman Stories: Legends of the Hopi Indians*. Tucson: The University of Arizona Press, 1979.

Ovid, trans. by Rolph Humphries. *Metamorphoses*. 1955.

Patricia Monaghan. *O Mother Sun!* Freedom, CA: Crossing Press, 1994.

Patterson-Rudolph, Carol. *On the Trail of Spiderwoman: Petroglyphs, Pictographs, and Myths of the Southwest*. Santa Fe: Ancient City Press, 1997.

Porphyry, trans. by Thomas Taylor. *On the Cave of the Nymphs*. Grand Rapids, MI: Phanes Press, 1991.

Regula, deTraci. *The Mysteries of Isis*. St. Paul, Minnesota: Llewellyn, 1996.

Shakespeare, William; textual editor G. Blakemore Evans. *The Riverside Shakespeare*. Boston: Houghton Mifflin Company, 1974.

Shinoda Bolen, Jean. *The Goddesses in Every Woman: A New Psychology of Women*. New York: HarperPerennial, 1985.

Sjoo, Monica and Mor, Barbara. *The Great Cosmic Mother: Rediscovering the Religion of the Earth*. San Francisco: HarperSanFrancisco, 1987.

Somé, Malidoma Patrice. *Ritual*. New York: Penguin Arkana, 1997.

"Ultraviolet Fly Trap." *Discover Magazine*, August 1990.

Vivekananda, Swami. *Jnana-Yoga*. New York: Ramakrishna-Vivekananda Center, 1955.

von Goethe, Johann Wolfgang; Stuart Atkins, ed. and trans. *Goethe: The Collected Works Faust I and II*. Princeton: Princeton University Press, 1984.

Weigle, Marta. *Spiders and Spinsters: Women and Mythology*. Albuquerque: University of New Mexico Press.

Wilde, Lyn Webster. "The Barraman and the Two Witches." *Celtic Woman* (1997).

Yeats, William Butler. *The Collected Poems of W. B. Yeats*. New York: Macmillan, 1933.

About the Author

Deborah Bergman is the author of *River of Glass*, a novel, and *Inner Voyager: A Journal for Intuitive Spiritual Discovery*. She has assisted a variety of prominent authors in telling their inspirational healing stories, and mentors knitters and handspinners in making their craft a spiritual practice. She lives in western Oregon, and grew up in Princeton, New Jersey.

She, along with color photographs of these projects and a bit more sacred wool-gathering, can be found at www.knittinggoddess.com.